About Island Press

Since 1984, the nonprofit organization Island Press has been stimulating, shaping, and communicating ideas that are essential for solving environmental problems worldwide. With more than 1,000 titles in print and some 30 new releases each year, we are the nation's leading publisher on environmental issues. We identify innovative thinkers and emerging trends in the environmental field. We work with world-renowned experts and authors to develop cross-disciplinary solutions to environmental challenges.

Island Press designs and executes educational campaigns, in conjunction with our authors, to communicate their critical messages in print, in person, and online using the latest technologies, innovative programs, and the media. Our goal is to reach targeted audiences—scientists, policy makers, environmental advocates, urban planners, the media, and concerned citizens—with information that can be used to create the framework for long-term ecological health and human well-being.

Island Press gratefully acknowledges major support from The Bobolink Foundation, Caldera Foundation, The Curtis and Edith Munson Foundation, The Forrest C. and Frances H. Lattner Foundation, The JPB Foundation, The Kresge Foundation, The Summit Charitable Foundation, Inc., and many other generous organizations and individuals.

The opinions expressed in this book are those of the author(s) and do not necessarily reflect the views of our supporters.

THE FARM BILL

THE
FARM BILL
A CITIZEN'S GUIDE

DANIEL IMHOFF
WITH CHRISTINA BADARACCO

ISLANDPRESS   Washington | Covelo | London

Library of Congress Control Number: 2018946760
All Island Press books are printed on environmentally responsible materials.

Manufactured in the United States of America
10 9 8 7 6 5 4 3 2 1
Keywords: agribusiness, Agricultural Adjustment Act, CAFO, commodity programs, conservation title, crop insurance, crop subsidies, ethanol, food stamps/SNAP, nutrition assistance, rural development

CONTENTS

FOREWORD

In 2011, I had the idea of teaching a graduate course on the Farm Bill to food studies students at New York University. As happens every four years or so, the bill was coming up for renewal, and I thought it would be useful for the students—and me—to take a deep dive into what it was about. I knew help was available. Dan Imhoff had laid out the issues with great clarity in his first book about this bill in 2007. I used that book as a text.

I wrote about this experience in "The Farm Bill Drove Me Insane" (*Politico*, March 17, 2016), which it most definitely did. The Farm Bill is huge, encompassing more than a hundred programs, each with its own acronym and set of interested lobbyists. The bill is unreadable, consisting mainly of amendments to previous bills; it is comprehensible only to lobbyists, a precious few congressional staffers, and occasional brave souls like Imhoff willing to take it on. It costs taxpayers close to $100 billion a year; most weirdly, 80 percent of this money covers the costs of the Supplemental Nutrition Assistance Program (SNAP, formerly food stamps), which is stuck in the Farm Bill for reasons of politics. The Farm Bill represents pork-barrel, log-rolling politics at its worst.

Imhoff explains the bill as a fully rigged system gamed by Big Agriculture in collusion with government. The public pays for this system thrice over: at the checkout counter, in subsidized insurance premiums, and for cleaning up the damage it causes to health and the environment. Despite these scandalous costs, the mere mention of the words *farm bill* makes eyes glaze over. Why? This is a forest-versus-trees problem. The bill—the forest—is far too big and complicated to grasp. We try to understand it by looking at the programs—the trees—one by one. Hence: insanity.

Imhoff's approach to the forest is to focus on the overriding issues that Farm Bills ought to address. A rational agricultural policy should promote an adequate food supply while protecting farmers against uncertain climate and price fluctuations. It should promote the health of people and the environment and do so sustainably. And it should provide incentives for people to farm and ensure a decent living for everyone involved. Instead, the Farm Bills encourage an industrial agricultural system incentivized to overproduce corn and soybeans to feed animals and to make ethanol for automobiles, to the great detriment of public health and environmental protection.

Nowhere are these problems more obvious than in the debates about the 2018 Farm Bill. As I write these words, the House of Representatives is working on a bill that seems less protective of health and the environment than any previous version. To cut costs while maintaining support of Big Agriculture, the House aims to reduce SNAP enrollments, eliminate conservation requirements, and cut out even small programs that support small farmers or promote production of fruits and vegetables, called "specialty crops" in US Department of Agriculture parlance.

At this moment, the outcome of the 2018 bill is uncertain, but *The Farm Bill: A Citizen's Guide* has a more generic purpose: to introduce readers to the big-picture issues. Imhoff relates the history of Farm Bills, their origins, and their subsequent growth. Imhoff describes the *system*: how Big Agriculture works, how food stamps ended up in the bill, what it all means for farming and food assistance, and what kind of legislation is needed to promote a healthier food system.

We should, Imhoff insists, rework the Farm Bill to promote public health by supporting an agricultural system that grows food for people rather than for animals and cars. We should legislate that crops be grown sustainably so as to reduce agriculture's contribution to greenhouse gas emissions, soil losses, and water pollution. Imhoff suggests twenty-five solutions to current agricultural problems. These should be required reading for anyone who cares about what we eat, today and in the future. It is too late to fix the 2018 Farm Bill, but there is plenty of time and opportunity to make the next one a true citizens' Farm Bill. To quote Imhoff, "It's time to question whether the industrial megafarm model is the only way to feed a growing global population or whether it's even possible for such a system to survive without costly government supports and unsustainable environmental practices." This book should inspire better, smarter solutions. Get busy.

Marion Nestle

PREFACE

In the late 1990s, I was particularly moved by a National Public Radio feature about US government programs that compensated farmers for maintaining unplanted fields. It was part of a concerted strategy to restore wildlife habitat across the country's farmlands. With the help of a lead biologist at the Natural Resources Conservation Service, I traveled extensively looking for the best examples of these government efforts. I saw grassland recovery in the Prairie Pothole Region, bayou and black bear restoration in Texarkana, panther habitat in southern Florida, riparian rewilding in the Sacramento Valley, and bobwhite quail reforestation in North Carolina, to name a few. This reporting provided a firsthand introduction to the pros and cons of US agriculture policy and formed an important chapter in my book *Farming with the Wild: Enhancing Biodiversity on Farms and Ranches*.

A few years later, I found myself sitting in a conference in Sacramento prior to the debates around what was the forthcoming 2007 Farm Bill. Speaker after speaker gave an astonishing account of negative consequences of the tens of billions of dollars spent every year on US agricultural and food assistance policies. It was stunning testimony: impacts to Mexican corn farmers due to years of dumping, a decade of record payouts primarily to large corporate farms that were forcing small- and medium-sized operations out of business, the subsidization of monocultures over vast areas where crops repeatedly failed one of every two years, and a spiraling crisis of diabetes and obesity fueled partially by a diet of cheap processed foods.

It was clear from this conference that the Farm Bill was perhaps the most important legislation that most citizens had never heard of—and one that affected them three meals a day—so I volunteered to be its translator. It proved to be a humbling task. The scale of the bill is so enormous that it's nearly impossible for one person to understand it all. A thick web of technical jargon and acronyms must be unraveled to break policies down to relatable concepts. Perhaps the short time frame was a blessing. It gave me little time to fret about what I had signed up for.

Food Fight: The Citizen's Guide to a Food and Farm Bill was published in early 2007. As the policy debates continued into 2008, I made many dozens of appearances around the country helping audiences understand how Farm Bill policies affected their regions and communities. The book's dynamic graphic approach gave readers easy access to extremely technical information. *Food Fight* was quickly adopted by university instructors and garnered wide mainstream media attention. It also directly inspired important efforts such as Wholesome Wave's farmers market food stamp incentives, health impact studies within the Centers for Disease Control and Prevention, and the City of Seattle's Farm Bill Principles.

A significant revision of the book was undertaken in anticipation of the 2012 Farm Bill reauthorization, which stretched into 2014. Since 1990, the legislation has been renewed every six years, often with significant new directions. In 2016, Island Press approached me about reintroducing the book with an even more direct and accessible format. Thanks to a concerted effort by Christina Badaracco, graphic designer Timothy Rice, and the team at Island Press, we are pleased to introduce a completely updated and revised primer on this most critical and timely matter.

How can we use the Farm Bill's precious funds to incentivize positive outcomes related to public health, a vibrant and regenerative agriculture, protection of wild nature, and the creation of landscapes resilient to climate change? We hope this book informs and inspires you to become a policy champion in your own life and community.

Dan Imhoff

ACKNOWLEDGMENTS

A book like *The Farm Bill* is only made possible with the careful management of a very large number of details and the help of true authorities in many wide-ranging fields. First, we would like to offer our sincere appreciation to Emily Turner and her team at Island Press. Emily was our editor and champion of this project, and her careful attention is evident throughout every chapter. Graphic designer Timothy Rice, a long-time collaborator, clocked long hours refining charts and illustrations. Many thanks go to Marion Nestle for her kind introduction to the book and many decades as a mentor, thought leader, and guiding voice for policies that promote public health, humane animal stewardship, environmental protection, and scientific and fiscal sanity.

We would like to particularly thank the following individuals, and we apologize in advance if we have somehow failed to acknowledge anyone's contributions. Ferd Hoefner from the National Sustainable Agriculture Coalition provided data about conservation programs. Timothy Wise from Tufts University offered continued support and insight about the impacts of NAFTA and corn dumping. Mary Hendrickson from the University of Missouri shared data and insight about consolidation in the livestock industry. Chris Brown and Patricia Carrillo guided us through ALBA's impressive farmer incubation program. Javier Zamora from JSM Organics gave a most gracious organic farm tour. Elanor Starmer of George Washington University and Rose Hayden-Smith from the University of California, Division of Agriculture and Natural Resources, provided key background about the KYF2 (Know Your Farmer, Know Your Food) initiative.

Thanks go to Honor Eldridge from the Soil Association for her sidebar and international perspective on crop insurance. Tricia Kovacs from USDA's Agricultural Marketing Service offered information about

USDA's Local Food Compass Map. Scott Shimmin from USDA's National Agricultural Statistics Service (NASS) helped in acquiring data about beginning farmers. Letitia Toomer-Jones from USDA's NRCS provided key information about conservation grant applications. Claudia Hitaj from USDA's Economic Research Service (ERS) helped with data about agricultural energy usage, and Marc Ribaudo from USDA's ERS provided data on nutrient management on croplands. Gary R. Keough and Rosemarie Philips from USDA's Natural Resources Conservation Service shared a map of the distribution of beginning farmers. Brenda Carson from USDA's Farm Service Agency shed light on agricultural disaster designations. John-Michael Cross from the Environmental and Energy Study Institute and Andy Olsen from the Environmental Law and Policy Center helped us better fathom the Farm Bill's renewable energy programs. Karen Hansen-Kuhn from the Institute for Agriculture and Trade Policy contributed up-to-date data on corn dumping as well as the sidebar she cowrote with Sophia Murphy.

Lynn Henning shared her unique investigative skills on Farm Bill programs and concentrated animal feeding operations in Michigan. Thanks go to Craig Cox from the Environmental Working Group for reviewing our chapter about ethanol and to Dan Rubenstein from Princeton University, Garrett Graddy-Lovelace from American University, and Nina Ichikawa from the Berkeley Food Institute, who facilitated this collaboration between two authors. Martha Noble again provided her invaluable expertise. Last but not least, thanks go to the supporters of Watershed Media, who for so many years have made this critical work possible. We could not have done it without all of you, and for that we will be eternally grateful.

PART 1

FARM BILL BASICS

1. What Is the Farm Bill?

> The path to reform ultimately leads to government policy.
> As the adage says, we reap what we sow, and in that regard there may be nothing more important than the Farm Bill.

GOVERNMENTS HAVE LONG PLAYED a role in food systems. Thousands of years ago, the stockpiles in palace granaries were distributed during times of need. Such policies may have been more a matter of self-preservation than altruism; passing out free bread, rice, or other staples goes a long way toward preempting rebellion.

Today, most countries accept that governments need to be involved in food production and hunger prevention. Just as a strong defense is regarded as national security, a diverse and well-developed agriculture is regarded as food security. In the United States, the Department of Agriculture (USDA) is charged with this dual mission: support the creation of an abundant food supply and ensure that all citizens receive basic nutrition. A primary mechanism for achieving this mission is federal legislation passed every five to seven years known as the Farm Bill.

Unlike during the Great Depression, when the Farm Bill was first written, the United States is no longer a country interlaced with millions of small, diversified family farms set amid vibrant rural communities. Today the United States is the world's leading industrial agriculture powerhouse, but a large share of production has shifted to nonfamily farms and larger family farms. About 1 percent of US farms are nonfamily farms that account for 10 percent of agricultural production. Large-scale and mid-sized family farms made up 9 percent of all US farms in 2016 but accounted for 60 percent of the value of US agricultural production. Small-scale family operations (less than $350,000 gross cash farm income) accounted for only 26 percent of production but represented 90 percent of US farms.[1]

Feeding more than 320 million citizens is just one part of the contemporary job assignment. The American farmer is also expected to help counter the mounting trade deficit and feed the rest of the world (or so we are told) with a steady stream of exports. Then there's the additional task of supplying feedstock for ethanol, bioplastics, and other products used as replacements for fossil fuels.

To promote this massive farm output, the government has embedded complex subsidies in various sections of the nearly 1,000-page Farm Bill. Land payments, crop insurance, research assistance, export marketing, and many other programs serve to maintain an ample supply of certain foods and commodity crops. The scale of government intervention is such that talk of "free markets" is merely rhetorical. Conventional farmers stay afloat by farming the system rather than growing what might best serve their particular tract of land for the long term or provide for more well-rounded, healthy diets. If the government removes all financial risks from growing corn, offers generous tax breaks to ethanol producers, and writes six-figure checks to feedlot operators, for example, farmers will plant corn and lots of it—even when the real winners are the agribusinesses and food manufacturers that buy it.

This scenario plays out each spring during what's called the fight for dirt, when American farmers decide how much land to devote to each commodity crop. Corn wins easily and is grown on upward of 90 million acres of farmland, an area roughly the size of the entire state of Montana. Figure 1 highlights many of the effects of this massive production.

Then, because American farmers export 40 percent of the world's corn and almost 40 percent of the soybeans, these choices ripple across global commodity markets.[2] Farmers who grow corn, cot-ton, wheat, rice, or soybeans in countries without strong subsidy programs can be severely disadvantaged. According to Tufts University agricultural researcher Timothy Wise, the dumping of subsidized US corn on the Mexican market, for instance, cost Mexico's farmers as much as $200 per acre per year from the passage of the North American Free Trade Agreement in 1994 until 2010.[3] An estimated 2.3 million small farmers in Mexico were forced to look for other work in the burgeoning maquiladoras—manufacturing factories and sweatshops of US corporations in cities like Juarez and Matamoros—or in fields, orchards, vineyards, slaughter plants, and other sectors across the border to the north. At the same time, subsidization of corn for ethanol drove up prices of corn exports in Mexico, increasing food prices and resulting in food insecurity. Although Mexico grows predominantly white ("food") corn that is distinct from American yellow ("field") corn, their prices are closely correlated.[4] Rising prices prevented further dumping in subsequent years, but recent evidence suggests that low prices are again driving US dumping in export markets.[5]

Massive farm worker migration is just one of the social costs of the government subsidizing an oversupply of corn. Others are harder to measure. For instance, most corn that American farmers grow isn't eaten by people. Instead, it is fed to animals in livestock warehouses and feedlots. It is fermented into ethanol (with the residual grains fed to animals) or turned into sweeteners and hundreds of other manufactured food ingredients. It contributes to a food system that relies heavily on farm chemicals, processing, packaging, and fossil fuels.

The irony is that all this work conflicts with the government's other major tasks in overseeing the

Figure 1

Effects of Cornification

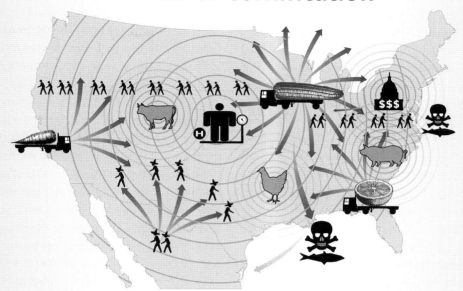

Taxpayer Subsidies. Direct payments and crop insurance totaling nearly $2.4 billion helped make corn the predominant crop in 2014. Many small- and medium-sized farmers depend on subsides to survive while large operators use subsidies to get bigger.

Corn Surpluses. 15.1 billion bushels were produced on more than 86 million acres in 2016. This created a surplus stock of 2.1 billion bushels. Very little of the corn is actually fed directly to humans. Most goes to animal feed or is processed into starches, corn oil, sweeteners, or ethanol for our gas tanks.

Concentrated Animal Feeding Operations. Confinement facilities, largely made possible and profitable through the low costs of subsidized feed, house tens of thousands of hogs, chickens, or cattle. Heavy concentrations of animal wastes, odor pollution, reliance on antibiotics, and dangerous workplaces are just a few of the many health concerns.

Food Deserts. Monoculture specialization of corn and other grains for export is the reason we see "so much agriculture, so little food" in farming areas. Impoverished inner-city areas, where access to supermarkets or farmers markets is limited or nonexistent, also become food deserts.

Dead Zones. Nutrient and chemical runoff from farms in the Corn Belt flow through the Mississippi River watershed and have created a dead zone in the Gulf of Mexico, decimating fish and other marine life. There are dozens of other agriculturally induced hypoxic zones, including in the Chesapeake Bay.

Food Miles. Processed foods now travel more than 1,300 miles and fresh produce travels more than 1,500 miles from farm to table. California, Florida, and a number of other states (and a growing number of countries) supply the nation's supermarkets with fruits and vegetables. Relatively little of this specialty crop production is supported by federal programs.

Immigration. After the implementation of NAFTA in 1994, an estimated 1 .3 to 2.3 million Mexican campesinos were forced to leave their lands and move elsewhere in Mexico or in the US to attain employment. Subsidized US corn, combined with the NAFTA trade agreement, had a catastrophic effect on Mexican farmers.

Rural Exodus. The farmer replacement rate has fallen as the number of beginning farmers replacing aging farmers has decreased by more than 23% in the last five years. Farmers are now 17 years older than the average American worker, and we have more farmers over the age of 75 than between 35 and 44. Many wonder if the United States may permanently lose the skills and productive farmland to remain an agricultural leader.

Obesity Crisis. The proportion of Americans who are overweight or obese climbed to 70.7% in 2014 and the child obesity rate has more than tripled since the 1970s (now at 17%). Lack of physical activity and poor nutrition—linked to subsidized and super-sized processed foods high in sugar, fat, and sodium—lie at the root of the epidemic.

food system: establishing healthy dietary guidelines and doling out nutrition assistance to those who are hungry. It might seem that subsidizing an industrial food system would make food inexpensive and abundant for everyone. The reality, however, is that enrollment in the Supplemental Nutrition Assistance Program, or SNAP (formerly called food stamps), hit an all-time high of almost 48 million participants in 2013.[6] In 2016, more than 41.2 million people were living in "food-insecure" households, implying that they lacked consistent and sufficient food for active, healthy lives.[7]

What's more, all the mountains of cheap food haven't made us healthy, either. Indeed, our epidemic of obesity hits the poor hardest. Fresh fruits, vegetables, and whole grains—the foods most recommended by USDA dietary guidelines—are largely ignored by Farm Bill policies. We have become overeaters of the wrong things, and many critics say that Farm Bill policies are at least partially at fault and can play a dynamic role in reversing this crisis.

Today's global headlines reflect crops unable to adapt to rising temperatures, spiking health costs due to high obesity rates, food shortages in certain areas of the world, and disease outbreaks emanating from ever-larger meat-, milk-, and egg-producing animal factories. The number of people affected, and worried, about these problems is growing, and, increasingly, they are realizing that the path to reform ultimately leads to government policy. As the adage says, we reap what we sow, and in that regard there may be nothing more important than the Farm Bill.

2. Why Does the Farm Bill Matter?

As a result of the Farm Bill, citizens pay a national food bill at least three times: (1) at the checkout stand, (2) in taxes that subsidize commodity crop production, and (3) in environmental cleanup and medical costs.

ON ONE LEVEL, we could make this a very short read by simply stating that although the Farm Bill does matter to the average US citizen, it is a fully rigged game run by the immensely powerful farm lobbies and monopolies that profit mightily from how our food is grown, processed, marketed, and distributed. Concerned citizens who do want to change an unfair and unhealthy system for the better are going to fall short of reform. Sadly, that may be all too true. The next Farm Bill will probably continue to prop up the industrial agriculture complex with tens of billions of taxpayer dollars annually, as it has done for decades. But our nation's food and farming system is far too important to us all to forgo serious debate and the hard work needed to achieve urgent reforms.

Here's why.

If you eat, pay taxes, care about biodiversity, worry about the quality of school lunches, or notice the loss of farmland and woodlands, you have a personal stake in the Farm Bill. If you're concerned about escalating federal budget deficits, the fate of family farmers, working conditions for immigrant farm laborers, the persistence of hunger and poverty, or how we support local and organic and pasture-raised food, you should pay attention to the Farm Bill. There are dozens more reasons the Farm Bill, and its attendant tens of billions of dollars, is critical to our land, our bodies, and our children's future (figure 2 gives a full list of problems and solutions). They include:

- The twilight of the cheap oil age;
- The onset of unpredictable climatic conditions;
- Looming water shortages;
- Increasing dead zones caused in part by agricultural runoff;

Figure 2

COURSE CORRECTION

Americans deserve a Farm Bill that addresses the challenges of the times. Current Farm Bill programs shovel money to the largest producers and don't properly support the small- and medium-sized growers, otherwise known as the "agriculture of the middle." Our system is overloaded with animal products and processed foods and short on fresh fruits and vegetables.

With record budget deficits, rising energy costs, an unpredictable climate, and skyrocketing health costs driven largely by preventable diseases, we can't afford not to act. Future Farm Bills must look forward to ensure that we have a farmer population actively engaged in growing healthy foods, conservation incentives that protect our natural resources from contamination and overexploitation, research that gives farmers valuable tools, and nutrition programs that ensure healthy and affordable food for all.

PRESENT CHALLENGES

Consolidation and concentration in the hands of a few corporate agribusinesses

Soil and biodiversity loss

Converging national healthcare crises

Childhood obesity at an all-time high; chronic hunger and inadequate nutrition that affect almost 45 million Americans

Sprawl into prime farmland

Record budget deficits

World Trade Organization rulings declaring US export subsidies illegal

Devastated farm communities

Rapidly aging US farmer population

Fluctuating energy costs

Increasing dependence on commodity exports and imports of "fresh" food

Water contamination and water shortages

Global warming

Increasing outbreaks of infectious diseases related to confined livestock production

Declining honeybee and native pollinator populations

Costly ethanol program

SOLUTIONS PROPOSED BY FARM BILL REFORMERS

Limit payments to individual recipients to level the playing field for all farmers; reform meat-packer regulations to break monopoly control of livestock industry; protect small and mid-sized farmers

Include requirements for on-farm conservation for all insurance and subsidy programs; make no net soil loss a goal of farm programs through fully enforced Sodsaver, Sodbuster, and Swampbuster provisions

Better align crop supports with the most recent Dietary Guidelines for Americans; launch nationwide farm-to-school, farm-to-college, and other fresh food distribution programs that also include a strong educational and fitness component

Maintain food assistance programs including improved access to healthy foods; expand funding for SNAP-Ed and SNAP at farmers markets; ensure that every American has access to affordable, healthy food

Increase funding to keep farmland and ranchland in agricultural use and open space rather than subdivisions and sprawl

Make spending serve as true public investment with targeted results; combine funding sources

Shift subsidies toward green payments, such as the Conservation Stewardship Program, which rewards farmers for environmental caretaking rather than overproducing export crops

Invest and offer loans to revitalize and diversify the rural sector; rebuild livestock processing infrastructure

Add 100,000 new farmers and ranchers over the course of the next Farm Bill

Expand research into energy-effective farming systems and increase support for on-farm energy conservation and renewable energy infrastructure

Invest in value-added processing and flexible supports for more diversified local and regional "specialty crops"; increase funding for efforts like the Fresh Fruit and Vegetable Program in schools

Increase incentives for farming systems that protect watersheds; research alternatives to synthetic fertilizers

Incentivize energy conservation, carbon sequestration, and pasture-based agriculture; implement cap-and-trade

Expand grass-pastured livestock operations; place a moratorium on new CAFO creation; eliminate EQIP funding for CAFO waste management; phase out nonveterinary, preventative antibiotic use in livestock

Expand wild habitat for native pollinators in and around farms; adapt new programs for beekeepers

End Renewable Fuel Standard that mandates corn ethanol use; evaluate role for advanced biofuels; increase fuel efficiency

- An aging farm population and lack of opportunity for young farmers;
- Expansion of corn ethanol production;
- Escalating medical costs related to obesity with a food system deficient in nutrition education and access to healthy foods;
- Taxpayer subsidies to corporate farms regardless of economic need;
- 44 million Americans, including 15 million children, who don't get enough to eat.[1]

The Farm Bill matters because it makes some big mega-farms scandalously rich while it drives family farmers out of business. It makes us fat, yet at the same time it produces a fragile (rather than a resilient) food system. It supports destructive monoculture farming practices and then spends billions trying to put bandages on the damage. It artificially sets prices while officials tout the virtues of "free markets" and "fair trade." Its consequences contribute to poverty, rural exodus, and famine.[2]

Subsidies, now predominantly in the form of insurance, do provide a critical safety net in some years to family farms that continue to grow commodity crops, helping them survive in unpredictable weather conditions and a competitive global economy. But the biggest beneficiaries are absentee landlords, tractor dealers, and banks and insurance companies that service farmers as well as the corporate agribusinesses, grain distributors, animal feeding operations, and ethanol producers that purchase subsidized crops. What started as an ambitious temporary effort to lift millions of Americans out of economic and ecological desperation during the Great Depression and Dust Bowl (supported initially by a tax on food processors) devolved over decades into a corporate boondoggle. As a result of the Farm Bill,

citizens pay a national food bill at least three times: (1) at the checkout stand, (2) in taxes that subsidize commodity crop production, and (3) in environmental cleanup and medical costs related to the consequences of industrial commodity-based agriculture.

Most analysts, most legislators, and even many farmers agree that our present course leaves the United States unprepared to meet many of the urgent twenty-first-century challenges outlined above. The silver lining is that Americans *actually have* a substantial food and farm policy to debate. Conditions for change are ripe, but a national movement with the political power to demand progressive reforms has been slow to materialize.

Our challenge is not to abolish government support; rather, it is to make certain we are investing in a viable future for our food system.

The Farm Bill matters because much-needed funds can drive small-scale entrepreneurship, on-farm research, species protection, nutritional assistance, healthy school lunches, job creation, and habitat restoration. Our challenge is not to abolish government support; rather, it is to make certain we are investing in a viable future for our food system. That responsibility now rests primarily with the parties who control the House and Senate Agriculture Committees that write the Farm Bill. Will they continue massive giveaways to corporations and surplus commodity producers, or will they reward stewardship, promote healthy diets, enhance regional food production, support family farms, address climate change, and make it easier for hungry families to eat healthy foods?

3. Who Benefits from the Farm Bill?

> Omnibus legislation: a law that addresses multiple issues simultaneously.

THE FARM BILL IS DECEPTIVELY SIMPLE SHORTHAND for the gargantuan package of legislation about food and farming that the US Congress drafts, debates, and ultimately passes every five to seven years. Each bill, as well as the drafts now under consideration, actually has a formal name—such as the Food and Agriculture Act of 1977; the Federal Agriculture Improvement and Reform Act of 1996; the Farm Security and Rural Investment Act of 2002; the Food, Conservation, and Energy Act of 2008; the Agricultural Act of 2014—but people generally refer to each as simply "the Farm Bill." Since its origins in 1933 as the Agricultural Adjustment Act, the bill has snowballed into one of the most—if not the most—significant legislative measures affecting land use in the United States.

The Farm Bill is an omnibus legislation because it simultaneously addresses multiple issues. However, modern Farm Bills traditionally have three primary thrusts: (1) food nutrition programs (now about 80 percent of gross outlays), (2) income and price supports for commodity crops and other forms of crop insurance (about 13 percent), and (3) conservation incentives (about 6 percent). In addition, the Farm Bill organizes its spending categories into "titles." These categories include trade and foreign food aid, forestry (because forests and woodlots are important components of farms), agricultural credit, rural development, research and education, nutrition, conservation, commodity programs, energy, horticulture, crop insurance, and miscellaneous (such as disease monitoring in aquaculture)[1] (figure 3). A number of policies, such as food assistance, conservation, agricultural trade, credit, rural development, and research, are actually governed by both the Farm Bill and a variety of separate laws, which are sometimes renewed or

Farm Bill Titles

The order and total number of Farm Bill titles vary from bill to bill. In the 2014 Farm Bill, the titles run as follows:

Title 1: Commodities

Title 2: Conservation

Title 3: Trade

Title 4: Nutrition

Title 5: Credit

Title 6: Rural Development

Title 7: Research, Extension, and Related Matters

Title 8: Forestry

Title 9: Energy

Title 10: Horticulture

Title 11: Crop Insurance

Title 12: Miscellaneous

Mandatory Spending

Programs with mandatory funding are generally assured, whereas programs with discretionary funding survive and perish at the hands of the House and Senate Appropriations Committees. Certain program categories have achieved baseline levels of funding over the decades.

Commodity Programs (1930s)

Nutrition Assistance Programs (1960s)

Conservation (1980s)

Rural Development, Research, and Horticulture (late 1990s)

Crop Insurance (2000)

Farm Bill Names

Each Farm Bill is actually a reauthorization of the programs dating back to the 1930s as well as an authorization of new programs.

Agricultural Adjustment Act of 1933

Agricultural Adjustment Act of 1938

Agricultural Act of 1948

Agricultural Act of 1949

Agricultural Act of 1954

Agricultural Act of 1956

Food and Agricultural Act of 1965

Agricultural Act of 1970

Agricultural and Consumer Protection Act of 1973

Food and Agriculture Act of 1977

Agriculture and Food Act of 1981

Food Security Act of 1985

Food, Agriculture, Conservation, and Trade Act of 1990

Federal Agriculture Improvement and Reform Act of 1996

Farm Security and Rural Investment Act of 2002

Food, Conservation, and Energy Act of 2008

Agricultural Act of 2014

modified as stand-alone bills. (The Child Nutrition Act, the Clean Water Act, and the Food Safety Modernization Act are recent examples of stand-alone legislation that addresses food and agriculture issues.) Increasingly, though, Congress prefers to combine many of these laws into a single, mammoth reauthorization of multiple statutes at the same time it renews the farm commodity programs.[2] This omnibus nature of the Farm Bill keeps the public in the dark: it's nearly impossible for any one person to understand the full extent of everything that's covered.

Although more than three-fourths of the Farm Bill budget is currently devoted to safety net nutrition programs, it is commodity subsidies, crop insurance, and price supports that most people equate with the heart of the legislation.[3] At their noblest, subsidy payments to farmers are intended to provide an income safety net in this economically and meteorologically volatile profession, thereby protecting the food supply and strengthening rural communities. Some programs genuinely invest in the long-term stability of the food supply and stewardship of the land. That was particularly true in the 1930s and 1940s, when the bill's defining goals involved idling land to prevent oversupply of crops and installing contour strips to protect the soil in exchange for loans and price supports for storable foods.

Along the way, though, the Farm Bill became an engine driving surplus production of commodity crops and a gravy train for powerful corporations that purchased and traded them. The bill's original focus on the public good was derailed. After modest reforms over five decades, political realities and global economics collided in the 1980s. Increased

global trade, the call for less government spending, the concentration of food distribution and processing centers, and low commodity prices took a toll on the farm sector and rural communities. Corporate agribusinesses and mega-farms then succeeded in tilting subsidies completely in their favor. Although control of today's agriculture is concentrated in a small number of corporate operations, the public perception of US agriculture is still rooted in nostalgic notions like the father and daughter in Grant Wood's classic painting *American Gothic*, the illustrations of Norman Rockwell, and the iconic images of the Western cowboy.

Many Americans believe, for example, that the tens of billions of dollars the government spends on agriculture primarily support farms where a husband and wife work from dawn to dusk growing crops, with roosters crowing from fence posts and cows grazing on rolling pastures. The real picture is not so idyllic. Commodity payments primarily go to large monoculture operators who grow corn and other feed grains, wheat and other food grains, rice, peanuts, sugar, cotton, soy, and oilseeds as well as to dairy producers. Three in four farmers get no commodity payments at all. Meanwhile, the top 5 percent of subsidy recipients (often producer cooperatives, Native American tribes, and large corporate entities) averaged more than $700,000 each between 1995 and 2016.[4,5] Another common perception is that Farm Bill subsidies that pay farmers not to grow crops have made soil erosion a relic of the Dust Bowl. Less than 10 percent of the US Department of Agriculture (USDA) budget is linked to conservation practices, however. According to the USDA's Natural Resources Conservation Service, nearly 2 billion tons of cropland soil—our most valuable nonrenewable

Figure 3

HOW THE FARM BILL

NUTRITION, FARM, AND CONSERVATION SPENDING

Gross Outlays Averaged Over Twelve Distinct Appropriations 2014–2018

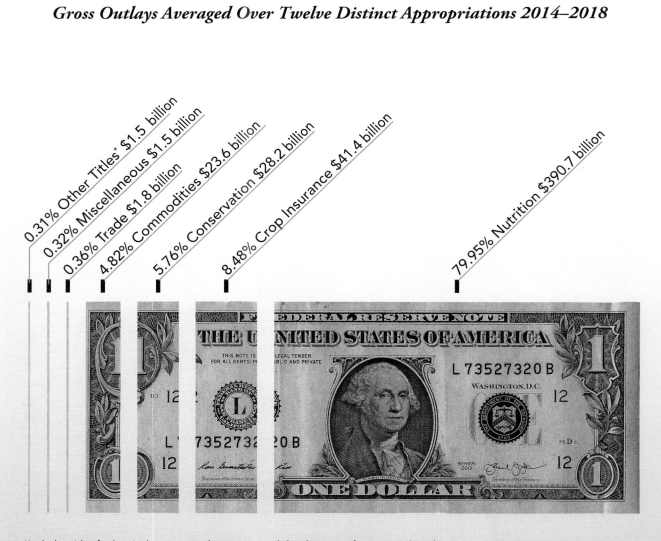

0.31% Other Titles* $1.5 billion

0.32% Miscellaneous $1.5 billion

0.36% Trade $1.8 billion

4.82% Commodities $23.6 billion

5.76% Conservation $28.2 billion

8.48% Crop Insurance $41.4 billion

79.95% Nutrition $390.7 billion

*Includes titles for horticulture, research, energy, rural development, forestry, and credit.

SPENDS A TAX DOLLAR

TAKING SNAP OUT OF THE EQUATION

Gross Outlays Averaged Over Eleven Distinct Appropriations 2014–2018

1.55% Other Titles* $1.5 billion

1.58% Miscellaneous $1.5 billion

1.82% Trade $1.8 billion

25.10% Commodities $23.6 billion

28.75% Conservation $28.2 billion

42.27% Crop Insurance $41.4 billion

Source: Renée Johnson and Jim Monke, "What Is the Farm Bill?," Report RS22131, Congressional Research Service, 2017.

Crop Subsidies at a Glance

Taxpayer-funded programs have taken most of the financial risks out of modern farming in the United States. Growers plant all they want and have a government security blanket for guaranteed income.

Crop insurance—Taxpayers pay about 60 percent of crop insurance premiums that cover nearly 80 percent of insurable acres.[a] This system of risk-free farming is rapidly expanding. Critics say that it encourages expansion of crop production into highly sensitive marginal lands and is just another taxpayer-financed income transfer. A new Stacked Income Protection Plan for upland cotton covers a portion of the expected revenue in each county. This plan was instituted in response to a World Trade Organization ruling brought by Brazil against US cotton subsidy payments.[b] In addition, the Supplemental Coverage Option subsidizes premiums for commodities that are covered by other plans.

Counter-cyclical payments—Also repealed by the 2014 Farm Bill, counter-cyclical payments formerly compensated farmers when the price of commodity crops dropped below a target price established by Congress. They were also tied to historical commodity base acres. Producers could even receive payments for crops they no longer grew.

Dairy subsidies—The Dairy Producer Margin Protection Program (DPMPP) replaced the former Milk Income Loss Contract program, which compensated dairy producers when the average monthly price of milk fell below government targets. DPMPP protects dairies from low operating margins that are set by the producers themselves. A new Dairy Product Donation Program also purchases dairy products to donate to nonprofit organizations when margins are low. Tariffs on dairy imports continue to limit supplies to boost milk prices.

Direct payments—Until repealed under the 2014 Farm Bill, landowners received direct payments according to historical land use—"base acres"—even in years of record income and even if they did not plant commodity crops that year. Direct payments were crop-specific. Half of US farms were ineligible for the $5 billion distributed each year because they did not grow commodity crops.

Disaster assistance—Average Crop Revenue Election was a revenue loss guarantee repealed by the 2014 Farm Bill. In recent years, the program had paid nearly $800 million per year to farmers enrolled in the program. Also now repealed, the Supplemental Revenue Assistance Payments Program reimbursed total crop revenue loss for the entire farm. These payments could be supplemented with ad hoc emergency disaster funding. Current programs include supplemental disaster assistance programs for livestock and fruit trees, emergency loans for crops and livestock, and lower-interest loans for farms not eligible for commercial credit.

Federal purchase programs—The US government purchases surplus meat, eggs, dairy, vegetables, fruits, grains, and other farm products for distribution to the National School Lunch Program and other various food assistance programs.

Livestock supports—The Environmental Quality Incentives Program offers hundreds of thousands of dollars in cost-share assistance to help concentrated animal feeding operations comply with clean air and water regulations. Food animal producers receive assistance through a suite of other programs: the Livestock Compensation Program, Emergency Livestock Feed Assistance, the Livestock Emergency Assistance Program, and the Livestock Indemnity Program.

Marketing assistance loans—Producers take out marketing assistance loans, using their commodity crops as collateral, and then hold the crops to sell as prices rise. If prices fall below the loan repayment rate, however, the government will accept crops as payment. Producers may receive a loan deficiency payment to cover any gap between the market price and the guaranteed price.

Risk coverage—New to the 2014 Farm Bill, Agricultural Risk Coverage and Price Loss Coverage are commodity payments that go into effect when a county-level crop revenue falls below a guaranteed amount or when the effective price falls below a reference price, respectively. They are expected to together cost taxpayers up to $5 billion per year.[c] Marketing Assistance Loans offer loan deficiency payments if prices fall below preset rates.

Sugar program—Quotas limit the amount of sugar that can be imported, and from where, to protect US corn and beet growers. These quotas can hurt unsubsidized farmers in other countries because putting the US market off limits deflates prices.

NOTES

a. "Crop Insurance Primer," Environmental Working Group, accessed March 5, 2018.

b. Renée Johnson, "Previewing a 2018 Farm Bill," Congressional Research Service, Report R44784, March 15, 2017.

c. Integrated Policy Group, "U.S. Baseline Briefing Book Projections for Agricultural and Biofuel Markets," University of Missouri Food and Agricultural Research Group, March 2015.

resource—are still lost every year.[6,7] Ethanol subsidies and generous crop insurance policies are encouraging an expansion of corn production and along with it risking a precarious escalation in soil erosion. More than one-half of agricultural counties in the United States were designated as disaster areas from 2012 to 2016.[8] This situation is simply unsustainable in the long term. There can be no farming without healthy soils.

Proponents frequently claim that the Farm Bill underwrites the cheapest and most nutritious food system in the world. But today's beneficiaries are truly large corporations, not consumers. The US food system encourages heart disease, diabetes, and other ills, which take a toll on individual lives as well as on our collective pocketbook. Healthcare costs for obesity alone are estimated to be between $147 billion and $210 billion per year in the United States.[9]

In essence, the Farm Bill has been hijacked by the powers dominating the industrial food system. What should be the government's best effort to invest in the finest food system possible for its people instead has created a concentration of wealth and production that we are frequently told is simply too big to fail.

Despite the dysfunction, however, the Farm Bill still represents one of our best chances to create a truly vibrant food system that fairly compensates family farmers, cares for those most in need, and conserves natural resources for future generations. More than anything, the Farm Bill is a snapshot of our democratic process in action, one that demands close attention from anyone who votes—or eats.

4. How Does the Farm Bill Work?

Flat-funding: when the moneys authorized for certain programs are cut in the appropriations process.

EVERY FARM BILL GOES THROUGH TWO DISTINCT PHASES. First comes the *authorization* of the bill itself—technically the reauthorization of the existing bill dating back to the 1930s, along with the introduction of any new programs. The Senate and House Agriculture Committees negotiate a balance among the many competing interests served by the Farm Bill and determine how taxpayer funding should be allocated. The result is essentially a set of promises made by Congress about the direction of US farming and food policy.[1]

Some programs acquire "mandatory funding" status in the reauthorization process, a signal that support for these programs should be made available throughout the term of the legislation. Other programs receive "discretionary funding" status, meaning that their fates rest on the Farm Bill's second phase—the yearly *appropriations* process (figure 4). The appropriations phase involves reinterpreting Farm Bill funding priorities every year with revised budgets, to create, in essence, a series of "mini Farm Bills."

The final say on whether a Farm Bill program actually receives money rests with the Agriculture Subcommittees of the Senate and House Appropriations Committees. These subcommittees set spending levels and thus determine the yearly survival of the discretionary Farm Bill programs. But their powers don't end there. The Appropriation Subcommittees can also pass changes in funding to the mandatory programs. If Congress approves such changes through the annual Agricultural Appropriations legislation, the Farm Bill's funding directives for that year are overridden. Flat-funding is one inside-the-Beltway term used to describe this process. ChIMPS, short for Changes in Mandatory Program Spending, is another. (So much for those

Figure 4

The Two Lives of Every Farm Bill

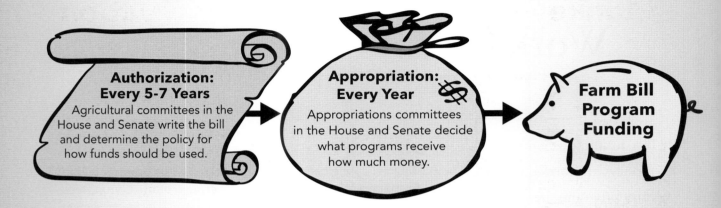

Authorization: Every 5-7 Years
Agricultural committees in the House and Senate write the bill and determine the policy for how funds should be used.

Appropriation: Every Year
Appropriations committees in the House and Senate decide what programs receive how much money.

Farm Bill Program Funding

mandatory dollars promised for land conservation, organic agriculture research, or expansion of farmers markets!)

As a rule of thumb, commodity price supports are the only untouchable spending categories in the appropriations process. If anything, commodity growers successfully lobby for more money, not less, through supplemental disaster payments in

---

Budget reconciliation: a budget-cutting exercise that can affect authorized program funding levels in the middle of a Farm Bill cycle.

---

response to floods, droughts, market fluctuations, or other circumstances. Programs that serve the broader public, however—conservation incentives, sustainable agriculture research funds, beginning farmer supports, farm-to-school distribution arrangements, food assistance for mothers and children, and so on—are historically the first on the chopping block.

Flat-funding, ChIMPing, and other forms of budget tinkering don't necessarily end with the annual appropriations process. In response to a projected deficit, Congress can also demand *budget reconciliation*, forcing committees to recalculate their budgets and further decrease spending for mandatory and discretionary programs. For example, after the 2002 Farm Bill passed, the reconciliation process tilted spending even further toward mega-agriculture, slashing conservation and farm-to-school programs while giving away billions in loan deficiency and counter-cyclical payments to compensate commodity growers for low market prices. It happened again during the 2014 Farm Bill, substantially reducing important conservation programs while continuing to fund commodity

Figure 5

Monkeying Around with Conservation

Nearly $2 Billion Cut from Farm Bill Conservation Programs 2011–2017

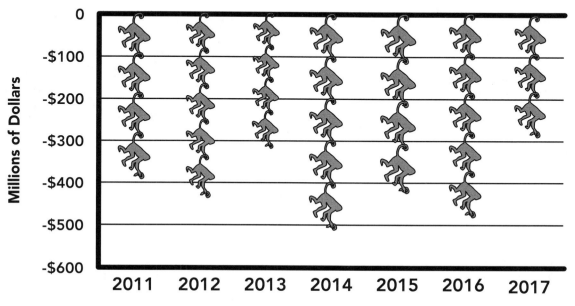

Changes in Mandatory Program Spending (ChIMPS)*

*ChIMPing figures include mandatory sequestration

Source: "Agriculture Appropriations Chart Fiscal Year 2015," National Sustainable Agriculture Coalition, 2014; "Agriculture Appropriations Chart Fiscal Year 2019," National Sustainable Agriculture Coalition, 2018.

supports. Such cuts have long-lasting budgetary effects. Reducing the baseline for a program in the middle of a Farm Bill can automatically trigger new lower spending levels in the next omnibus Farm Bill legislation.

The importance of the yearly money battles cannot be overstated. Regardless of promises in the Farm Bill, if no money is appropriated to carry out

the work, the program is dead. One example is the Conservation Stewardship Program (CSP), added in 2008. This initiative to reward farmers for environmental stewardship (rather than maximizing yields and acreage) was the primary concession offered to an alliance of conservationists and sustainable farming advocates during the 2002 Farm Bill negotiations. It was widely heralded as the best way to reform US farm policies, with new supports based on green payments—financial incentives for landowners to maximize environmental benefits like stable soil, clean water, and species protection. It represented a new conservation approach to farm support by "rewarding the best and motivating the rest" and offering subsidies to a population of small producers long ignored because of the focus on commodity agriculture. Among other practices, qualifying participants have to actively prevent manure from polluting waterways, limit fertilizers from entering streams, minimize or eliminate pesticide use, improve energy efficiency, and set aside habitat for wildlife.

But flat-funding of conservation programs has been sadly all too typical. The 2002 Farm Bill promised that the CSP would have equal funding status with the Commodities title and that all US farmers would be able to apply for conservation-related farm supports. That never happened. In fiscal year 2005, Farm Bill conservation programs were cut by nearly one-third, meaning that the backlog of qualified, underfunded applications seeking to protect habitat on both agricultural and nonagricultural lands far exceeded support. Further slices to the CSP budget occurred in 2007, with $113 million taken from what had been promised. As recently as 2015, 75 percent of qualified applicants to the CSP program were not able to enroll due to this same ChIMPing.[2] In 2018, some legislators were working to eliminate this green payments program altogether.

That's just the beginning. In 2014, the Environmental Quality Incentives Program funding was cut by $274 million due to ChIMPS, and an additional $126 million was slashed as part of an attempt to reduce the federal budget deficit. This sequestration process began in 2011 as the Office of Management and Budget mandated reductions to budgets across federal agencies.[3] Although this change applied to most programs funded by the Farm Bill, including commodity payments, other conservation program payments, such as for the Conservation Reserve Program, were actually exempt from mandatory cuts.[4] See figure 5 for ChIMPing estimates from 2011 to 2017.

It's not only conservation programs that are targeted. Renewable energy programs lost almost half of their funding in the 2014 Farm Bill, followed by additional cuts due to ChIMPing. The Rural Energy for America Program and the Biomass Crop Assistance Program, both intended to support renewable energy or biomass production on farms, were cut by 30 percent and 52 percent, respectively.[5]

In addition to budget slashing, appropriations committees often assume interpretive legislative powers. For example, the Agriculture Appropriations Committees pushed back the implementation of the mandatory Country of Origin Labeling, or COOL, program—established by the 2002 bill to inform consumers where their perishable foods originated—for four years, from September 2004 to September 2008. Congress repealed this law in 2015 in response to a World Trade Organization ruling that Canada and Mexico could place tariffs on US products because of these supposedly unfair labeling requirements. The Agriculture Appropriations Committees also tinkered with organic standards by voting to allow non-organic-certified additives and ingredients in certified organic processed foods. Changes to the organic standards were ultimately dropped due to significant public resistance. More recently, a 2017 bill changed or delayed some of the nutrition standards that schools must follow to be eligible to receive federal reimbursement for the meals they serve. Although unrelated to the amount of funding spent on the National School Lunch Program, these changes, such as loosening whole grain standards and delaying stricter sodium requirements, affect the food that ends up on school lunch trays. Suppliers and manufacturers continue to reformulate foods in response to these lowered federal standards, with important consequences for our children.

In short, authorization of the Farm Bill signals the beginning—not the end—of the annual appropriation struggles that ensue throughout the life of the legislation. If any constituency (besides that of commodity producers) hopes to see promised Farm Bill funds, they must be prepared to fight tooth and nail every year.

PART II

THE HISTORY OF FOOD POLICY

Migrant mother, Nipomo, California, 1936 © Dorothea Lange

5. Origins of the Farm Bill

America during the Great Depression was a hungry nation whose most valuable natural resource—the soil—was literally blowing away.

THE IDEA OF A NATION BUILT BY HARD-WORKING, God-fearing farmers taps a deep nerve in the American psyche. In 1801, when Thomas Jefferson became the United States' third president, 95 percent of the population of the young nation made a full-time living from agriculture. Jefferson envisioned the United States' democracy as orbiting around a citizenry of yeomen farmers. He wrote:

> Cultivators of the earth are the most valuable citizens. They are the most vigorous, the most independent, the most virtuous and they are tied to the country and wedded to its liberty and interests by the most lasting bonds. I think our governments will remain virtuous for many centuries so long as they are chiefly agricultural.[1]

Half a century later, Abraham Lincoln extended this vision by establishing the railroad land grants, the Morrill Land Grant College Act of 1862, and the Homestead Act of 1862, all intended to spread independence, encourage settlement, and foster stability.

As the decades wore on, though, wave upon wave of new settlers—bringing with them crops, domesticated livestock, and farming methods often not well suited to the land—exploited the continent's natural resources. By the early twentieth century, more than half the population had moved off farmland. It was becoming clear that Jefferson's notion of an agrarian democracy was giving way to an urban industrial society with fewer and fewer farmers growing its food. For many, fewer people working in agriculture was a sure sign of prosperity as it meant a growth of manufacturing and service sectors of the economy.

It took the Dust Bowl and the Great Depression to bring on total collapse of the agrarian-democratic ideal. By the 1930s, one in four Americans still lived on a farm, but increasing numbers of tenant farmers and sharecroppers were being forced from their land or pushed into desperate poverty. Farm foreclosures had become commonplace. Drought, searing heat, dust storms, floods, and monopolistic and unfair market practices also took a punishing toll. The nation's most valuable agricultural resource—the soil—was literally blowing away. On a single Sunday afternoon in 1935, for example, a storm barreling through the Texas Panhandle swept 300,000 tons of topsoil—twice the volume of soil excavated during the entire construction of the Panama Canal—into the air.[2] It ravaged the countryside—choking people and animals, blanketing houses and cars.

By most accounts, the United States was becoming a cauldron of civil unrest. In *The Grapes of Wrath*, John Steinbeck described the situation this way:

> And the dispossessed, the migrants, flowed into California, two hundred and fifty thousand, and three hundred thousand. Behind them new tractors were going on the land and the tenants were being forced off. And new waves were on the way, new waves of the dispossessed and homeless, hard, intent, and dangerous.[3]

Ironically, the farm crisis of the 1930s, like the Dust Bowl, had been triggered by overplanting. A decade of zealous and speculative field expansion, combined with technological advances such as tractors and nitrogen fertilizers synthesized from natural gas, resulted in chronic overproduction of most crops. Oversupply of crops also meant low prices. Falling income levels in rural areas and the rising economic power in the cities created an ever-widening gap in American society.[4]

The nation was rapidly changing. While low crop prices directly benefited distributors, processors, and monopolists who were increasingly controlling the food system, the US agrarian culture and economy were unraveling. To stay afloat, farmers and sharecroppers planted more and more acreage, but this further oversaturated the markets, exacerbated land abuse, and dropped crop prices below what it cost to produce them. Total farm income decreased by two-thirds between 1929 and 1932. Six of every ten farms had been mortgaged to survive, and many did not make it. In the single year of 1932, five of every one hundred farms in Iowa were foreclosed and sold at auction.[5] In 1933, the price of corn plummeted to $0 as grain elevators simply stopped buying surplus corn altogether.[6] In Le Mar, Iowa, a group of angry farmers dragged a judge from his bench and threatened to hang him unless he refused to rule on cases that would result in a family losing its farm. Leaders of the mob were eventually jailed. Even so, there were some advantages to living in the country at this time. After the Wall Street crash, at least farm families could grow most of their own food—something urban folks could not do.

From these extraordinary circumstances, the first Farm Bill emerged and became one of the most ambitious social, cultural, and economic programs ever attempted by the US government. On March 16, 1933, President Franklin Delano Roosevelt addressed Congress about this cornerstone of his New Deal agenda:

> I tell you frankly that this is a new and untrod path, but I tell you with equal frankness that an unprecedented condition calls for the trial of a new means to rescue agriculture. If a fair administrative trial of it is made and it does not produce the hoped for results I shall be the first to acknowledge it and advise you.

Administered by Secretary of Agriculture Henry A. Wallace, the early Farm Bill responded directly to a number of crises:

- Rock-bottom crop prices due to overproduction;
- Widespread hunger;
- Catastrophic erosion and soil loss due to prolonged drought and poor land stewardship;
- Unavailability of credit and insurance to subsistence farmers;
- Need for electricity, water, and infrastructure in rural communities;
- Unfair export policies prohibiting free and fair trade;
- Increasing civil unrest.

Henry Wallace was a gifted, lifelong farmer, a vegetarian, and a spiritual seeker whose father had also served as a secretary of agriculture. Under Wallace's direction, the US Department of Agriculture (USDA) blossomed into one of the largest arms of the government, with more than 146,000 employees and a budget of more than $1 billion. In 2017, its

yearly budget was about $150 billion (still less than 4 percent of the total federal budget).[7]

A driving principle of Wallace's administration was the creation of a farm support program based on a concept known as the Ever-Normal Granary. This initiative took its historical precedent from ancient times, traceable to both Confucian China and the biblical story of Joseph.[8] The idea was straightforward, but politically controversial. The government would purchase and stockpile surplus crops and livestock during good years as a protection against dwindling supply during lean times. Doing so helped accomplish two important goals: (1) raising market prices for farmers by contracting supply and (2) distributing meat and grain products in times of need.

In addition, in an attempt to prevent overproduction, farmers participating in federally supported programs were required to idle a certain percentage of their historical base acreage. Author Michael Pollan explained how the early programs, such as the early Marketing Assistance Loan, worked to regulate markets:

> For storable commodities such as corn, the government established a target price based on the cost of production, and whenever the market price dropped below the target, the farmer was given a choice. Instead of dumping the corn into a weak market (thereby weakening it further), the farmer could take out a loan from the government—using his crop as collateral—that allowed him to store his grain until prices recovered. At that point he sold the corn and paid back the loan; if corn prices stayed low, he could elect to keep

the money he'd borrowed and, in repayment, give the government his corn, which would then go into something that came to be called, rather quaintly, the "Ever-Normal Granary."[9]

Early Farm Bill programs were also attempts at maintaining fair markets by serving as a balance between farmers and large distributors. Because nonperishable commodities can be stored for a long time, large companies have the ability to withhold or flood commodity markets. By increasing supply, they can drive the price down when they want to buy commodities from farmers. Alternatively, they can drive the price up by making supply scarce when they want to sell. When commodity programs were first established, wrote Scott Marlow of the Rural Advancement Foundation International, the government acknowledged that without its intervention, companies could drive the price so low that it would be impossible for farmers to survive.[10] Thus, early commodity programs were designed in part to counteract the domination of powerful corporations in agricultural markets.

Government involvement in the food system, however, did not begin and end with credit, price supports, and grain warehousing. Wallace's vision for farm policy included a range of departments and programs that, taken together, made up an integrated food, farming, and stewardship platform. The Soil Conservation Service (originally the Soil Erosion Service and today the Natural Resources Conservation Service) addressed erosion control with alternative methods of tillage, cover cropping, crop rotation, and fertilization. In coordination with state agencies, more than three thousand soil demonstration districts were established, primarily at the county level, to promote agricultural practices to combat Dust Bowl conditions. Participation in government subsidy programs required farmers to sign contracts agreeing to production control and conservation programs. Land-use incentives helped regulate crop acreage and maximize the fallowing and recovery of fields. Programs were specifically tailored to assist sharecroppers and the rural poor. Credit and crop insurance programs met the early and late-season needs of farmers. Research into plant and animal diseases and new varieties and uses of crops were critical innovations. Hunger relief and school lunch programs were part of an overall policy to provide a baseline of nutritional assistance for an extremely needy population.

Despite a demonstrated seven-times "multiplier effect" whereby every government dollar spent generated seven more in the overall economy, New Deal agriculture reforms were controversial from the outset.[11] Many farmers considered hunger relief both a shameful charity and a threat to free markets. Helping the needy was somehow perceived as un-American. As a consequence, in the early years of the Farm Bill, millions of young hogs purchased by the government to restrict supply (to bump up prices) and feed the hungry never reached their intended beneficiaries. Instead, they were slaughtered and dumped in the Missouri River. Likewise, millions of gallons of milk were poured into the streets rather than nourishing the famished.[12] Not until the term *relief* was dropped from the name of food distribution programs and replaced with the Federal Surplus Commodities Corporation were these programs ultimately accepted by powerful farmer

Coon Valley, Wisconsin, 1930s
This historic photo documents the collapse of the Coon Creek Watershed in Coon Valley, Wisconsin, during the Dust Bowl era. The valley was also the site of the first Farm Bill conservation program.

coalitions. Surplus commodities could at last be distributed by the boxcar load to counties, schools, welfare agencies, and charitable institutions.

In 1936, the US Supreme Court ruled that initial programs to limit acreage and set target prices for upland cotton were unconstitutional, although marketing loans and deficiency payments (to boost farmer income up to a preset target price) were later upheld. Farmers themselves seem to have been conflicted about this emerging agricultural order. Historian Bernard DeVito wrote that "farmers throughout the West were always demanding further government help and then furiously denouncing the government for paternalism, and trying to avoid regulation."[13] A decade prior to the 1930s Farm Bill programs, H. L. Mencken said of American farmers, "When the going is good for him he robs the rest of us up to the extreme limit of our endurance;

when the going is bad, he comes up bawling for help out of the public till. . . . There has never been a time, in good season or bad, when his hands were not itching for more."[14]

Henry Wallace, meanwhile, moved on from secretary of agriculture to become vice president during Franklin Roosevelt's second term, and his vision for an integrated farm and food policy was never completed. A genuine attempt had been made to enact policies that brought balanced abundance to the people, protected against shortages, and buffered farmers against losses with loan and insurance programs. And the two foundations of today's Farm Bill—nutrition assistance and aid to farmers—were firmly established. Ultimately, however, these programs could not solve agriculture's looming challenge: overproduction in a rapidly globalizing and industrializing food system.

6. The Changing Face of Agriculture

Farmers who had maintained wild or semi-wild borders around and between fields (in accordance with the best practices of former administrations) tore out shelterbelts, windbreaks, filter strips, and contour terraces. Wetlands were drained and forests obliterated, often with direct technical assistance and financial aid from the USDA Soil Conservation Service.

AFTER WORLD WAR II, a great deal of America's five million farms remained alike in many respects: they were similar in size with a fair degree of surrounding natural habitat raising a diversity of marketable crops depending on the growing region, including livestock (for meat, dairy, eggs, and fertilizer), honeybees (for pollination and honey), and other products. Agricultural policy was likewise diverse: more than one hundred commodities received some form of federal price support, mainly in the form of loans. All that would soon change in ways few could have ever predicted.

The technological and industrial capacities developed during the war were unleashed upon the civilian economy, and agriculture became one of the primary outlets. Tractors replaced horses, taking on tank-like power. Chemicals were concocted into a slew of pesticides, herbicides, and synthetic fertilizers. Squadrons of crop-dusting planes were deployed in the Cold War effort to meet rising global demand for food. Plant breeding also evolved, creating high-yielding hybrid grains tailored to these shifts in chemical inputs and mechanical growing and harvesting. These unprecedented gains in farm productivity came to be widely known as the Green Revolution.

Even as yields improved, farming became more expensive to undertake—and not necessarily any more profitable, except for the largest operations. According to agricultural historian Paul Conkin, between 1950 and 1970, the workforce in agriculture declined by 50 percent, while the total value of farm output rose by 40 percent (figure 6).[1] Fewer people were necessary to harvest much more food. This situation created an oversupply that led to consistently low prices. Meanwhile, employment in the manufacturing and service sectors led to

Combines, NRCS

The "Green" Revolution

The precolonial famines of Europe raised the question: What would happen when the planet's supply of arable land ran out? We have a clear answer. In about 1960 expansion hit its limits and the supply of unfarmed, arable lands came to an end. There was nothing left to plow. What happened was grain yields tripled.

The accepted term for this strange turn of events is the green revolution, though it would be more properly labeled the amber revolution, because it applied exclusively to grain—wheat, rice, and corn. Plant breeders tinkered with the architecture of these three grains so that they could be hypercharged with irrigation water and chemical fertilizers, especially nitrogen. This innovation meshed nicely with the increased "efficiency" of the industrialized factory-farm system. . . . For openers, it disrupted long-standing patterns of rural life worldwide, moving a lot of no-longer-needed people off the land and into the world's most severe poverty.

Source: Richard Manning, "The Oil We Eat," *Harper's Magazine* 308, no. 1845 (February 2004): 41.

Figure 6

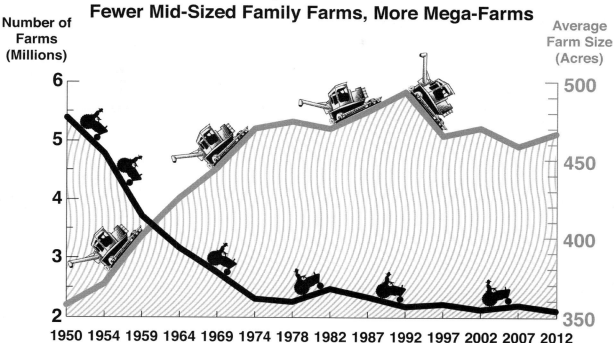

"Get Big or Get Out"
Fewer Mid-Sized Family Farms, More Mega-Farms

Number of Farms (Millions)

Average Farm Size (Acres)

1950 1954 1959 1964 1969 1974 1978 1982 1987 1992 1997 2002 2007 2012

Sources: National Agricultural Statistics Service. "2012 Census of Agriculture Highlights: Farms and Farmland." ACH12-3. US Department of Agriculture. September 2014. Albert R. Mann Library, Cornell University. "Census of Agriculture Historical Archive: 2002 Census Publication." US Department of Agriculture. Accessed August 17, 2017.

a time of unprecedented prosperity. In Washington, Congress struggled mightily to find an answer to the "farm problem": chronically low income across rural America.

Government policies provided an essential platform for these changes to take place. The Farm Bills of the New Deal era had opened the federal treasury's coffers to agriculture. Despite a few attempts to return to a free market system, the emergency price supports of the 1930s and 1940s grad-

ually became institutionalized and ultimately gave way to annual taxpayer support for an increasingly powerful farm lobby. For the next fifty years, the federal government maintained a system of production control and grain reserves along with loan benefits and price supports for farmers. Conservation programs continued and in some cases were expanded. But with continual gains in output due to mechanization and industrialization, even taking land out of production did little to limit surpluses or raise prices. Farms were growing in size through consolidation and becoming more prolific, with yields steadily breaking records. Like other businesses, agriculture was also becoming more specialized. In the decades following World War II, it became increasingly rare even for family farmers to keep chickens, hogs, or dairy cows for market. With so many employment opportunities outside of agriculture in the booming postwar economy, many people farmed part-time or left altogether. Retiring farmland was used for the suburban housing developments springing up around the country.

By the 1970s, government agriculture policy was shaped by a controversial US Department of Agriculture (USDA) secretary named Earl Butz. By the end of his career, he had earned a reputation for offensive racial and religious insults, had been convicted of tax evasion, and had launched a campaign to drive the final nails into the coffin of the American family farm culture. A secret "Soviet grain deal" in 1972 involved the sale of 10 million tons of American wheat to the Soviet Union, driving up domestic prices. Amid this rare period of surging prices and foreign demand, Butz decided that he had found the answer to the farm crisis. Supplying export markets was going to solve America's chronic problem of oversupply and low prices.[2] America would feed the world.

Under Butz, progress was measured by increasing yields, with little attention paid to any harmful environmental, health, or economic effects of monoculture and the industrialization of agriculture. He spurred on farmers to "get big or get out," "adapt or die," and "farm fencerow to fencerow." In addition to the existing production loans, a new form of income compensation—deficiency payments that

boosted income—was established. Larger operators were heavily favored in the new system. America's strategic grain reserves were nearly emptied out as the boom cycle continued. To add acreage and take advantage of the expanding markets, farmers leased lands or bought out smaller growers. Those who had maintained wild or semi-wild field borders (long encouraged by former administrations) tore out shelterbelts, windbreaks, filter strips, and contour terraces. Wetlands were drained and forests obliterated, often with direct technical assistance and financial aid from the USDA Soil Conservation Service. The rise of "clean farming" meant the loss of naturally buffered aquatic systems and uncultivated habitat for native pollinators and beneficial insects. The American farm assumed a factory-like efficiency.

Animal agriculture epitomized this shift in farming as the animals were taken off the land and housed in windowless buildings by the thousands or tens of thousands. Rather than grazing on pasture, animals were raised in factory-like warehouses. Feed was sometimes transported across vast distances. The heavy output of waste from such intensive concentrations of animals eventually became a toxic liability rather than a replenishing fertilizer as it was spewed across the landscape, often finding its way into groundwater and stream channels. By the mid-1970s, concentrated animal feeding operations (CAFOs) were identified by the Environmental Protection Agency as point sources of pollution affecting the country's rivers, lakes, and streams. Between 1980 and 2000, the percentage of US livestock produced from large operations increased dramatically. Nowhere was it more astounding than in the pork sector, where the number of US hog

Figure 7

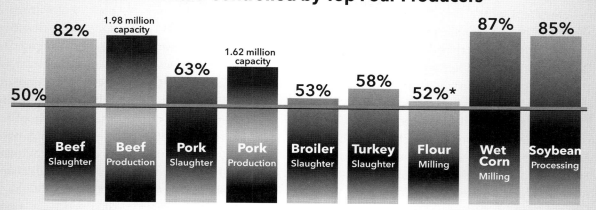

BIG AG
Market Share Controlled by Top Four Producers

- Beef Slaughter: 82%
- Beef Production: 1.98 million capacity
- Pork Slaughter: 63%
- Pork Production: 1.62 million capacity
- Broiler Slaughter: 53%
- Turkey Slaughter: 58%
- Flour Milling: 52%*
- Wet Corn Milling: 87%
- Soybean Processing: 85%

50%

*Just 3 firms.

Markets are considered concentrated if the share controlled by the top four producers exceeds 20 percent and very highly concentrated if the share approaches or exceeds 50 percent.

Source: Hendrickson, Mary. "Resilience in a Concentrated and Consolidated Food System." *Journal of Environmental Studies and Sciences* 5 (2015): 418–31.

operations fell by a factor of almost 10, from just under 500,000 to about 56,000 between 1982 and 2006, while the number of animals stayed roughly the same.[3,4]

It could be argued that these mid-twentieth-century changes in agriculture served a higher purpose. People all over the world were worried about an imminent shortage of global food stocks and potential famine, so the New Deal's Ever-Normal Granary programs of loan-based, county-by-county supply regulation, and grain reserves were eventually phased out in favor of payments designed to reward farmers for maximizing crop yields. Farmers

specialized their operations and plowed up more acreage, even on marginally productive lands. Debt leveraging became business as usual. When prices inevitably plummeted once again, bankruptcies and foreclosures followed, along with a rise in depression, suicides, and rural outmigration.[5]

By the early 1980s, large grain handlers like Cargill and Archer Daniels Midland and other agribusiness giants were essentially writing the Farm Bills for their own benefit.[6] With the elimination of price floors and acreage controls, they received a steady oversupply of cheap commodity crops that they could trade internationally or process into value-added products.[7] There was money to be made in agriculture, to be sure, but rarely for family farmers.

Despite a $20 billion program aiming to boost farm income in 1985, 16 percent of farms were financially stressed. That year alone, about 300,000 farmers sold out and left agriculture entirely.[8] The big got bigger, and the small and medium-sized independent farms—often referred to as the "agriculture of the middle"—disappeared.

The Butz era irrevocably changed the scale and face of agriculture. With the move from family farms to mega-farms, agriculture had become increasingly dominated by concentrated corporate interests in almost every sector. American farmers assumed a manufacturing mentality. They became low-cost producers of the industrial ingredients of modern processed food. As with manufacturing, economies of scale allow the largest operations to spread fixed costs over a large swath of assets. With industrialization came whole new sets of problems: carbon-intensive production; widespread damage to soil, air, waterways, and marine life; the shuttering of entire farm communities; overuse of antibiotics for diseases and hormones for growth in animal factory operations; disappearing grasslands, forests, and wetlands; and a rise in the number of endangered species and impacted fisheries.

During this time, a sustainable agriculture movement also began to take root in the United States as a counter to the trend toward agribusiness. Inspired by the promise of living self-sufficiently on independent farms and concerned about an oil crisis, thousands of Americans went to work on farms, communes, and other arrangements during the late 1960s and 1970s. This back-to-the-land movement was led by innovative, organic producers motivated by the ideals of chemical-free farming methods, healthy food, and vital communities. Their efforts were not funded by Farm Bill programs and were based on sharing of information between growers rather than profit making and market domination. In the end, many back-to-the-landers found self-sufficient farm life extremely difficult or unsustainable without some sort of economic safety net—either strong markets or the type of taxpayer support that commercial farmers had received for decades. Ironically, many were replaced by yet another wave of rural refugees: immigrants from Mexico and Latin America unable to earn a living as farmers and farm workers in their respective countries.

In the decades after the sustainable agriculture movement began, those organic farmers who did remain succeeded in launching a modern food and farming revolution of their own. Organic products accounted for 5.5 percent of food sales in 2017, increasing 6.4 percent from 2016 to 2017 to reach a new record, and have become one of the fastest-growing market segments in the food industry.[9] The organic movement is now global and has finally been acknowledged with some degree of USDA Farm Bill funding, reaching almost $170 million in 2017.[10] The 2014 Farm Bill also doubled mandatory funding to assist growers and handlers to achieve organic certification and increased funding for organic research to $100 million.[11]

Based on the 2012 Census of Agriculture, 3.2 million farmers operate 2.1 million farms in the United States, but only one-fourth of them—about 515,000 operations—report sales of $50,000 or more.[12] Of course, food production doesn't only take place at the farm level; it also involves increasingly complex systems for processing, marketing, and distributing. According to the USDA Economic Research Service, these systems together consumed a record high of 88 cents of every dollar spent on food in 2016, meaning that 12 cents of every food dollar (in real dollars) actually return to the farm sector.[13] The top three or four conglomerates in grain handling, corn exports, beef packing, pork packing, pork production, turkey production, broiler chicken production, and flour milling control at least 40 percent of their respective markets (figure 7).[14] In 2012, 145 operations with at least 50,000 pigs owned 62 percent of the national total, and 200 operations with at least 20,000 cattle owned 8 percent of the national total.[15] Oligopolies also dominate the crop insurance industry, the seed business, food retailing, food processing, fertilizer production, and ethanol manufacture, among many others.[16]

Even conservative financial institutions recognize that commodity subsidies have led to excessive corporate concentration that is failing rural communities. The Federal Reserve Bank of Kansas City, hardly a liberal think tank, reported in 2005 that "commodity programs wed farming regions to an ongoing pattern of economic consolidation. It should not be surprising, therefore, that the very places that depend most on federal farm payments also happen to be places where economic consolidation is happening apace. . . . Traditional programs simply do not provide the economic lift that farming regions need going forward."[17] It also found that between 2000 and 2003, in nearly two-thirds of the counties that received heavy farm subsidies, the growth rate for job creation fell below the national average. A majority of heavily subsidized counties also lost population.

Recent experience confirms that farm support programs tie rural regions to specific types of farming with broad implications for the quality of life there. Since 2012, with the number and size of farms nearly steadying, farmers have had to respond to low crop prices and income by cutting corners in capital investments and daily purchases, seeking more work off the farm, and relying more heavily on the crop insurance programs that make up for the losses due to these low prices.[18] According to Traci Bruckner at the Center for Rural Affairs:

> In its current state, federal crop and revenue insurance subsidy programs contribute to the consolidation of farms by providing a competitive advantage to the nation's largest farms at the expense of small, mid-sized, and beginning farmers. That problem arises because insurance subsidies are unlimited. At the same time, federally subsidized crop insurance fails to provide fair access for diversified, organic, and beginning farmers and it discourages conservation practices that could benefit the environment and increase the resiliency of farms to climate change.[19]

In other words, what's good for mega-farms and mega-processors is usually not good for local and regional economies or their communities. And so it goes: the lingering damage of Farm Bills under Earl Butz.

7. The Changing Face of Hunger

Having witnessed rural poverty firsthand on the presidential campaign trail, President Kennedy signed an executive order in the early months of his administration that revived the food stamp program.

EVEN MORE CONTROVERSIAL THAN GOVERNMENT INTERVENTION in agricultural markets was the other side of the Farm Bill equation: public food distribution and financial assistance for the needy. Until 1932, that responsibility lay solely at the feet of local communities and charities. Critics of food assistance programs believed that hunger relief would lead the country irreversibly toward socialism and the dole. Even as crop surpluses and global competition drove food prices to record lows and as displaced farmers and sharecroppers waged protests and joined the staggering unemployment lines during the Great Depression, no resolution appeared to the paradox of want in the midst of overabundance.

The Federal Surplus Relief Corporation, created in 1933 as part of the Agricultural Adjustment Act (the first Farm Bill), was charged with purchasing, storing, and processing surplus food to relieve the hunger stemming from unemployment and to stabilize prices for farmers.[1] Although the distribution of surplus food didn't always function perfectly, this legislation established a lasting connection between Americans' nutritional health and the nation's agricultural policy. As the Great Depression wore on, the federal government initiated the first food stamp program in 1939. Recipients purchased one dollar's worth of orange stamps for $1 and exchanged them for any foods they wanted. In addition, they received 50 cents' worth of blue stamps. Relief came in the form of these free blue stamps that could only be spent on select, seasonally available government surplus foods such as dairy products, eggs, fruits, vegetables, and wheat flour.

America's entry into World War II effectively wiped out agricultural surpluses and mass unemployment as food exports to the Allied powers increased and jobs became available.[2] The New Deal food distribution and assistance programs were thus phased out by 1943.[3] Policy makers remained acutely aware, however, of the hazards of undernourishment. During wartime, 40 percent of draftees had been rejected from military duty because of malnutrition.[4] Hunger was no longer simply a moral or social issue, but a threat to national security. With broad bipartisan support, the federal government passed the National School Lunch Act in 1946. As its name implied, the act established school lunch programs—which included distribution of surplus commodities—throughout most public schools. It remains one of the largest and most heavily relied-upon public food assistance programs, serving lunches to more than thirty million children every school day.[5]

Otherwise, the strong postwar economy coupled with flagging political and public awareness of the lingering problem of hunger in the United States led the government to largely abandon food assistance programs for years. Not until the late 1950s did John F. Kennedy and a few other senators pick up the torch for federal hunger and nutrition assistance. Having witnessed rural poverty first-hand on the campaign trail, President Kennedy signed an executive order in the early months of his administration that revived the food stamp program in select counties.

In the spring of 1961, unemployed West Virginia miner Alderson Muncy and his wife, Chloe, were driven 25 miles to a grocery store where they were met by Secretary of Agriculture Orville Freeman and a television crew. The Muncys ceremoniously received $95 in food stamps to feed their family, including thirteen children, and the modern era of nutrition assistance was born.

Hunger in America. Among the first acts of the Kennedy administration was to reinstate the food stamp program, which eventually changed the nature of Farm Bill politics.
Kennedy, West Virginia, © Cecil Stoughton/JFK Presidential Library

Tensions remained high, however, between Cold War conservatives and Great Society liberals over the acceptability of persistent income supplements to farmers on the one hand and government food giveaways on the other. As in the Depression era, the initial 1960s food stamps were offered at a discount rather than given free of charge. This "copayment" arrangement was intended to dignify recipients and deflect the idea that it was an act of welfare. (Food stamps without restrictions seemed to some legislators too much like "free money" that could be used to buy whatever one wanted, even though alcohol, tobacco, and imported foods were ineligible.) Congress eventually passed the Food Stamp Act of 1964, which expanded the program to reach half a million people. More important, however, was the decision to place the responsibility for food assistance within the US Department of Agriculture (USDA). This decision would ultimately change the political dynamics of negotiations in future decades as Farm Bills evolved. Farm programs benefited rural states with relatively low populations. Nutrition assistance programs were increasingly popular among legislators representing large urban areas. These two lobbying forces would largely shape food and farm policies moving forward.

In 1968, a groundbreaking *CBS Reports* documentary, "Hunger in America," hosted by Charles Kuralt, exposed appalling scenes of poverty and malnutrition across the country, among whites in Virginia, blacks in Alabama, Navajos in Arizona, and Latinos in Texas. This airing heightened the cause of advocates working on issues of hunger, nutrition, and civil rights, although leadership on food stamps came primarily from Congress. Senators George McGovern, a liberal Democrat, and Bob Dole, a conservative Republican, spearheaded the Senate Select Committee on Nutrition and Human Needs. Nutrition assistance soon became an integral part of Farm Bill politics as both annual appropriations and direct payments to families steadily increased. By 1971, public-interest lobbying organizations such as the Food Research Action Center and the Community Nutrition Institute formed to defend these hard-fought gains during legislative negotiations.

Renamed the Supplemental Nutrition Assistance Program (SNAP) in 2008, this program has been part of every subsequent Farm Bill. It attempts to ensure that eligible low-income Americans receive a monthly stipend that affords them a nutritionally adequate diet until their economic situations improve. By the mid-1970s, nearly 20 million Americans, or around 10 percent of the population, received assistance. In 1977, during the Carter administration, Congress stopped requiring recipients to purchase stamps and distributed them for free. Eliminating the purchase requirement aimed to increase access to low-income recipients and reduce administration and fraud-related expenses.[6] Eligibility was determined by a work requirement and income limit. The program would come under assault at various times in subsequent administrations—during the Reagan administration and in the Republican-led Congress of the mid-1990s, in particular—with enrollment rising and falling along with economic realities and the political perception of food assistance.

The Nutrition title accounts for by far the largest chunk of money spent on Farm Bill programs (figure 8), with an estimated budget of $73 billion in 2016 alone.[7] The title allocates funding predominantly for SNAP as well as for other programs such as child nutrition assistance and emergency food distribution. The stamps themselves (and some of the social stigma attached with food relief) are now a thing of the past, having been replaced with plastic debit cards using an electronic benefits transfer, or EBT, system. Conservatives are currently calling for stricter work requirements despite some evidence that most recipients have jobs and that SNAP functions as a safety net rather than permanent welfare assistance.

One striking difference exists between the farm lobby and the hunger lobby. As Thomas Forster, formerly with the Community Food Security Coalition in Washington, DC, explained: "Along the way, benefits to farmers got subverted as the [crop] subsidies were increasingly channeled to the very largest producers, absentee landowners, and agribusiness and insurance corporations—often masquerading

Figure 8

Hunger Safety Net for the Poor

SBP
$3.6 b
3.6%

NSLP
$9.6 b
9.6%

Other*
$5.4 b
5.4%

WIC
$6.3 b
6.4%

SNAP
$74.1 b

74.8%

Average Annual Food and Nutrition Spending, 2014

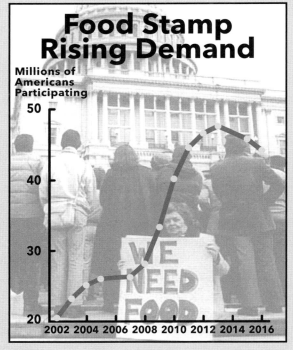

Food Stamp Rising Demand

Millions of Americans Participating

50

40

30

20

2002 2004 2006 2008 2010 2012 2014 2016

*Other programs include the Commodity Supplemental Food Program, Special Milk Program, Child and Adult Care Food Program, Summer Food Service Program, Food Distribution Program on Indian Reservations, NSIP Elderly Feeding, TEFAP Emergency Food Assistance, Disaster Assistance, administrative costs, and other programs.

Nutrition Assistance Programs. The Nutrition title is by far the largest Farm Bill spending category. Also funded by the Child Nutrition Act, food and nutrition programs make up more than 70 percent of all USDA spending. There is a valid reason for that: the number of households classified as food-insecure increased significantly most years in recent history in response to economic downturn. Supplemental Nutrition Assistance Program (SNAP) participation also rose stead-

ily during that period. According to the USDA Food and Nutrition Service, in an average month of 2016, 44.2 million Americans received SNAP benefits. Total spending for SNAP reached $68.1 billion in 2017, down almost $3 billion from 2016. The hunger crisis could be far worse than these figures suggest. An average of up to 30 percent of eligible individuals may not register for and receive SNAP benefits.

Sources: Supplemental Nutrition Assistance Program Data System, Time-Series Data; Annual Summary of FNS Programs. Food and Nutrition Service. "Supplemental Nutrition Assistance Program National Level Annual Summary." Updated February 2, 2018. Pringle, Peter (Ed.). *A Place at the Table: The Crisis of 49 Million Hungry Americans and How to Solve It.* New York: PublicAffairs, 2013.

as family farmers. By contrast, food policy has not been subverted from its original intent to serve as a hunger safety net for the poor."

While hunger advocates continue to fight to make sure food reaches populations in distress, a bitter irony remains: Farm Bill programs make sure Americans are *fed*, but not necessarily *nourished*. Addressing hunger is now widely recognized as not simply a matter of delivering calories. Rather, it means providing consistent access to nutrient-dense foods, including daily servings of fresh fruits, vegetables, and whole grains. Improving the diets of the more than 41.2 million Americans classified as food-insecure may be the largest challenge and opportunity for Farm Bill reforms in the decades ahead.[8] (Note: The number considered food-insecure doesn't directly parallel the number eligible for SNAP.)

By far the largest federal nutrition assistance program, SNAP plays a critical role in ensuring that basic caloric needs are met. Without SNAP, tens of millions of Americans—more than half of whom are children—could be suffering from hunger-related diseases. Indeed, 69 percent of SNAP participants are families with children.[9] Many studies suggest that positive effects of receiving SNAP benefits on children include increasing their well-being, reducing or preventing food insecurity, improving birth outcomes, and raising test scores and the likelihood of graduating from high school.[10,13] Figure 9 shares quotes from parents struggling to feed their families on SNAP benefits.

Yet the program could be improved to serve its recipients better. It is important to recognize that SNAP does not reach all who need it or who are eligible for assistance.[14] In addition, many studies suggest that it does not provide enough money to purchase a diet based on the USDA Thrifty Food Plan[15] upon which benefits are calculated.[16] Perhaps most alarming, a recent systematic review of the analysis of dietary quality and SNAP participation suggested that although most participants are able to consume enough calories, they usually have lower dietary quality than comparison groups, and this discrepancy may be due to greater consumption of energy-dense foods.[17] Furthermore, analyses of national data suggest that SNAP participants are more likely to be obese, putting them at greater risk for type 2 diabetes, hypertension, cardiovascular disease, and certain types of cancer.[18] Although this area continues to be actively researched, these findings highlight the potential benefits of improving the nutritional quality of food purchased with SNAP benefits.

Although not included in the Farm Bill, the National School Lunch Program and the Special Supplemental Nutrition Program for Women, Infants, and Children (WIC) now have more stringent requirements on the nutritional quality of food that recipients may purchase. In the case of school lunches and breakfasts, school food service directors must ensure that the meals they sell meet strict nutritional requirements, according to national legislation, to receive federal reimbursement. In addition, WIC benefits can only be used for specific food packages, depending on the health and needs of a woman or her infant. These specifics are updated periodically, based on recommendations from the Food and Nutrition Board of the National Academies of Sciences, Engineering, and Medicine, to improve nutritional quality.

Figure 9

Struggling to Cope

SNAP Is a Lifeline for 42 Million Americans

Recipient: Miracle B.

I was taking a friend to do our bottles and cans, so we have enough to make up the difference since the Food Stamp cuts. Eleven dollars has been taken out by the cuts, and sometimes bottles and cans don't make up that difference, sometimes not even half.

Mother: Crystal S.

With the money food stamps provide, I was able to feed her breakfast that morning. Without it what would she have eaten? I wanted to show that with the help she was able to eat breakfast that morning. She had cereal. She had milk. She didn't have to go without.

Mother: Melissa H.

My son, he's already on the small side and he needs every bit of food that he can get to make him healthy, keep him healthy. He has failure to thrive. He has a bone deficiency that doesn't allow him to grow. He's only thirty pounds. And the kids know my food stamps got cut off. Because when they came home from school today, they didn't have their snacks. So they know that I didn't go to the market. I really didn't tell them why or anything like that, because I don't think they understand. But it affected them.

Mother: Imani S.

He was asking the caseworker for something to eat. I don't have childcare, so I have to take him to my appointments. If he was in day care I wouldn't have to have lugged him early in the morning to an appointment to the welfare office to try to get food stamps and medical coverage. I can't help it if my baby's hungry. I was thinking 'I'm not going to lie to you miss, he's hungry.'

The Witness to Hunger Project allows mothers and caregivers of young children to document their experiences with hunger.

Source: Center for Hunger-Free Communities. "Witnesses to Hunger Sites." Accessed August 18, 2017. Drexel University.

Regulations for SNAP may be less stringent because policy makers want to avoid overburdening business owners and government agencies that oversee purchases or because of a lack of efficient data collection. WIC participants must also be deemed to be at "nutritional risk," directly motivating more of a nutrition prescription. School meal standards are likely also more stringent because children may not yet have the knowledge to select healthy and balanced meals and are also subject to more intense marketing of unhealthy food and beverages.

Some advocates for SNAP reform are taking a "carrot" approach, calling for an increase in programs that double the purchasing power of recipients to buy fresh produce in farmers markets or stores. Others argue for a "stick" approach, such as restricting the use of benefits for sugar-sweetened beverages. The anti-hunger community has largely rebuffed any attempts to limit the free choice of recipients as an assault on personal dignity. Improving diets for SNAP recipients, however, could improve not only their health and well-being, but also their economic status. While it remains to be seen whether restrictions could improve diet and health, the potential to boost productivity and reduce healthcare costs by investing in chronic disease prevention warrants serious consideration.

Today more than ever, we understand that how we grow and process our crops affects the nutrients they provide and thus determines their long-term impacts on public health. The Farm Bill truly is a Food Bill. One of its stiffest challenges is offering a basic nutritional safety net that meets the Dietary Guidelines for Americans, jointly produced by the USDA and the Department for Health and Human Services, and at the same time involving the nation's farmers in that food system.

8. The Conservation Era

Well-directed conservation efforts are arguably some of the very best tax dollars we can spend. When large continuous habitats are restored, they provide resilience against species loss, catastrophic weather events, and water shortages.

THE 1972 DEAL TO SELL US SURPLUS GRAIN TO THE SOVIET UNION— and the subsequent commodity crop price spike—set off a decade-long fury of borrowing, speculation, and agricultural expansion (followed by the inevitable overproduction and price collapse). Particularly caught up in the euphoria were farmers in the Prairie Pothole Region, which spans parts of Iowa and Minnesota, North Dakota, South Dakota, northeastern Montana, Saskatchewan, and Alberta. The Pothole Region—rolling hills and grasslands pocked by wetlands—is also called North America's duck factory, because up to 60 percent of waterfowl are hatched in this habitat.[1] The region is also important for storing water, filtering water, and storing carbon in soils.

Farmers began draining wetlands to expand their harvest potential in the great plow-up inspired by the promise of new foreign grain markets. A prolonged drought in the Pothole Region in the early 1980s laid bare the damage that had been done. The loss of vital habitat, combined with severe weather conditions, reduced the populations of ducks, pheasants, grouse, deer, and other species to record-low levels.

Legislators responded with new conservation programs in the 1985 Farm Bill that was formally titled the Food Security Act of 1985 but was frequently referred to as the Environmental Farm Bill or the Environmental Act. Funds were made available to enroll up to 37 million acres—approximately 10 percent of total US farmed acreage—in the Conservation Reserve Program (CRP). It was, in essence, a contract with farmers to idle a certain amount of highly erodible land as set-aside acreage. That same Farm Bill included "Swampbuster" and "Sodbuster" provisions. These disincentive programs immediately withdrew federal payments from farmers who drained wetlands (Swampbusters) or plowed up protected grasslands (Sodbusters).

The global grain conglomerates hotly contested these conservation initiatives, which had been championed by hunting, fishing, and environmental groups, insisting that they would result in massive crop shortages. The next two decades, however, proved them wrong. Until the ethanol boom started in 2005, corn surpluses persisted and global commodity prices stayed low. Every year, there were more farmers willing to idle fields than conservation funds available. According to Farm Bill conservation program expert Ferd Hoefner at the National Sustainable Agriculture Coalition, three out of every four farmers and ranchers who applied to participate in Farm Bill conservation programs in 2015 were rejected due to lack of funds (figure 10). Of the total amount available through the En-

vironmental Quality Incentive Program (EQIP), only 26 percent of eligible applicants actually received funding in 2016.[2] In addition, this percentage has varied greatly across states, with some accepting as few as one out of six applicants.[3] This variation indicates not only differences in demand, but also in state ranking criteria and levels of promotion by state Natural Resources Conservation Service (NRCS) offices and partner groups.[4]

Meanwhile, a study by the NRCS estimated an increase of nearly 26 million ducks and waterfowl in the Prairie Pothole Region between 1992 and 2003, a success largely attributable to CRP land idling.[5] The 2014 Farm Bill included new provisions particularly relevant for this region, including expansion of a partnership between Ducks Unlimited and NRCS

Figure 10

Excess Demand for Limited Conservation Funds

Program	Year	Unfunded Applications	Unfunded Application Dollars	Unfunded Application Acreage
Environmental Quality Incentives Program (EQIP)	2015	72,104	$1,900,000,000	780,538
Conservation Stewardship Program (CSP)	2015	14,200	No Data	164,369
Conservation Reserve Program (CRP)	2016	21,437	No Data	1,449,227
Agricultural Conservation Easement Program (ACEP)	2015	809	$233,000,000	258,777
Watershed Rehabilitation Program (WRP)	2015	203	$426,000,000	No Data

Sources: Data for unfunded EQIP and CSP acreage came from personal communication with Letitia Toomer-Jones, Coordinator of Strategic Information Team in Resource Economics and Analysis Division at Natural Resources Conservation Service on July 20, 2017. Stubbs, Megan. "Agricultural Conservation: A Guide to Programs." June 2016. Congressional Research Service; "The Conservation Reserve Program: 49th Signup Results." USDA Farm Service Agency.

to develop a carbon credit marketing system to discourage tilling of grasslands. In total, it provides $25 million annually in Conservation Innovation Grants through EQIP.

After 1985, each successive Farm Bill added conservation programs (see descriptions in the "Alphabet Soup" feature). In 1990, the Wetlands Reserve Program (WRP) provided money to set aside and restore 1 million acres of wetlands.[6] Although it could in no way compensate for the losses—500,000 acres per year—that had been occurring since the 1950s, the program targeted critical habitats for restoration that benefit a variety of species and protect the nation's aquatic systems.[7,8] More than 2.3 million acres of wetlands were restored under the WRP, most under permanent or long-term easements.[9] It was arguably the most successful Farm Bill conservation program.[10]

Pilot programs introduced in 1996 furthered the emphasis on conservation. The Wildlife Habitat Incentive Program (WHIP) provides assistance for protecting sensitive species and restoring or maintaining critical habitats in farming regions. EQIP offers funds for a wide variety of environmental "improvements" and efforts to meet clean air and clean water regulations. Incentives and cost sharing cover measures such as soil erosion and air pollution reduction, forest replanting and thinning, and stream bank restoration. Some areas specifically support beginning or disadvantaged farmers, transition to organic certification; or other related goals. The highest-funded conservation practice is cover cropping, which does indeed help promote good soil and water quality. Thanks to lobbying from meat, egg, and dairy industries in the 2002 Farm Bill, however, hundreds of millions of precious EQIP dollars have been used to fund the

Conservation Milestones in Farm Bills

1985   Conservation Compliance ("Swampbuster" and "Sodbuster" provisions); Conservation Reserve Program; National Sustainable Agriculture Information Service; Low-Impact Sustainable Agriculture

1990   Sustainable Agriculture Research and Education Program; Integrated Farm Management Program; Wetlands Reserve Program; Water Quality Incentives Program; National Organic Program; Outreach Program for Socially Disadvantaged Farmers

1992   Beginning Farmer and Rancher Development Program; set-aside of loan funds for beginning farmers and ranchers

1996   Planting Flexibility; Environmental Quality Incentives Program; Farm and Ranch Lands Protection Program; Farmers and nongovernmental organization representatives added to Natural Resources Conservation Service State Technical Committees; Fund for Rural America; Community Food Grants

1998   Initiative for Future Agriculture and Food Systems

2000   Insurance Non-Discrimination Policy for sustainable and organic agriculture; Risk Management Education Program

2002   Conservation Security Program; Conservation Partnership and Cooperation; Wetlands Reserve Program increase; Increase in Value-Added Producer Grants to pay for local, sustainable, and organic marketing and processing; Beginning Farmer Credit Reforms; Organic Farming Research; Organic Certification Cost Share; Farmers Market Promotion Program; Contract Agriculture Reform; Small- and Mid-Sized Farm and Rural Research

2008   Conservation Stewardship Program; Biomass Research and Development

2014   Agricultural Conservation Easement Program; Conservation Compliance for Crop Insurance Recipients; Regional Conservation Partnership Initiative

Source: National Sustainable Agriculture Coalition, "Farm Bill Programs and Grants—Overview," accessed June 15, 2018.

Pay Now or Pay Later
Hidden Costs of Industrial Agriculture

Figure 11

WATER CONTAMINATION
Pesticides; Nitrates; Phosphates; Bacteria; Dead Zones

AIR EMISSIONS
Methane; Ammonia; Nitrous Oxide; Carbon Dioxide

BIODIVERSITY LOSS
Wildlife and Habitat Loss; Hedgerow and Woodlot Loss; Bee Colony Decline; Vanishing Crops and Breeds

Costs Above the Price of Food at the Checkout Counter

SOIL LOSSES
Erosion; Loss of Organic Matter and Carbon Sinks

HUMAN HEALTH
Pesticide Toxicity; Asthma; Bacterial and Viral Diseases; Antibiotic Resistance; MRSA and E. Coli; Exogenous Hormones; Obesity and Diabetes

DISAPPEARING WETLANDS
Tile Drainage; Dewatered Rivers; Impact on Species

Source: Pretty, Jules. "The Real Costs of Modern Farming," *Resurgence,* Issue 205 (2001).

construction of expensive manure lagoons along with other dubious solutions to the problem of vast quantities of concentrated animal waste at industrial dairies, hog factories, and feedlots.[11] Figure 11 gives examples of the negative environmental effects. After 2014, EQIP became much larger and now includes other programs, such as WHIP.

The 2002 Farm Bill also included a new Conservation Security Program, which was expanded and improved as the Conservation Stewardship Program (CSP) in the 2008 Farm Bill. One of the most significant changes to CSP in the 2008 Farm Bill was that it became available in all states and counties every year. That structure was preserved by the 2014 Farm Bill.

While demand for conservation programs has soared, funding has remained modest, and such programs remain a prime target for the hatchets of appropriations committees and budget reconcilers. During the 2008 Farm Bill, the WRP, which mostly bought permanent easements to save and restore large swaths of critical habitat, suffered steep cuts, as did EQIP. The WRP, along with the Farm and Ranchlands Protection Program and the Grassland Reserve Program, were repealed by the 2014 Farm Bill and replaced by the Agricultural Conservation Easement Program (ACEP) (which maintained contracts from the previous programs).[12] This program provides both technical assistance and grants to governments or nongovernmental organizations to prevent conversion of agricultural land to other uses and to protect and restore wetlands. ACEP only approved 22 percent of incoming easement applications in 2017.[13] Because the authorized funding was slashed in half in 2018, that percentage will likely continue to fall.

The 2014 Farm Bill cut CRP and CSP by 2 million and 28 million acres to save $3.3 billion and $2.3 billion from the budget, respectively.[14] Although EQIP was authorized to receive $1.6 billion in that Farm Bill, it only received $1.3 billion in 2016.[15] In addition, as markets for exportable commodities and biofuels grow, farmers are quick to beg release from land-idling contracts so as to cash in on high prices. (So much for the social contract between farmers and taxpayers when there is money to be made.)

Overall, $6.1 billion was cut from conservation funding budgets for the subsequent ten years, including the amount subtracted due to sequestration mandated by the Budget Control Act of 2011.[16] Sadly, it was the first time that conservation funding had been cut since it was incorporated into the Farm Bill in 1985.

Paying landowners to *not* grow crops may seem a counterintuitive use of tax dollars, unless it is viewed as a long-term investment in soil protection, habitat conservation, preservation of healthy water systems, and supply control. In fact, well-directed conservation efforts could arguably be some of the very best tax dollars we can spend. When large contiguous habitats are restored and permanently protected, they provide resilience against species loss, catastrophic weather events, and water shortages. All these efforts are vital for safeguarding our natural legacy for future generations, especially around lands being used for productive agriculture.

The market does not currently take into account the total costs of food production, known to economists as externalities. Conservation measures were, in fact, a requirement for all farmers enrolling in early Farm Bill programs, a policy well worth reviving. As the old saying goes, there is no free lunch. If we don't invest in our soils, streams, and habitats now, we will surely pay later.

Paying the Polluters

Taxpayers are footing the bill for concentrated animal feeding operations (CAFOs). These massive dairies, mega-sized hog farms, poultry factories and battery operations, and other livestock feeding facilities house thousands (often tens or even hundreds of thousands) of animals, producing outputs of waste equivalent to the sewage volumes of small cities. The late Brother David Andrews of the National Catholic Rural Life Conference described the problem as "a fecal flood."[a]

The 2002, 2008, and 2014 Farm Bill Conservation titles each showered hundreds of millions of dollars on CAFOs, not only to clean up existing pollution, but also to fund new feedlots and expand old ones without accounting for their overall impacts on the environment. These Farm Bills mandated that 60 percent of the Environmental Quality Incentives Program (EQIP) budget be allocated to animal agriculture operators with the largest potential impact for remediation, which means that preference is given to the most egregious bad actors rather than to healthy operations that might still have a need for some improvements. In fact, CAFOs (along with other recipients) are eligible for up to 75 percent of costs up to $450,000 per owner (increased from the 2008 Farm Bill cap of $300,000). This public money can pay for hauling fees, building storage facilities for animal waste, and other costs of complying with regulations. In the long run, these large subsidies underwrite the increased loading of animal waste on land in many of the nation's watersheds. Meanwhile, projects with organic production benefits are capped at $20,000 annually or $80,000 over any six-year period.

CAFOs first became eligible to receive EQIP funding at the same time that the Clean Water Act was expanded to address CAFO pollution issues in 2002. Thanks to hefty campaign contributions from agribusiness lobbies and the support of a few antipollution advocacy groups, Farm Bill conservation dollars are being diverted to build and fortify manure lagoons on corporate feedlots, even as landowners eligible to protect wetlands, conserve invaluable habitat for wildlife, and provide other critical environmental services are turned away due to a lack of funding.[b]

Because there is an abysmal lack of public data about the amount of money distributed to CAFOs through the EQIP program, it is extremely difficult to understand the full scope of this government-funded pay-the-polluter policy. Where information on specific contracts to industrial operations is available, it is troubling. Texas receives more payments than any other state, reaching more than $700 million between 1997 and 2015. During this same period, 1,072 contracts received more than $250,000 to support projects such as installing irrigation systems and constructing infrastructure and fencing. The median contract payment has steadily increased from $1,355 in 1997 to more than $5,000 today.[c]

Many of these recipients are simultaneously the worst polluters. In Michigan, more than 15 percent of the state's 238 CAFOs have owed $1.3 million in fines and penalties for Clean Water Act violations since 1996. Yet the owners and operators of those facilities received $26 million in subsidies between 1995 and 2011, according to a report by the Less=More Coalition.[d] The National Sustainable Agriculture Coalition estimates that CAFOs received more than $100 million in EQIP funding in 2015 alone, mainly for waste storage and handling.[e]

The issue raises a number of important concerns about the unwholesome connections between large livestock operations and Farm Bill subsidy programs.

1. **Taxpayer-funded CAFO infrastructure.** Although enhancing water and air quality is indeed in the public's best interest, it is questionable whether taxpayer funds should be used to build the infrastructure for agribusiness to comply with regulations. Unfortunately, some politicians and even a few environmental organizations believe that the only way massive hog farms, beef and poultry feedlots, and dairies will comply with regulations is if we pay them to do so. Construction loans and other financing mechanisms are one thing. But these cost-share programs are corporate giveaways for some of the country's most horrendous polluters.[f]

2. **Compliance versus conservation.** EQIP funds come out of the Conservation title of the Farm Bill. Misconstruing end-of-pipe factory farm pollution compliance as conservation is twisted logic. There is little or no net environmental benefit from EQIP funding that perpetuates and expands ecologically damaging feeding operations. In addition to causing water and air pollution, a 2006 study by the United Nations Food and Agriculture Organization revealed that animal feedlots (the largest of which include CAFOs) are a major contributor to climate change and are causing land and water degradation on a global scale.[g]

3. **CAFOs and energy production.** One of the largest emissions from CAFOs is methane, a potent greenhouse gas, which can produce energy when captured. The Farm Bill offers incentives for farmers to invest in methane digesters that convert animal waste into combustible fuels and residual solids and liquids. The current limitation on incentive payments for methane

Manure lagoon, NRCS

digesters under EQIP is $450,000. This is a reduction of payments from under previous Farm Bills but still provides a large financial incentive for the establishment of a CAFO operation. Methane digesters can be effective at producing fuel on a small scale (particularly in developing countries), but they have not proven an effective way to reduce waste.

4. **Support for pasture operations.** EQIP is used by many livestock and crop producers to carry out important practices that may help limit negative environmental impacts. But the disproportionate flow of EQIP funds to large-scale

Cows, Helen Reddout, Socially Responsible Agriculture Project

animal factories can result in a net increase in overall pollution. This fundamental flaw in the policy may jeopardize its long-term effectiveness. EQIP funds can better help solve the CAFO pollution crisis by directing support solely to perennial, grass-pastured, integrated livestock farms, as was the program's original intent. Not only would this approach be better for land, water, air, and human health, but it would also promote production systems that need not rely so heavily on external funding for nutrient inputs and pollution remediation.

NOTES

a. Martha Noble, "Paying the Polluters," in *The CAFO Reader: The Tragedy of Industrial Animal Factories*, ed. Dan Imhoff (Healdsburg, CA: Watershed Media, 2010), 222.

b. Suzie Greenlaugh, Mindy Selman, and Jenny Guiling of the World Resources Institute quote the following sources for conservation program spending: (1) Environmental Quality Incentives Program funding allocation; Edward Brzostek, USDA Natural Resources Conservation Service, personal communication, June 2006; (2) Conservation Reserve Program funding allocation 29th signup; (3) Grassland Reserve Program funding allocation; (4) Wetlands Reserve Program funding allocation; (5) Wildlife Habitat Incentives program funding allocation; and Albert Cerna, USDA NRCS, personal communication, June 2006.

c. "Environmental Quality Incentives Program in the United States," Environmental Working Group, updated 2017.

d. "Restoring the Balance to Michigan's Farming Landscape," Sierra Club, Michigan Chapter, February 15, 2013.

e. "CAFOs and Cover Crops: A Closer Look at 2015 EQIP Dollars," National Sustainable Agriculture Coalition, November 20, 2015.

f. Suzie Greenlaugh, Mindy Selman, and Jenny Guiling, "Paying for Environmental Performance: Investing in Farmers and the Environment," World Resources Institute, July 2006.

g. FAO Newsroom, "Livestock a Major Threat to Environment: Remedies Urgently Needed," November 29, 2006, web edition.

Alphabet Soup:
Deconstructing the Conservation Program Palette

Understanding Farm Bill conservation programs requires delving into a parallel universe of acronyms. First and foremost are the Natural Resources Conservation Service (NRCS) and Farm Service Agency (FSA)—the conservation arms of the US Department of Agriculture, which administer programs.

Set-aside and easement programs such as the 1985 Conservation Reserve Program (CRP), 2014 Agricultural Conservation Easement Program (ACEP), and 2014 Healthy Forests Reserve Program (HFRP) pay landowners to take land out of production and restore functional grasslands, wetlands, or forests. They are either permanent buyouts or long-term (thirty-year) contracts, and the most effective ones target large areas of contiguous and high-priority habitat.

Habitat-building programs offer cost-share assistance to restore land and protect declining species, including the Wildlife Habitat Incentives Program (WHIP) and the Conservation Reserve Enhancement Program (CREP).

Stream buffer, Appomattox River Watershed, Dan Imhoff

Compliance-oriented programs like the Environmental Quality Incentives Program (EQIP) have more questionable conservation value. They often pay large amounts of money to polluting corporations, such as massive confinement hog and dairy farms, to comply with the Clean Water Act, the Clean Air Act, and other regulations by which most businesses have to abide on their own. However, EQIP has also been used to a lesser extent to provide habitat for fluvial Arctic graylings, lesser prairie chickens, sage grouse, and bobwhite quail. Sodbuster, Swampbuster, and Sodsaver programs prevent many program benefits when conservation requirements are not met.

Stewardship-oriented incentives such as the Conservation Stewardship Program (CSP) combine both ecological farming and long-term care for the land. CSP encourages and supports conservation on farming and ranching operations of all types in all regions and comprehensively addresses soil, water, wildlife, energy, and other resources as bases of healthy agriculture rather than as side issues or through costly remediation. For these reasons, it is also called a working-lands program.

Source: Megan Stubbs, "Agricultural Conservation: A Guide to Programs," Congressional Research Service, June 2016.

PART III

KEY POLICY ISSUES

9. Crop Subsidies

> Freedom to Farm triggered the largest government payouts in history, the opposite of its policy objective.

RHETORICALLY, THE 1996 FARM BILL—known as "Freedom to Farm"—was supposed to signal the end of the subsidy era and a return to free-market agriculture not seen since the early days of the New Deal. It was passed by a Republican-controlled Congress in a time of strong crop prices and tight federal budgets and on the heels of a World Trade Organization (WTO) agreement in which developed countries committed to eliminating their agricultural subsidies. Congress claimed that Freedom to Farm would wean US agriculture off federal support over the following seven-year period. Instead, it triggered more than a decade of the largest agribusiness payouts in history and is the main reason politicians and citizens alike cringe when they hear the words *farm subsidies*.

Among heralded legislative improvements was the concept of "decoupled payments." These subsidies were no longer linked, or coupled, to growing a specific crop. Instead, decoupled payments rewarded landowners on the basis of their subsidy history, whether or not they grew commodity crops. The intent of these base acreage lump payments was to afford farmers flexibility to transition to new crops and alternative approaches to farming while the sun slowly set on the Washington subsidy game.

Freedom to Farm also eliminated the previous acreage set-aside requirements, which served as both a soil conservation measure and a supply management strategy. In addition, the government shuttered the remnants of its decades-old strategic grain reserve. Without county-by-county management of crop acreage or a relief valve for surpluses, farmers now flooded markets with their entire harvests.

Phasing out subsidies did not go according to the script. Unusually favorable weather conditions promoted large yields, and an international financial crisis reduced demand for exports. These unforeseen factors led to oversaturated markets, and the farm economy fell into another tailspin.[1] Commodity prices plummeted, and Washington reneged on the phase-out plan. The few preceding years of high crop prices had reduced the cost of commodity subsidy programs down to $3 billion to $4 billion per year. After the passage of Freedom to Farm, however, the cost soared to $15 billion to $25 billion, ballooning with multi-billion-dollar "emergency market loss" bailouts on top of subsidies. Loan deficiency payments were also intended to supplement the difference in price between a county's applicable loan rates and posted market prices for individual crops.[2] These moves, originally intended to reign in government spending, shifted the advantage to buyers. The beneficiaries became an elite group of mega-farms along with the food processors, confinement feeding operations, grain distributors, and others that purchased the glut of corn, cotton, wheat, rice, and soybeans at prices that sometimes fell below what it cost to grow them.

By the turn of the millennium, the farm economy rebounded, yet the next Farm Bill, the Farm Security and Rural Investment Act of 2002, continued the trend of generous subsidies. In fact, it became the most lavish yet. The president boasted that this mammoth legislation "preserves the farm way of life for generations."[3] Onlookers across the country were appalled. The *Washington Post* called it "a shockingly awful farm bill that will weaken the nation's economy." The *Wall Street Journal* labeled it "a 10-year, $173.5 billion bucket of slop." North Car-

olina's *Greensboro News Record* deemed it "a gravy-train for mega-farms and corporations."[4] At the same time, the United States began a trajectory of growing national deficits (figure 12).

The 2002 Farm Bill made permanent Freedom to Farm's temporary transition slush fund—the decoupled payments—in the form of direct payments. They became an instant entitlement program that reeked more of eighteenth-century feudalism than twenty-first-century democracy. Growers received direct payments just for owning land with a particular commodity production history. It didn't matter if they had lost money that year or even if they were planting commodity crops. Direct payments were also favored by lenders financing the expansion of farming operations, and they were not limited by WTO agriculture guidelines. In addition, the blockbuster disaster bailouts of the late 1990s became normal budget items in the 2002 Farm Bill, this time as counter-cyclical payments that fluctuated depending on global market prices to ensure that farmers didn't lose money in oversupplied markets. In fact, this type of deficiency subsidy to ensure that farmers received at least a preset target price based on estimated production costs had been around at least since the 1970s. Under the 2002 Farm Bill, however, the subsidies reached new heights.

To satisfy environmentalists and the outdoor "hook and bullet" constituencies, the 2002 Farm Bill also set a record for conservation spending, at least theoretically. It included a new program aimed at transitioning agricultural subsidies into green payments, the Conservation Security Program, and new Grassland Reserve Program funds to protect rare remnant prairies and grassland habitats. As

Figure 12

Government Debt Is Your Debt
1995-2018

NOMINAL DOLLARS*
(BILLIONS)

Chart shows annual surpluses and deficits from 1995 to 2018, with bars labeled "surplus" or "deficit." Administrations marked: CLINTON ADMINISTRATION, G. W. BUSH ADMINISTRATION, OBAMA ADMINISTRATION, TRUMP ADMINISTRATION. Y-axis from -1,800 to 400. X-axis years 1995 through 2018.

The End of Entitlements? The mounting costs of the prolonged wars in Afghanistan and Iraq and rising costs in Syria; recovery from a global economic downturn; rising costs of Medicare, Medicaid, and Social Security; and unexpected natural disasters like Hurricane Sandy have forced legislators to scrutinize all spending. The hard and honest truth is that—with the exception of record payouts for commodity producers—many programs have already been cut to the bone through the annual appropriations process. Unfortunately, the price of doing nothing to address the complex interrelated challenges of current food and farm policy in the long run may be unaffordable.

*Nominal dollars are not adjusted for inflation.

Sources: Congressional Budget Office. "Budget and Economic Data." Accessed August 18, 2017. Collender, Stan. "2018 Budget Deal Is the Start of 'The New Normal' in U.S. Politics and Economy." *Forbes*. February 9, 2018.

so often happens, however, these promises were eventually broken. Conservation programs wound up drastically underfunded (flat-funded or even cut altogether) during the annual appropriations process. As many as four out of five applicants were turned down for programs due to lack of support over the course of the 2002 bill. Ducks Unlimited and other conservation groups warned of another aggressive expansion into Prairie Pothole habitats that were previously uneconomical or impractical to farm, with up to 22 million acres at risk of being plowed. These fears proved to be well warranted. The lack of funding meant that Natural Resources Conservation Service field offices failed to enforce conservation compliance provisions or provided too many exemption waivers. Nearly half of all field offices failed to implement at least one provision, according to the US Government Accountability Office.[5]

With so little money dedicated to environmental stewardship and diversified agriculture, farmers were incentivized to "farm the system" by planting as much as possible. The largest and most aggressive operators received the most benefits and used subsidies to drive up cash rents and arable land values, exerting even more financial pressure on smaller and beginning farmers. For example, corn farmers received $2 billion in federal direct payments in 2007, a year during which they experienced record yields and strong prices.[6]

Farmers could now plant as much as they wanted while being guaranteed government bailouts if they experienced low yields, low market prices, unfavorable weather conditions, or crop failures because they planted on marginal lands. Counter-cyclical payments, crop insurance, disaster

The Failure of "Freedom to Farm"

When Freedom to Farm was passed in 1996, conditions on the farm and in government included high farm prices and a tight federal budget. In addition, developed countries had just started feeling pressure from the World Trade Organization to eliminate subsidies. With that year's Farm Bill, Congress aimed to permanently phase out farm subsidies, but its plan backfired. For example:

- In 1996, Freedom to Farm eliminated land idling requirements and the grain reserve program.
- The lack of idling requirements resulted in a combined increase of 15 million harvested acres of corn and soybeans between 1995 and 1997.
- Without a grain reserve program, farmers flooded the market with their surplus crops.
- Due to oversupply, between 1996 and 1999 the price of corn fell by 50 percent and soybeans by more than 40 percent.
- Farmers planted more acres to make up for low prices, which resulted in larger surpluses and even lower prices.
- Congress established disaster payments to supplement falling farm incomes.
- Congress made disaster payments permanent in the 2002 Farm Bill, perpetuating the cycle of oversupply and compensation.

As Congress develops the next Farm Bill amid rapidly falling farm income yet tightening spending, it will need to decide how it will intervene to regulate loss to farmers or rising prices for consumers.

Source: "Farm Subsidies 101 Fact Sheet," *Food and Water Watch*, February 2011.

relief, and other price supports, along with ethanol tax incentives, virtually eliminated most risks for commodity agriculture operators.

Many of these archaic programs (including direct and counter-cyclical payments) were repealed by the 2014 Farm Bill, which replaced them with Price Loss Coverage and Agricultural Risk Coverage. Again targeting commodities, these programs allow farmers to receive payments when market prices fall below a reference price or revenue falls below a certain threshold. Although automatic payments have been eliminated, the concentration of power continues at the expense of small and medium-sized farms. Fueled by taxpayer dollars, the bulk of the benefits still go toward supporting crops produced by conventional agribusiness.

Debate about Farmers' Crop Insurance Heightens

Some say subsidized payments are necessary; others contend they should end. Years of drenching rainstorms in several northern farm-belt states have caused payments under a popular type of government-subsidized crop insurance to nearly triple in the past decade, heightening debate about whether farmers should be compensated when they can't plant their fields.

Payments for "prevented plantings" exceeded $2 billion annually in both 2011 and 2013 and are nearing $1 billion for 2014, with some claims still being processed. Although these payments are available to farmers nationwide, the lion's share of the 2014 payouts, as in previous years, went to farmers in the Prairie Pothole Region—which includes parts of North Dakota, South Dakota, Minnesota, Iowa, and Montana. This area contains pockets of wetlands that some say are largely unsuitable to farming.

Craig Cox, an agricultural expert at the Environmental Working Group, said the payments encourage farmers in the region to take risks they wouldn't normally take. "These seasonal wetlands are called seasonal because they're wet in the spring" when planting often takes place, he said. "If farmers didn't have that sort of risk protection—and they actually lost money—I don't think we'd see the same sort of behavior."

Mark Formo, president of the North Dakota Grain Growers Association, said it is unfair to use recent history to judge the effectiveness of the prevented-plantings system. "A lot of the land that's farmed now has been farmed for generations, [but] normal just hasn't been normal," he said. "My dad is seventy-five and he's always saying this is the wettest he's ever seen it."

A report released this week by the Environmental Working Group, a frequent critic of agricultural subsidies, said farmers in the Prairie Pothole Region received about 60 percent of all prevented-planting payments between 2000 and 2013, equal to about $5 billion. That allocation dropped to 40 percent in 2014, according to the group. The analysis, based on US Department of Agriculture (USDA) data, covers years of record-high crop prices, which resulted in higher payments to farmers.

After last year's wet spring prevented Doyle Lentz from planting 10 percent of his acreage, the Rolla, North Dakota, farmer filed a claim under his crop-insurance policy and received 60 cents on the dollar for the insured value of wheat, barley, and soybeans he had intended to plant. "Farmers don't want to have to file for this," Mr. Lentz said. "They're not set up to not plant."

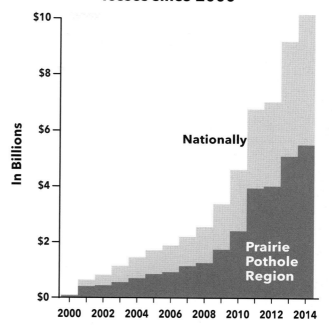

Reaping Benefits
Cumulative payouts for prevented-planting losses since 2000

Others aren't so sure. Some environmentalists say the wetlands aren't fit for farming and farmers are abusing the system. Critics are calling on Congress to stop subsidizing this type of coverage. Prevented-planting policies, which are overseen by the USDA but sold by insurance companies, became a part of crop insurance in 1995. The federal government, in addition to subsidizing farmers' premiums, also shoulders some of the claim-related losses.

The government picks up the tab for an average 60 percent of farmers' insurance premiums. The policies generally kick in when crop yields or revenue come in lower than expected, or, in the case of prevented-planting payments, when farmers can't get their crops in the ground.

Since its rollout, the program has come under fire from both the Government Accountability Office and the USDA's internal watchdog. In 2013, the department's inspector general cited hundreds of millions of dollars in potentially excessive payouts and said the program discouraged farmers from planting other crops later in the season when their first choice was no longer an option.

USDA spokeswoman Gwen Sparks said the prevented-plantings payments help preserve the environment. "These provisions protect the soil by providing a safety net when conditions are not suitable for planting, such as when there is too much or too little water," she said.

The debate about prevented plantings is taking shape as a broader fight about agricultural subsidies simmers on Capitol Hill. Farm-state lawmakers contend growers need to be protected from forces beyond their control, often weather related, while nonfarm representatives and fiscal conservatives maintain that the government is providing a needless and costly form of income support.

"We should not be forcing taxpayers to foot the bill for expensive subsidies to big businesses that don't need it," said Senator Jeanne Shaheen (D-NH). Ms. Shaheen was part of a group of senators earlier this year who proposed to limit government-subsidized crop insurance.

Senator John Thune (R-SD) said the number of prevented-planting claims should drop in coming years as new conservation compliance requirements deter farmers from trying to plant in areas known for being seasonal wetlands. The latest statistics "fail to recognize how recent important policy and legislative improvements will likely reduce future prevented-planting claims and protect marginal lands, including wetlands," Mr. Thune said.

So far this year, the region is getting less-than-average rainfall, suggesting that flooding won't be as big of an issue. The White House proposed new limits on prevented-planting payments in its 2016 budget. The USDA, meanwhile, is rolling out new eligibility standards specifically for Prairie Pothole farmers. Starting last year, farmers have had to show that they were able to harvest a crop at least once in the past four years. According to the National Oceanic and Atmospheric Administration, three of the ten wettest years on record in North Dakota have occurred since 2010. The situation is similar in South Dakota.

Source: Tennille Tracy, "Debate about Farmers' Crop Insurance Heightens," *The Wall Street Journal*, April 30, 2015.

10. Nutrition, SNAP, and Healthy Eating

With the nation entrenched in recession, the Food, Energy and Conservation Act of 2008 became largely a Food Stamp Bill.

THROUGHOUT 2007 AND 2008, Farm Bill negotiations were dominated by discussions of the country's deepening nutrition crises. One-third of US adults and 17 percent of children were classified as clinically obese. The ranks of citizens affected by food insecurity swelled to more than 50 million people. Nutrition programs, which already made up 50 percent of Farm Bill spending, were eventually awarded another $10 billion from Congress. The goal was to boost consumption of fruits and vegetables and increase benefits for the Supplemental Nutrition Assistance Program (SNAP) over the next decade. In the midst of the greatest economic downturn since the Great Depression, record numbers of Americans applied for government assistance each month, and SNAP received 80 percent of that increase.[1] Per-meal allowances, also known as the Thrifty Food Plan, were raised modestly, after not being updated in more than a decade.

With the nation entrenched in recession, the Food, Energy and Conservation Act of 2008 became largely a Food Stamp Bill. By 2010, with a huge infusion from the Stimulus Bill, the SNAP program would account for more than 70 cents of every dollar spent by the US Department of Agriculture.

When the next Farm Bill was passed in 2014, health statistics had not gotten much better. About 14 percent of the national population was food-insecure, which was only slightly lower than during the peak of the recession despite significant recovery in the national economy.[2] Meanwhile, almost 38 percent of the population was classified as obese. SNAP participation continued to increase until the 2014 Farm Bill was passed and has declined by several million as the economy has slowly recovered.

The 2014 bill increased funding to a few specific programs. One initiative tried to help recipients find jobs, and another established a grant program to encourage the purchase of fruits and vegetables with SNAP dollars. Although $8 billion was cut from all nutrition programs during the appropriations process, these programs overall received an additional 13 percent of the Farm Bill's budget.[3,4]

The 2014 Farm Bill also increased cooperation between nutrition and local food advocates, a partnership that began in earnest in 2008. Forceful lobbying led to the creation of the Farmers Market and Local Food Promotion Program, which received triple the funding of a similar, earlier program. Half of the program's funds go to intermediaries such as processors and distributors, generating opportunities for local farmers and consumers alike. Other improvements include more funding for Value-Added Agricultural Product Market Development Grants and Specialty Crop Block Grants as well as development of the Healthy Food Financing Initiative, which aims to expand acceptance of SNAP benefits by retailers.[5]

This merger of the public health and local food communities is an important evolution in Farm Bill discussions. It has supported innovative urban and rural food distribution networks, with the broader goals of creating jobs, increasing public access to healthy foods, and fighting hunger. One victory involved a regulatory change that required no extra spending: a geographic preference rule gives K–12 schools that receive federal funds through the National School Lunch Program the flexibility to choose local vendors rather than simply pick the lowest-cost producers.

Policy makers can improve the nation's nutrition not only through hunger prevention programs, but also by shaping what kinds of crops are grown. Specialty crop farmers—growers of fruits, nuts, and vegetables—received a slice of the Farm Bill pie for the first time in 2008. In 2014, funding for the Specialty Crop Block Grant Program increased by more than a third to $72.5 million per year and expanded to include funding for multistate projects related to marketing and research. Other specialty crop funds were used to increase supplies of vegetables and fruits in school snacks and meals and double the purchasing power of SNAP recipients who buy fruits and vegetables at farmers markets (mentioned in chapter 8). Initiatives included pilot programs for procuring fruits and vegetables in the National School Lunch Program, competitive research grants for disease research, and collection of data about local food production and regulatory compliance.[6]

A diverse food system also depends on healthy markets, which in turn require fair competition among a wide range of producers. For decades, urgent reforms have been needed to overturn unfair and abusive practices in the livestock industry. This particularly applies to the poultry sector, which is dominated by a few large companies in nearly every step of production and where one-sided contracts often keep farmers in perilous economic straits. Congress made steps toward protecting independent livestock, swine, and poultry producers from unfair contracts and practices in the 2008 Farm Bill through regulations known as the GIPSA rules. (See the "GIPSA" feature.) But due to years of intensive lobbying efforts by livestock industry associations, the revised rules remained blocked by Congress and were eventually abandoned in 2017.

GIPSA: The Fight to Restore Fair Competition to the Livestock Industry

For years, the US meat-packing industry—the small number of enormous corporations that buy and slaughter nearly all the country's livestock and poultry—has taken unfair advantage of America's independent family farmers and ranchers. This industry rigged the game to benefit huge feedlots and concentrated animal feeding operations (some of which they themselves own) and pay small poultry, hog, or cattle producers less for their animals, even when the quality of the animals is exactly the same.

Meat-packers have also turned the job of raising animals, particularly swine and poultry, into a contract arrangement more like running a factory or sweatshop. The livestock integrators own the animals, and the contractors raise them to exact specifications; responsibility for mortalities and disposal of waste lies with contractors. Smaller producers have either accepted corporate control or have left the livestock sector altogether. The agency charged with regulating anticompetitive behavior in the meat-packing industry is called the Grain Inspection, Packers and Stockyards Administration, or GIPSA. It's housed within the US Department of Agriculture (USDA). Until recently, GIPSA had not performed its intended function of regulating fair markets. Congress gave GIPSA the power to prevent large corporations from using unfair contracts, price manipulation, self-dealing, and other anticompetitive practices to gain monopoly control over the industry under the Packers and Stockyards Act of 1921, but the USDA did not issue regulations needed to implement the act until 2010.

A coalition of family farmer and rancher, food justice, antitrust, and consumer groups lobbied Congress to require the USDA to write new rules for GIPSA as part of the 2008 Farm Bill. As a result, the USDA along with the Department of Justice examined the meat-packing industry to determine the extent of anticompetitive activity in livestock markets. A new set of rules was drafted. According to those new rules, packers would have to keep records detailing why premiums are paid.

Contract terms would have to be transparent. Packers would be prohibited from retaliating against contract growers who voice concerns or seek improvements. The USDA would be required to more clearly define unfair and discriminatory practices.

The big meat-packers immediately pressured Congress and the USDA not to finalize the rules, arguing that such changes would cost the industry and consumers billions. They demanded an economic analysis, a common stalling tactic. Congress blocked the USDA from implementing the new rules for fiscal year 2012. In the meantime, the meat-packing industry marshaled all its forces to maintain unfair domination of animal food production in the next Farm Bill. Appropriations acts in subsequent years weakened the GIPSA rules. Finally in 2017, with support from industry members who actually argued they would lead to greater consolidation, the USDA decided to withdraw the revised rules.

In a similar vein, the USDA released Farmer Fair Practice Rules at the end of 2016. But due to continued opposition, implementation was delayed and eventually discarded in late 2017 following the transition in administration. Although a loophole for companies to continue operations with a "legitimate business justification" left small farmers worried about enforcement, this rule could have given contract farmers more power to sue the corporations that unfairly control nearly every aspect of their businesses.[a]

The 2008 and 2014 Farm Bills gave the USDA more power to police anticompetitive behavior by meat-packers. So far, however, a minority of powerful meat and poultry industry interests has fought off these long overdue reforms, squashing any hope for a more diversified, competitive, and fair food system.

NOTE

a. Siena Chrisman, "Long-Delayed Rules to Protect Small Farmers Might Be Too Little Too Late," *Civil Eats*, January 11, 2017.

In contrast, the organic industry has had more success in furthering its inroads into the Farm Bill. Demand for organic foods continues to exceed supply in the United States, with sales rising to $43 billion and 5 percent of the food market.[7,8] Americans buy organic foods for many reasons, including to avoid toxic synthetic fertilizers, pesticides, and growth hormones. Organic products are typically priced higher to cover the costs of certification and production methods and because supply is more limited. A recent *Consumer Reports* study of one hundred foods suggested that organics are, on average, 47 percent more expensive (and highly variable).[9] Many Americans are also willing to pay more for these products because they believe the products are healthier. Increasingly, studies suggest that some organic foods may be more nutritious than nonorganic food. A 2016 meta-analysis, for example, which looked at evidence from 170 peer-reviewed studies, found significantly higher levels of essential fatty acids, vitamin E, and iron—all critical to human health—in organic cow's milk.[10] That is at least partially because organic cows are primarily grazed, adding yet another reason we would be wise to consume products from animals raised on biologically appropriate diets. As we learn more about such benefits, perhaps the national Dietary Guidelines for Americans can one day account for the ways in which our food is grown and produced.

Organic farming has traditionally received less support than conventional production, with research, insurance, and market data collection largely ignored by Farm Bill programs, but there were some signs of progress in the 2014 bill. Importantly, almost $60 million in mandatory funding has helped producers afford the cost of organic certification, allowing them to market and price their products as organic. Increased funding for enforcement of certification standards is a double-edged sword. Reducing fraud protects consumers, but it can also create burdens, such as increased paperwork, for already overstretched farmers. California has acted progressively to update the state's own organic program, capping fees and streamlining the certification process, setting an example for other states and the National Organic Program.

Recent gains in programs supporting organic farming, specialty crop production, and nutrition education cannot be assumed to be renewed automatically. They will have to be continually championed against the forces of mainstream resistance to be included and appropriated in future Farm Bills.

Organic's Fair Share

By 2014, the organic food movement was reaping the benefits of more than three decades of pioneering work from farmers, retailers, and consumers across the country. While economic growth in much of the food industry remained static, the market for certified organic products was experiencing brisk yearly expansion. Annual sales of organic foods exceeded $43 billion by the time of the 2014 Farm Bill reauthorization, capturing more than 5 percent of all food sales. "Organic food was moving into the mainstream, but not in terms of federal support," said Bob Scowcroft, founder and former director of the Organic Farming Research Foundation. "Our strategy was simple. We wanted our fair share of research dollars and other production support from national Farm Bill programs."

The "fair share" strategy started during the lead-up to the 2002 Farm Bill. At that time, organic farming was not included in the definition of "good farming practices" that qualified farmers for federal crop insurance benefits. With a legislative champion in the farmers' corner, an amendment was introduced to include organic farming under that provision. Although it ultimately passed into law, there would be further reforms necessary to tailor crop insurance premiums to the high value of organic crops.

This small victory was symbolic of the growing influence of the organic food and farming movement on the political process. Organizational capacity had been steadily increasing over the years. Consumers had once generated more than 300,000 public responses to defeat an attempt to allow sewage sludge, genetically modified organisms, and nuclear irradiation under the national organic standards. Groups such as the Organic Trade Association, National Organic Coalition, Organic Farming Research Foundation, Organic Consumers Union, Center for Food Safety, and National Sustainable Agriculture Coalition as well as grower cooperatives and others presented a formidable voting block.

It helped to have sympathetic allies in Congress with aides willing to craft language that their legislators could champion. A bipartisan "Organic Caucus" consisting of three Democratic and three Republican representatives formed in 2003 to drive the movement's legislative agenda. A primary focus was on research dollars to develop innovative strategies and markets for organically produced crops. The 2002 Farm Bill had introduced a modest pilot research program: $15 million over five years.

The Organic Caucus wanted to expand that research purse devoted exclusively to organic and sustainable agriculture to 2.5 to 3 percent of the $1 billion annual US Department of Agriculture research budget. (In the end, $78 million in research funding was devoted to organic farming over the five-year course of the bill.) A second policy objective was to help farmers with third-party certification, a time-consuming and costly part of verifying that something is actually grown according to standards. (That effort netted $22 million over five years. Individual farms can receive up to 75 percent of certification costs, with a $750 limit.) Funds were also approved to assist farmers transitioning from conventional to organic production, a process that typically takes three years to complete.

Champions like Sam Farr (D-CA) and Tom Harkin (D-IA) ultimately pushed these programs into the law and budget. There is still a long way to go to actually defend organic's fair share of the Farm Bill budget. In the short term, however, there has been a push for more crop insurance that takes into consideration organic's high cost and value in the marketplace (known as price elections), along with better market data collection to improve trending and forecasting. Finally, conservation programs such as the Environmental Quality Incentives Program (EQIP) now recognize organic production as an environmental benefit.

After membership and interest began to wane, the Organic Caucus was revived in 2010 when freshman Representative Richard Hanna (R-NY) joined three long-time Democratic members. Today, membership includes ten Republicans and thirty-three Democrats.[a] Before passage of the 2014 Farm Bill, some of the caucus's top priorities included better integration of organic systems and requirements into EQIP and the Conservation Stewardship Program, improving oversight, national data collection, and requiring price elections for organic crops.[b] Only the first one has not yet been advanced.[c] The organic industry celebrated many other victories in 2014, including nearly doubling the certification cost-sharing program from $4.4 million to $11.5 million per year, strengthening aspects of the National Organic Program, and maintaining funding for research and data collection. One hopes that the Organic Caucus can continue to leverage its share of Farm Bill funding to focus on the real goal: helping organic farming practices become the standard for agriculture in a country focused on health, a clean environment, energy conservation, and food security.

Lessons from the Organic Caucus

1. Assess Your Organizational Capacity. Be honest. How much time do you and your organization have to devote to the Farm Bill? Are there other nongovernmental organizations with which you can collaborate? Among the coalition, who has connections in Washington, DC? Who has media skills? Can you forge a strategy together?

2. Determine Your Congressional Allies. Do you know anyone on the Agriculture or Agriculture Appropriations Committees? Can you find a sympathetic staff person who can help with the long, hard work ahead?

3. Create a Media Strategy. Identify influential publications and key reporters on the national and regional agricultural policy beat, such as the *Washington Post*, the *New York Times*, and *Politico*. Look for charismatic spokespeople—farmers, doctors, policy makers, school lunch directors—to carry your message to the media. Help reporters in your area tell Farm Bill stories (good and bad) that can influence local representatives and voters.

4. Generate Funding to Support Your Effort. A combination of special events, corporate support, and grant writing can help you pay people, including interns, for the hard work that this Farm Bill lobbying entails. Budgets may include travel to Washington, DC.

NOTES

a. "Is Your Representative a Member of the Organic Caucus?," National Organic Coalition, 2018.

b. Price elections allow organic producers with crop insurance to receive a payout rate higher than the conventional price in case of loss. As of 2017, 79 crops had premium price elections.

c. "Organic in the Farm Bill," National Organic Coalition, February 19, 2014.

11. Agribusiness versus Family Farms

Of the hundreds and even thousands of plant and animal species cultivated for human use, the Farm Bill favors just four primary groups: food grains, feed grains, oilseeds, and upland cotton. Most are either fed to cattle in confinement or processed into oils, flours, starches, sugars, other industrial food additives, or ethanol.

BILLIONS OF FARM BILL DOLLARS flow into America's rural communities each year to boost income for farmers, who continue to face cycles of financial, environmental, and agricultural challenges. But are the farmers and landowners who cash those subsidy checks the ultimate beneficiaries of these programs, or are other interests being served? Following the money trail involves understanding the complex circumstances surrounding what it means to be a "farm." It also requires focusing on why the government singles out so few crops for the majority of subsidies. Finally, it means drilling down into deep divides: family farms versus corporate mega-farms, producers versus buyers, and commodity versus diversified agriculture.

Farm Bill funding is undoubtedly skewed toward a narrow group of crops and the handful of congressional districts where those crops are grown. Of the $323 billion US taxpayer dollars spent on subsidies between 1995 and 2014, almost 70 percent went to the production of just five crops: *corn, wheat, cotton, soybeans*, and *rice*. More than half of that money went to the eight states that produce most of those commodities.[1] These statistics did not improve with the end of direct and counter-cyclical payments; the top six crops still accounted for 94 percent of all outlays, and the basic structure continues to favor the same monoculture crops.[2] Furthermore, the system is easily exploited. Between 1995 and 2014, fifty billionaires from the Forbes 400 list of wealthiest Americans received $6.3 million in subsidies.[3] Although the 2014 Farm Bill prevented subsidy payments to farmers earning more than $900,000 per year, it did not include restrictions on crop insurance premium subsidies.

With these broad-brush strokes, it's easy to demonize commodity farmers. The media frequently cite this statistic: the richest 10 percent of farm subsidy recipients take in more than three-fourths of payments. Although the system certainly suffers from rampant abuse, those numbers must be unpacked to get a more accurate assessment of the financial state of the American farm.

The US Department of Agriculture (USDA) identifies approximately 2.1 million farms in the country. In fact, the agency's definition of a farm is quite broad: "any place from which $1,000 or more of agricultural products were produced or sold, or normally would have been sold, during the census year." When the USDA averages farm income, it includes a sizable category called "rural residence farms": households that may own a cow or a few sheep but do not list their occupation as "farmer." Only 45.8 percent of farms actually grow enough crops or animals to earn more than $100,000 a year, and 22 percent are producing so little that they don't even clear $1,000 a year.[4] Such mini-farms generally do not receive subsidies, and their households rely primarily on off-farm income, yet they represent two-thirds of all "farms" surveyed by the USDA. The paychecks these people get from other jobs are also taken into account when the USDA tallies "average farm income." This practice makes it appear as if the majority of American farmers do not receive subsidies and have above-average income.

Just a fraction—around 10 percent—of all farms generates nearly 75 percent of the agricultural output, primarily because they have specialized in commodity crops (figure 13). The family farm is a dying breed. Although the average American farm measures about 415 acres, farms of that size are, in fact, becoming increasingly difficult to find. Although mega-farms and so-called hobby farms are increasing, it is the medium-scale operations, with acreage between 50 and 2,000 acres, that are declining.

Focus on that slice of small and mid-sized farms that make up less than 10 percent of all operations—those that gross between $100,000 and $250,000 from farming and whose operators claim farming as their primary occupation—and a far different picture develops. According to an analysis of USDA farm data by Tufts University researcher Timothy A. Wise, in 2003, these commercial family farms earned an average net income of $30,000 a year from farming, more than half of which came from subsidy payments. Based on USDA data from 2014, small family farms earned an average net income of about $42,000.[5] Of all small and mid-sized farms in this income segment, 82 percent received some sort of government payment. In other words, contrary to popular belief, a significant majority of family farmers receive benefits from farm programs and rely on them to keep their operations afloat.

Even when commodity prices reached record highs in 2007, family farmers continued to struggle. While corn prices increased 87 percent between 2003 and 2007, fertilizer costs jumped 67 percent. Fuel costs doubled. Since then, the price of corn has fallen to just over half of that peak, and fertilizer prices have fallen as well. As a result, the new Price Loss Coverage and Agricultural Risk Coverage, designed to guarantee revenue, won't lead to substantial decreases in payments to farmers. Total government farm payments were just above $11 billion—only 7 percent lower in 2017 compared

Figure 13

Only the Mega-Farms Succeed
Average US Farm Household Income

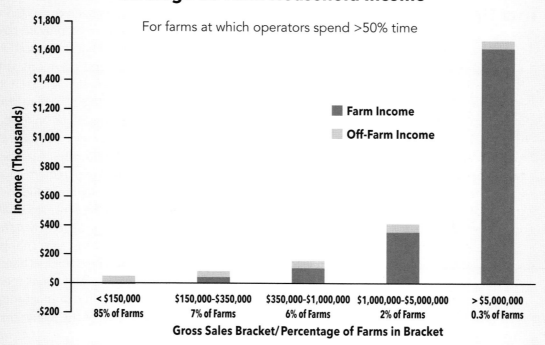

Sources: Hoppe, Robert. "Structure and Finances of US Farms: Family Farm Report, 2014 Edition." Bulletin 132. December 2014. USDA Economic Research Service; Economic Research Service. "Farming and Farm Income." 2017. US Department of Agriculture.

to 2008.[6] As both national net farm income and median farm income have fallen since 2014, median off-farm income also continues to rise and help buffer against a more significant loss.[7]

The elite group of mega-farms felt no such squeeze. These large commercial farms that earn more than $350,000 per year control vast acreages and benefit from farm payments tied to land ownership and historical production. According to Wise's analysis of USDA data, very large commercial farms were responsible for 44 percent of commodity crop production and received 32 percent of commodity payments in 2003. "The concentration of farm payments," Wise wrote, "is caused primarily by the concentration of land and production in the hands of a relatively small number of large farmers. It may be necessary to address the root causes of this concentration in order to meaningfully address inequities in US farm programs."[8] This concentration is reflected in figure 14.

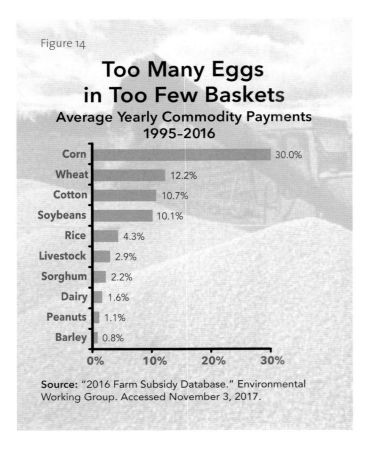

Figure 14

Too Many Eggs in Too Few Baskets
Average Yearly Commodity Payments 1995–2016

Commodity	Payment
Corn	30.0%
Wheat	12.2%
Cotton	10.7%
Soybeans	10.1%
Rice	4.3%
Livestock	2.9%
Sorghum	2.2%
Dairy	1.6%
Peanuts	1.1%
Barley	0.8%

Source: "2016 Farm Subsidy Database." Environmental Working Group. Accessed November 3, 2017.

Starting in the 1970s, federal law technically capped annual subsidy payments at $50,000 per farm, but farmers and landowners easily circumvented it by morphing into multiple entities (sometimes referred to as Christmas trees), each eligible for payouts. Even among those "wealthy farmers" at the top of the scale, however, the statistics can be somewhat misleading. None of the top 20 recipients of government farm and conservation payments between 1995 and 2010 was an individual family farm. Instead, their ranks included corporations, Native American tribes, cooperatives that distributed payments among their members, and, to a lesser extent, conservation organizations.[9]

It is important to keep in mind the type of agriculture—for both plants and animals—that the federal subsidy system has intentionally perpetuated. The farm sector has been converted to a manufacturing model, designed to provide buyers with a lowest-cost product. Labor is replaced with energy-intensive machinery and chemicals whenever possible. Those are extremely high costs that are most economically beneficial when spread over a maximum number of acres or animals. For example, a new modern tractor or combine may cost upward of $300,000 (not including accessory equipment and upgrades) and then require an average of $200 for every hour it operates (due to fuel, repairs, maintenance, etc.).[10,11] Once invested in such a capital-intensive system, it is extremely difficult for an operator to make any significant change in the scale or approach to farming. In fact, as harvests and production become more and more mechanized, the main response, like in manufacturing, is simply to try to grow the scale of the operation.

LOOPHOLES

It's understandable that we want to ease the plight of the family farmer, but as we can see from the discussion above, drawing a line between what constitutes a family farm and a corporate mega-farm has become extremely complicated. One recurring problem with farm subsidies is the lack of practical limits on how much a single farming operation can receive. Thanks to numerous legal loopholes, lax enforcement, and loose definitions of what it means to be actively engaged in farming, essentially no caps currently exist.

In 1986, the Prince of Liechtenstein infamously collected more than $2 million in cotton and rice subsidies as absentee landowner and half-owner in a Texas farming operation.[12] In response, Congress created the so-called three-entity rule in 1987.

Under this provision, a farmer could collect $50,000 in subsidies in his own name and, as half-owner, up to $25,000 for each of two other entities.[13] Since those limits were enacted, however, new subsidy programs have proliferated and new loopholes have further eroded subsidy caps. Farmers and landowners creatively form complex family partnerships with associated limited liability companies that grow new tentacles into the subsidy gravy train. Lawyers and accountants opportunistically exploit these loopholes, offering "payment limitations planning" services that stretch the legal definitions of "actively engaged in farming." According to a report in the *Atlanta Journal-Constitution*, for example, in 2005 at least 195 US farming operations—or, more accurately, landowners—collected more than $1 million each from taxpayers.[14] That same year, 100,000 farms nationwide received between $25,000 and $100,000 each.

European princes haven't been the only sources of indignation. The Scotty Pippin Rule—drafted after the multimillionaire professional basketball player's farm subsidy receipts made headlines in 2002—determined that no one with an adjusted gross income of more than $2.5 million (of which less than 75 percent came from farming) could receive program supports. Enforcing such rules has become a bureaucratic nightmare, though, and the payment system is easily scammed. In 2004, a Government Accountability Office study found that USDA Farm Service Agency field offices failed to use their own tools to determine eligibility at least half of the time.[15]

Today, commodity payments are capped at $125,000 per year per individual. Only those earning up to $900,000 in adjusted gross income (which is reduced by deductions and exemptions) qualify.

This limit no longer distinguishes between on-farm and off-farm income, as did the 2008 Farm Bill, and no longer includes an exemption for farmers earning most of their income on the farm. The current subsidy system still provides too much leniency for big earners because crop insurance subsidies do not have payment limitations. In the 2016 report by the Congressional Budget Office (CBO), "Options for Reducing the Deficit: 2017 to 2026," one option is lowering the government's subsidy of premiums from 60 percent to 40 percent. By decreasing payments primarily to mega-farms, spending would decrease by $27 billion over ten years.[16] However, again according to a CBO estimate, crop subsidies (excluding insurance premiums) between 2016 and 2018 will exceed initial estimates by $7.5 billion.[17]

A lot of nonfarmers receive subsidy payments. According to a 2015 *Economist* article, the federal government paid $3 million between 2007 and 2011 in subsidies to landowners who did not farm any crops.[18] Congress members past and present have also been beneficiaries, sometimes raking in sizable yearly payments. According to the Environmental Working Group, thirty-six members of Congress or their immediate family members received farm subsidies between 1995 and 2014, some totaling millions of dollars and overall reaching $9.5 million.[19] Between 2008 and 2012, $10.6 million went to farmers who had passed away at least a year before.[20]

THE TRUE BENEFICIARIES

Today's Farm Bill subsidies represent a complete departure from the price-stabilization policies that dominated the first four decades of these bills. In general, the government purchased grain from farmers during harvest time when it was plentiful and sold it off when grain was scarce. Other programs, such as land set-asides, also helped manage supply, boost prices, and impose some fundamental soil conservation practices.

These programs were slowly dismantled beginning in the 1970s, when globalization began to shape the political and economic agenda. The US government encouraged its farmers to plant fencerow to fencerow to generate exports. By 1996, the grain reserve program was eliminated by a Republican-dominated Congress. With the government out of the supply management game, farmers once again planted as much as they could, hoping to get ahead. The result was oversupply that resulted in a market free fall. In the ensuing years, the price of corn fell to an average of 23 percent below the farmers' cost of production. As rural communities foundered, Congress instituted so-called emergency payments in 1998 to help keep farmers afloat. Those payments were made permanent in the 2002 Farm Bill.

With that move, the United States completed its shift away from policies designed to stabilize commodity prices for farmers to a system that encourages low market prices and then attempts to make up the difference with subsidies, revenue insurance, and disaster assistance programs. Meanwhile, policies continue to support primarily monoculture crops that promote land and water degrading practices and poor diets.

In the meantime, the companies that buy commodity crops have been riding high. According to researchers Timothy Wise and Elanor Starmer, Tyson, the country's largest chicken producer, saved nearly $300 million per year in the decade after the 1996 Farm Bill because it could buy chicken feed at a price lower than what farmers (and the government) paid to produce it. Smithfield, the

world's largest hog producer, saved nearly the same amount. In total, the top four chicken companies saved more than $11 billion in the decade after the 1996 Farm Bill, and the top four hog giants saved nearly $9 billion on their feed costs.[21]

Big processed food manufacturers have also fared well following the dismantlement of USDA supply management programs that attempted to promote fair minimum prices for farmers. According to a 2011 paper by Food and Water Watch and Public Health Institute, corporations like Coca-Cola reap huge capital benefits when high-fructose corn syrup (HFCS) is cheap and abundant. That's because just 2 cents of every consumer dollar spent on soda returns to the pockets of farmers who grow the corn that becomes HFCS. The remaining 98 cents goes to the beverage manufacturers and marketers. The authors report that soda companies have saved an estimated $100 million each year on their corn bill since supply controls were dismantled. Going back to the 1980s when HFCS began to replace cane sugar as a sweetener of choice, those total savings reached $1.7 billion.[22] An often-quoted USDA study revealed that the overall revenue farmers receive from every dollar of an average food item purchase is closer to 15 cents.[23] So, Coca-Cola represents a rather extreme, although not isolated, example. It is important given the growing emphasis on taxation and reduction of soda consumption by public health advocates. Should our farm supports enable the manufacture of cheap unhealthy products or invest in other more profound public health outcomes?

Another sticky issue is that farmers who grow the perishable produce necessary to support a balanced diet have been kept out of the subsidy game for decades. With 20,000 miles of waterways, nearly 80,000 farms, and more than $33 billion in annual on-farm crop revenues (even following two years of intense drought), California tops all states in terms of agricultural sales, yet 90 percent of its growers receive no subsidies. California contributes almost 12 percent of the total US agricultural market value, including two-thirds of fruits and nuts, one-third of vegetables, and 20 percent of dairy, yet its farmers receive less than 4 percent of agricultural subsidies.[24,25] Florida is another prolific food producer, with extensive citrus, row crop, dairy, and calf breeding operations, yet only 10 percent of Florida's farms and ranches receive agricultural subsidies.[26] If farm payments were based on overall contributions to the nation's specialty crops rather than the narrowly targeted commodity groups, ten other states with large, but mostly unsupported, farm sectors would also immediately benefit (figure 15).[27] Other regions traditionally left out would also get their due on par relative to their food and fiber output: all of New England (from Maine to Connecticut), the Mid-Atlantic (from New York to Maryland), most of the upper Midwest, and states scattered across the South and West.[28]

A FAIRER SYSTEM

In understanding the subsidy game, it's often more important to know who ultimately benefits from policies rather than who gets the money directly. The real winners in the subsidy explosion have been the animal feedlot operators and the largest corporate mega-farms along with input suppliers like Monsanto, a host of service industry providers, and the big grain traders: ADM, Bunge, Cargill, and Dreyfus. Small and mid-sized growers depend on subsidies to stay afloat, sometimes even in highly profitable years. Meanwhile, big industrial growers

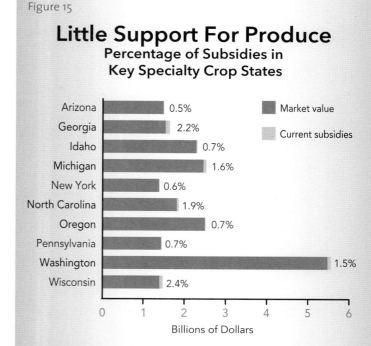

Figure 15

Little Support For Produce
Percentage of Subsidies in Key Specialty Crop States

After California and Florida, each of these states produces more than one billion dollars-worth of specialty crops per year but receives less than five percent of our national subsidies.

Source: "2014 Farm Subsidy Database." Environmental Working Group. "2012 Census of Agriculture: Specialty Crops, Volume 2 Part 8." USDA National Agricultural Statistics Service.

thrive. Isn't there a better system to qualify who actually needs support and under what conditions?

The answers may require a fundamental shift away from twentieth-century policies that encourage overproduction and low prices. Policies should be reoriented toward a holistic system that focuses on community well-being—one that helps qualifying family farmers earn a fair price for their products, caps payments, rewards stewardship, and incentivizes more resilient and regenerative farming methods.

Subsidy Tracking

1. From 2007 to 2011, 2,300 farms that didn't grow any crops received a total of $3 million in subsidies.[a]

2. In 2015, US taxpayers funded approximately $20 billion in agricultural subsidies. As farm prices have continued to fall and price and revenue coverage make up for this difference, this amount will surely increase.[b]

3. Of the farms that receive payments, those selling less than $1,000 get 9.36 cents per dollar of output, but those selling more than $1 million get 2 cents per dollar of output.[c]

4. Farms that are large or grow commodities are more likely to receive payments from multiple programs than are farms that are small or grow specialty crops. This discrepancy may have a negative unintended consequence of increasing price risk among these farmers.[d]

5. Another unintended consequence results from planting restrictions among farmers who receive payments for commodities: fruit and vegetable acreage falls by 4.26 for every 100 acres of those that are subsidized.[e]

6. Economist Julian Alston estimates that government spending on research would be more effective in supporting farm income than are subsidies. Although farmers receive 50 cents per dollar spent on subsidies, they could benefit by up to $10 if that dollar were spent on research and development.[f]

7. Over a five-year period, participants receiving the ten highest crop insurance premium subsidies insured an average of 39,000 acres and collected an average of $2.6 million in premium subsidies and approximately $2.5 million in claims payouts.[g]

8. The new Agricultural Risk Coverage and Price Loss Coverage programs are now predicted to pay more than $24 billion, which is $2.4 billion more than the direct payments they replaced, over the five years of implementation in response to falling food costs.[h]

9. Under the Agricultural Risk Coverage program, most counties in Ohio, Iowa, Minnesota, and Kansas are projected to receive between $60 and $200 per acre—a drastic increase from the average of $24 per acre for direct payments—just for corn.[i]

10. Crop insurance subsidies are predicted to reach $85 billion—a 27 percent increase over the previous decade—over the next ten years of implementation.[j]

NOTES

a. "Milking Taxpayers," *The Economist*, February 12, 2015.

b. "Milking Taxpayers."

c. Jayson L. Lusk, "The Evolving Role of the USDA in the Food and Agricultural Economy," Mercatus Research at George Mason University, June 2016.

d. Lusk, "The Evolving Role."

e. Joseph V. Balagtas et al., "How Has US Farm Policy Influenced Fruit and Vegetable Production?," *Applied Economic Perspectives and Policy* 36, no. 2 (2014): 265–86.

f. Julian M. Alston, "Efficiency of Income Transfers to Farmers through Public Agricultural Research: Theory and Evidence from the United States," *American Journal of Agricultural Economics* 91, no. 5 (2009): 1281–88.

g. Government Accountability Office, "Crop Insurance: Reducing Subsidies for Highest Income Participants Could Save Federal Dollars with Minimal Effect on the Program," GAO-15-356, March 2015.

h. Integrated Policy Research Group, "U.S. Baseline Briefing Book Projections for Agricultural and Biofuel Markets," University of Missouri Food and Agricultural Policy Research Institute, March 2015.

i. Anne Weir Schechinger, "Crop Subsidies Soar under 2014 Farm Bill 'Reforms,'" Environmental Working Group, March 13, 2015.

j. Integrated Policy Research Group, "U.S. Baseline Briefing."

12. Job Creation

Farmers over age sixty-five now outnumber those under thirty-five by a ratio of more than six to one. From 2015 to 2020, 91.5 million acres of agricultural lands—an area larger than the amount of land set aside in all our national parks combined—will be transferred to new owners.

"IF WE ARE NOT CAREFUL, WE COULD LOSE THE FARM AND THE FOOD SYSTEM ON OUR WATCH." That drastic warning came from A. G. Kawamura in 2005, when he was secretary of the California Department of Food and Agriculture.

Kawamura was not only alluding to how important forward-thinking policy is to the food system; he also knew that people who grow food for a living are becoming a dying breed. Already, agriculture is greatly diminished in terms of economic measures: it represents just 1.2 percent of the US gross domestic product (GDP); services make up 77 percent and manufacturing 22 percent of GDP. Farming has become a forgotten career path as well.

Farmers over age sixty-five now outnumber those under thirty-five by a ratio of more than six to one (figure 16). From 2015 to 2020, 91.5 million acres of agricultural lands—an area larger than the amount of land set aside in all our national parks combined—will have been transferred to new owners,[1] but who will be those new owners? Youth continue to migrate out from the corn-rich heartland and leave agriculture altogether. Many interested younger Americans simply can't afford the costs of entry into farming. Others won't accept the economic instability of the job. For many, food production seems less appealing than opportunities in business and technology. Meanwhile, the United States edges toward becoming a net importer of foods. The country already imports $119 billion in agricultural products each year[2] (figure 17).

In short, we don't have enough people becoming farmers, and we're importing food to fill the gap. Yet few people are debating our flagging national food security with the fervor expressed about manufacturing jobs shipped overseas.

Figure 16

Young Farmer Deficit
Share of Beginning Farmers* by County

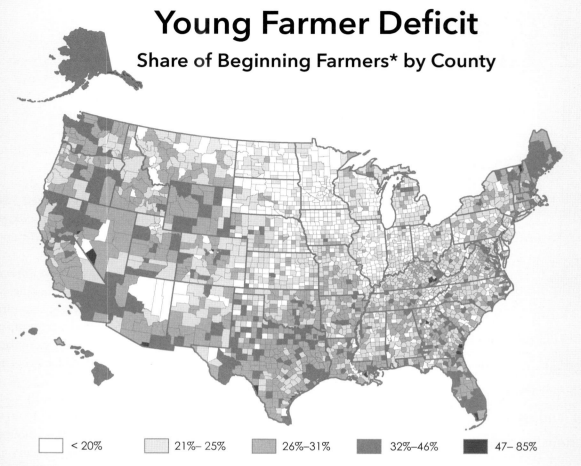

☐ < 20%   ☐ 21%– 25%   ▨ 26%–31%   ▨ 32%–46%   ■ 47– 85%

*Beginning farmers are here defined as having worked on any farm for less than ten years.

As the average age of farmers continues to rise, so have concerns about a pending farmer shortage and diminished innovation on the farm. There are several reasons why fewer people are choosing to become farmers: the cost of entry is very high, the lifestyle is difficult, and it has become increasingly hard to make a living as a farmer. This map shows just how few beginning farmers there are in the United States. There were 20 percent fewer beginning farmers in the 2012 Census of Agriculture than the previous 2007 census. The largest percent increases occurred in Alaska, Rhode Island, and Maine, and the smallest occurred in much of the Midwest—that is, where the predominant volume of agricultural production occurs. However, it is important to keep in mind that beginning farmers are not necessarily young farmers. In fact, in 2012, 36 percent of beginning farmers were age fifty-five years or older.

Source: "USDA Census of Agriculture." 2012. US Department of Agriculture. "2012 Census of Agriculture." May 14, 2014. Farmland Information Center.

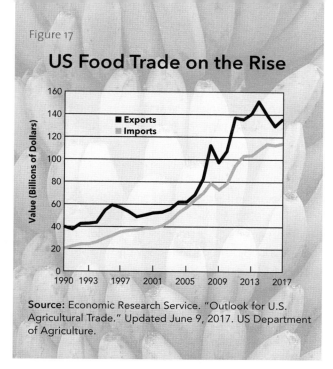

Figure 17

US Food Trade on the Rise

Value (Billions of Dollars)

■ Exports
■ Imports

1990 1993 1997 2001 2005 2009 2013 2017

Source: Economic Research Service. "Outlook for U.S. Agricultural Trade." Updated June 9, 2017. US Department of Agriculture.

Even our domestic foods are processed and distributed by an ever-smaller group of corporations.[3] Today, the majority of our food supply is in the hands of a combination of foreign producers and corporate executives as opposed to family farmers and a diverse corps of processors and regional distributors.

With just 1 percent of the US population producing food for the remaining 99 percent, the efficiency of the existing food system is staggering. In 1900, it took 147 hours of human labor to grow 100 bushels of wheat. By 1990, that number had shrunk to 6 hours. Similarly, the amount of human labor required to produce 1,000 pounds of broiler chickens fell from 85 hours to less than 1 hour between 1929 and 1980.[4] Imagine someone raising 1,000 pounds of chicken meat—from baby chicks to slaughter—with less than 1 hour of labor. It can be hard to comprehend the scale, mechanization, and infrastructure of a system that can produce almost nine billion meat chickens every year.

Although such efficiency is impressive, it comes with costs and trade-offs. Fewer hours of labor means fewer jobs for farmers. Fewer farmers means more consolidation, less diversity of crops, declining rural communities, and reduced food security.

In 2010, former Secretary of Agriculture Tom Vilsack introduced the idea of using Farm Bill programs to add 100,000 new farmers (an echo of a Clinton-era program to add 100,000 police officers to the nation's streets). The 2014 Farm Bill increased funding to $20 million annually for training and outreach for beginning farmers and ranchers. Also in 2014, the US Department of Agriculture (USDA) launched a "New Farmers" website, intended to help new (and especially minority) farmers learn about resources available to them to pursue agriculture. Given current population trends, these newcomers would barely begin to replace an aging farming generation. Still, it's a step in the right direction. More farmers and food systems workers could mean a new generation of stewards of the land and a vessel for the skills and traditions of agriculture that are at risk of being lost. A concerted new farmer program could help increase the number of small and mid-sized farms, boost food entrepreneurship, and reverse poverty in rural areas. Job creation—increasing the number of farmers—will continue to be central to future Farm Bills. It will surely become part of Farm Bill rhetoric to justify ongoing agricultural policies as well, especially as budget constraints take center stage.

The push for more farmers is finding support in the surging nationwide interest in local food production. These local food systems cover a great deal of ground: farmers who grow food; school and institutional cafeterias that purchase it; processing facilities that add value to fruits, vegetables, and meat and dairy products; new markets and distribution networks that link producers and eaters; and now even gleaning and other repurposing initiatives to reduce waste and feed the hungry. Rebuilding local or regional food systems does not mean ending international food trade, as some suggest. It merely means restoring some geographic and seasonal balance to food production. As populations become more urbanized and the climate increasingly uncertain, boosting regional farming capacities is seen as one way to provide jobs, increase access to healthy food, and create some degree of self-sufficiency.

THE FOOD HUB

Consumers could do their part in local farm job creation by eating their daily recommended allotment of fruits and vegetables. The Centers for Disease Control and Prevention estimated that only one in ten Americans actually eats five daily servings of fruits, nuts, and vegetables.[5] Depending on the season, many Americans increasingly rely on farmers from other countries to keep them supplied year-round with tomatoes, apples, and berries. According to the USDA, if Americans increased their consumption of fruits and vegetables to meet the Dietary Guidelines for Americans, we would need an additional 13 million acres of "specialty crops"—and that was estimated at a time when almost one in five ate the recommended daily servings. That's about two times what the country currently devotes to fruit and vegetable production and three times the acres in California currently under fruit and vegetable production.

What if we made a concerted effort to increase the amount of fruits, nuts, and vegetables on a regional basis? The regional food hub, a centralized facility where local produce and animal products are aggregated, stored, processed, and distributed, is gaining traction in Farm Bill circles. There are already more than 350 operational food hubs around the country, with large clusters in the Midwest and Northeast. The average food hub generates nearly $1 million in annual sales and an estimated thirteen jobs. Food hubs mean new marketing opportunities for local farmers: the average food hub is supplied by forty small and mid-sized farms. They are prime examples of applying new approaches to management, technology, marketing, and infrastructure to revitalize traditional food production arrangements. Farmers receive a fair price for their products, and consumers value the quality of their food as well as the experience of interacting directly with local farmers. Support from the 2014 Farm Bill comes from the Farmers Market and Local Food Production Program, which helps these various enterprises expand marketing and distribution.

There are other signs of hope for the next generation of farmers. Innovative partnerships are combining local, state, and federal programs to establish revolving loan funds and forgivable loan funds to help new growers get started. The past three Farm Bills contained several provisions to assist beginning farmers and ranchers, and USDA leaders have shown a renewed interest in young farmers. One of the most prominent programs, the Beginning Farmer and Rancher Development Program, received $20 million per year from 2014 through 2018 in addition to the $75 million allocated by the 2008 Farm Bill from 2009 to 2012 (see the "Beginning Farmer Incubator Programs" feature).

To keep agriculture healthy into the future, however, subsidies will need to be more responsive to the next generation of farmers. Our current subsidy system is based on insurance and price coverage that reward established mega-farms and risky behavior rather than good land stewardship. An alternative payment scheme that better rewards hard work, crop yields, and conservation practices would draw more beginning farmers to the trade.

Beginning Farm Programs
Initiated by Recent Farm Bills

Beginning Farmers and Ranchers Individual Development Accounts (BFRIDA): Provides beginning farmers of limited means with business and financial education and matched savings accounts. The 2014 Farm Bill again directed the US Department of Agriculture (USDA) to start pilot projects in at least fifteen states, but this program has yet to receive funding.

Beginning Farmer and Rancher Development Program (BFRDP): Funds education, extension, outreach, and technical assistance initiatives for beginning farmers and ranchers. The 2014 Farm Bill gave the program mandatory funding of $20 million per year, with an emphasis on veterans.

Office of Advocacy and Outreach: Established to improve access to USDA programs for small farms and ranches, beginning farmers and ranchers, and socially disadvantaged farmers and ranchers. The 2014 Farm Bill added eligibility for veterans.

Outreach and Technical Assistance for Socially Disadvantaged Farmers and Ranchers ("Section 2501"): Provides grants to organizations that assist minority farmers in owning and operating farms and participating in agricultural and USDA-specific programs. It received $10 million per year—less than half that in the 2008 Farm Bill—in mandatory funding from the 2014 Farm Bill.

Conservation Reserve Program—Transition Incentive Program (CRP TIP): Creates incentives for CRP contract holders to sell or lease to beginning or minority farmers to begin sustainable practices to transition to organic production. It received $33 million in mandatory funding from the 2014 Farm Bill.

Land Contract Guarantee: Provides assurance of selling land through a multiyear contract for retiring farmers. Established by 2002 Farm Bill and reauthorized in 2014.

Down Payment Loans: Helps beginning or minority farmers purchase property through low-interest loans. It was reauthorized with a lower interest rate and allowing land of higher value in 2014.

Direct and Guaranteed Farm Loans: Supports start-up costs and guarantees commercial loans for family farmers. The 2014 Farm Bill eliminated term limits, among other changes that added flexibility.

Microloans: Provides loans up to $50,000 to cover annual operating expenses or investments related to operations. The 2014 Farm Bill permanently reauthorized the program and also made changes to add flexibility.

Source: "Farm Bill Programs and Grants—Overview," National Sustainable Agriculture Coalition, accessed July 4, 2017.

Beginning Farmer Incubator Programs

At a time when American farmers are aging and mega-farms are gobbling up medium-sized operations, the Agriculture and Land-Based Training Association (ALBA) has a bold mission: bringing new faces to agriculture. It is no small task. Farming remains one of the most challenging professions, requiring experience, planning and business skills, start-up capital, and access to land.

ALBA is dedicated to breaking down those barriers to becoming a farmer. Three hundred and fifty farmers have graduated from its rigorous farmer education program in the Salinas Valley, which is referred to as the nation's salad bowl because nearly two-thirds of all leafy greens grown in the United States come from this one valley. Farm Bill dollars and nonprofit foundation grants provide about one-third of the funding for ALBA's farmer incubator project, and a burgeoning organic produce distribution business provides the rest.[a]

"ALBA is like a school that invests in human development today and will provide returns well into the future," said executive director Patricia Carrillo. "Unlike a school, the payback is also immediate. ALBA incubates thirty to forty farm businesses in any given year, employing around seventy people and growing organic strawberries and vegetables worth over $2 million. Alumni farming off-site are greater in number and size, generating far more economic output. ALBA Organics itself has sold over $25 million in organic produce in the last decade, driving start-up farm sustainability. Needless to say, the economic impact resulting from USDA programs far exceeds the grant funding awarded."[b] Beyond the Beginning Farmer and Rancher Development Program, ALBA relies on funding from the Environmental Quality Incentives Program (EQIP), the Socially Disadvantaged and Veteran Farmer and Rancher Development Program, and other USDA sources.

To enter the ALBA farmer incubator program, known as the Farmer Education and Enterprise Development Program, students must first complete a nine-month basic training, which includes both classroom and farm training and field days, culminating with writing a farm plan and applying for a plot of ALBA's land to cultivate. This education takes place in the evenings and on weekends so that participants can maintain their regular jobs. Each year, at least thirty-five students farm on ALBA's 100 acres of organic land during many stages of their training. ALBA Organics, ALBA's food hub, distributes products to markets throughout the Bay Area to help grow its businesses.

ALBA is designed to nurture a beginning farmer for five years. After that, the training and below-cost land rentals end. Graduates have to make it on their own in the marketplace and pay the going rate for land rentals.

Many of ALBA's graduate growers are finding success. Among the graduates, "160 have launched an organic farm business at ALBA. Nearly half of these farms are still in operation, providing economic independence to workers who had relied on low-paying, seasonal fieldwork," said Carrillo. "Others used the skills gained at ALBA to find more gainful employment in Monterey County's thriving agriculture sector, which is rapidly transitioning to organic farming practices. Either way, ALBA's goal is to connect hard-working, limited resource farmers to opportunities in the sector."[c]

ALBA also focuses on a sector of the farming population often overlooked by many policy programs—low-income, primarily Hispanic communities—believing that the Latino community will play a strong role in the next generation of farmers. According to Carrillo, "ALBA serves immigrant field workers, developing their skills to advance their employment prospects or help them pursue the dream of farm ownership."[d]

Mendoza Family at ALBA

They include farmers like Javier Zamora, who grew up on a family farm in Mexico. Zamora came to the United States in 1986 but did not return to farming for more than two decades, at which point he returned to school to study horticulture production and learned about ALBA. After graduating, he rented about 1.5 acres with support from ALBA and began his first venture in organic farming. He finally purchased his ranch, with more than 200 acres, in 2017, and his operation earns more than $1 million per year. He employs twenty-six people and states that they "are all paid very well." "I am very blessed but I work very hard," said Zamora. "I have been successful because of ALBA giving me technical assistance and people who have shown me what I need to do."[e] He has also utilized funding from EQIP and other Natural Resources Conservation Service programs to support conservation practices that he learned about from ALBA.

Zamora is eager to pass along the mentoring spirit as he hosts local students and mentors smaller farmers. His next goal is to further open his farm to the surrounding community to "see how crops are grown and learn about nature" as they harvest strawberries and cut flowers on his organic land. Most importantly, he looks forward to continuing to "supply very good organic food to the local community."[f]

Javier Zamora of JSM Organics

The Beginning Farmer and Rancher Development Program is a testament to how long it can take to transplant a Farm Bill program from inside the Beltway into the ground. It took fifteen years—three Farm Bill cycles—from the time this program was first floated as a marker bill on the House floor until it was finally championed by representatives, written into law, and funded by the Appropriations Committee.

The 2014 Farm Bill reauthorized the program, and future Farm Bills can build on these important investments in beginning farmers.

NOTES

a. Robert Walch, "Small Farms Hatch from Salinas Valley Ag Incubator," *(Salinas) Californian*, August 9, 2015.

b. Patricia Carrillo, email communication, August 9, 2017.

c. Carrillo, email communication.

d. Carrillo, email communication.

e. Javier Zamora, personal communication, July 28, 2017.

f. Zamora, personal communication.

13. Trade

Brazil successfully argued that US direct payments to cotton farmers were "trade-distorting." These payments, the dispute panel found, artificially depressed global prices and stimulated overproduction, thereby costing Brazilian cotton farmers hundreds of millions of dollars in sales.

THE PROGRAMS AND POLICIES SET OUT IN EACH FARM BILL don't exist in a domestic bubble. They also affect, and are affected by, global food demand, shifting prices, and, increasingly, international trade agreements. Most nations are both food importers and exporters out of necessity, economic globalization, and dietary affluence, yet conditions for farmers vary widely, especially between northern industrialized countries and the developing world. In wealthier countries, a small number of subsidized producers grow most of the crops. In countries where farming is far less mechanized, agriculture employs large percentages of the population, often at subsistence levels.

The World Trade Organization's (WTO's) Agreement on Agriculture, an international convention forged between 1986 and 1994 to establish the rules of trade between countries, attempts to level a highly uneven economic playing field for farmers throughout the world. Agricultural subsidies and trade barriers (such as tariffs) are designed to boost income and carve out markets for producers at home, but they can have an extremely disruptive effect on prices in the international arena. Many Farm Bill programs have been specifically designed to pay for some of the costs of growing cotton, corn, and milk or to shield domestic cane and sugar beet producers from other countries that produce at a lower cost. The United States also consistently exports 20 percent of its agricultural output. So, Farm Bill programs that promote the overproduction of corn, cotton, wheat, soybeans, rice, meat, and dairy products can glut the market, undermine prices, and harm competing farmers in other countries.

Market distortions caused by agricultural subsidies in wealthy countries served as a point of bitter contention until commodity markets heated up in 2007. Nobel Prize–winning economist Joseph Stiglitz explained why: "When subsidies lead to increased production with little increase in consumption, as is typical with agricultural commodities, higher output translates directly into higher exports. Higher exports translate directly into lower prices for producers. And lower prices translate directly into lower incomes for farmers and more poverty among poor farmers in the Third World."[1]

The dumping of heavily subsidized commodity crops on international markets remained a key tripping point in 2001 as the latest Doha Development Round of WTO negotiations started and stalled (see the "Trade Talk Timeline" feature). The farm lobby, with its tremendous power, continually subverted both the US trade position and domestic concerns about rising deficit spending as payment programs inflated between 1996 and 2007. This discrepancy points to the perhaps irreconcilable tensions between an export-driven farm economy on the one hand and, on the other hand, the dire need for a new agricultural order that promotes fair markets so that countries can protect their farmers who feed their citizens while continuing to trade.

At the WTO Ministerial Conference of December 2015, members from developed countries decided to eliminate export subsidies for agricultural products by 2018. This decision exemplifies the effort to reduce distorted market prices, surplus commodity production, and dumping in developing countries.[2]

THE US COTTON CASE

Writing about US cotton export supports in particular, Stiglitz asserted that "seldom have so few done so much damage to so many."[3] Frustrated by the United States' continual refusal to reform its cotton program, Brazil brought a case before the WTO, arguing that US market deficiency payments and export subsidies to cotton farmers were "trade-distorting." On March 3, 2005, a WTO Appeals Panel upheld a ruling against the United States, concluding that market loans and export subsidies to US cotton farmers (part of 2002 Farm Bill programs) artificially depressed global prices and stimulated overproduction, thereby costing Brazilian cotton farmers hundreds of millions of dollars in sales.

> The United States agreed to pay the Brazilian Cotton Institute $147.3 million per year for "technical assistance and capacity building."

The 2005 Appeals Panel ruling allowed Brazil to respond through "cross-sectoral retaliation." That meant it could compensate for the losses in its cotton industry by imposing tariffs on American goods such as food, electronics, pharmaceuticals, and technology. The United States filed another appeal, and in August 2009, the WTO once again ruled in Brazil's favor, authorizing it to impose import tariffs on American goods and intellectual properties to the tune of $820 million. Rather than expose US technology, pharmaceutical, and biotech firms to costly economic reprisals, the two countries reached an interim agreement in April 2010, and the United States agreed to pay the Brazilian Cotton Institute $147.3 million per year for "technical assistance and capacity building."

Trade Talk Timeline

In late 2001, the World Trade Organization (WTO) began a series of talks—the Doha Round—to assist developing countries by reducing government subsidies and opening markets for agricultural and manufactured goods.

November 2001, Doha, Qatar: WTO trade talks start two months after the September 11 attacks. Developing countries complain about subsidies and US cotton payments in particular.

September 2002: Brazil sues the United States through the WTO appeals process, claiming cotton subsidies lower world prices by encouraging overproduction and excess exports.

September 2003, Cancun, Mexico: Talks disintegrate as poor countries protest refusal of affluent countries to reduce or eliminate farm subsidies.

September 2004: The WTO rules in Brazil's favor regarding US cotton subsidies. The United States is required to halt a few direct payment subsidies immediately and to reduce or eliminate certain major subsidy programs.

March 2005: The WTO Appeals Panel rules against the United States and sets a timeline for action.

October 2005: US trade negotiators propose significant subsidy cuts if Europe lowers tariffs and developing countries open markets wider to US exports. No changes materialize.

July 2006, Geneva, Switzerland: Talks are suspended with affluent countries, the United States in particular, criticized over their continuation of subsidies.

August 2009: A WTO arbiter rules that Brazil can take countermeasures against the United States, up to $143.7 million annually, including suspending international property right protection, for such things as genetically engineered seeds.

August 2010: The United States and Brazil reach an agreement in which the US Commodity Conservation Corporation would pay the Brazilian Cotton Institute $143.7 million annually for technical assistance until a resolution is reached.

May 2011: Further talks are held in Geneva as the Doha Round remains in limbo.

December 2011: Russia, the only remaining major economy outside of the WTO, officially joins the organization.

February 2013: The United States and the European Union develop the Transatlantic Trade and Investment Partnership in an effort to liberalize trade between the two entities. Moving forward, this partnership will influence and interfere with WTO negotiations, although it remains to be finalized.

December 2013: WTO ministers agree on the first global trade deal at a meeting in Bali, although many remain unsatisfied with the outcomes. To facilitate trade, the agreement reduces import tariffs and improves customs procedures.

December 2015: A final WTO ministerial meeting is held in Kenya, where many believe the Doha Round will die. Export subsidies are phased out in developed countries, although developing countries meanwhile increasingly impose domestic agricultural support, adding to global market distortions.

February 2016: Twelve nations sign the Trans-Pacific Partnership, the largest international trade agreement to date, which will supersede the North American Free Trade Agreement.

January 2017: The United States ends the Trans-Pacific Partnership in an effort to end its involvement in multinational trade agreements.

May 2017: The United States and China sign a trade agreement to formally recognize China's growing international influence as bilateral trade (including US beef exports) will liberalize between the two countries.

July 2018: President Trump announces plan to provide $12 billion in supplemental support to US commodity farmers to compensate for market losses due to tariffs.

Sources: Katie Allen, "World Trade Organisation: 20 Years of Talks and Deadlock," *The Guardian*, December 15, 2015; Can Chapman and Michael Dabrowa, "Cotton Bailout: An Ocean Apart, but Interwoven, Record US Exports Dampen World Cotton Prices," *Atlanta Journal-Constitution*, October 8, 2006; Simon Lester, "Is the Doha Round Over? The WTO's Negotiating Agenda for 2016 and Beyond," Cato Institute, *Free Trade Bulletin* no. 64, February 11, 2016; Joshua P. Meltzer, "The U.S.-China Trade Agreement—A Huge Deal for China," *Brookings Institution*, May 15, 2017.

Nearly $150 million per year is a lot of money, and public outcry over this deal was immediate and forceful. In June 2011, a defiant House of Representatives voted to eliminate these payments to Brazil, threatening to put the United States out of compliance with the WTO ruling. Withdrawing could have resulted in significant economic payback by Brazil against, for example, biotech giants like Monsanto and Pioneer whose patented genetically engineered seeds are popular among Brazilian commercial growers.

Instead, changes made by the 2014 Farm Bill to conform cotton subsidies to WTO obligations ultimately ended the costly dispute with Brazil. Revenue payments for the United States' 9,000 upland cotton farmers, so strong in the previous two Farm Bills, were shifted to insurance protection, mainly through the Stacked Income Protection Plan.[4] This program provides a buffer against low revenue by limiting indemnities to between 10 and 30 percent of expected revenue and subsidizes 80 percent of insurance premiums. The substantial costs of administering the insurance program are covered as well. Even with these modifications, cotton received 8 percent of crop insurance premium subsidies in 2016.[5] Upland cotton is also still eligible for marketing assistance loans. The Environmental Working Group recently reported that, despite soaring market prices, the USDA revived its Cotton Ginning Cost Share Program in 2018. Each farmer can receive up to $40,000 through this subsidy program that cost taxpayers more than $330 million just two years earlier.[6]

Of course, the United States is not alone in subsidizing its agriculture in ways that distort free trade. Japan, South Korea, and many European governments (France, Norway, Switzerland, and other Group of Ten industrial nations) have been propping up farm sectors for decades, often to a far greater extent than the United States does. Theoretically, open markets should help "float all boats" and create a more prosperous world for all, but trade negotiators of developed countries appear to be deadlocked in a high-stakes game of chicken. No one wants to be the first to cut its commodity growers off from production supports.

"Most countries recognize that some level of financial support and tariffs are necessary to promote food security," explained Ben Lilliston, director of rural strategies and climate change at the Institute for Agriculture and Trade Policy (IATP) in Minneapolis. "Countries need to be able to protect and support domestic food production. Developing countries need to be able to support their farmers, and at the same time, protect their farm economy from dumping, which has traditionally come from American and European-based agribusiness corporations."

New Zealand is a rare exception. That country removed its subsidy system in 1984, following years of industrialization and significant government support (see chapter 14). Although farmers initially protested, the country's agricultural economy eventually recovered, diversified, and expanded. Environmental management student William Miao argued that New Zealand's predominance of family farms, robust exports, and continued success of livestock production prove that removal of government supports may be not only feasible, but beneficial, for many smaller countries.[7] Eliminating production subsidies, however, should not necessarily mean ending supports for conservation, stewardship, and ongoing research.

THE THREE SUBSIDY BOXES

The WTO's Agreement on Agriculture established rules to govern farm protection and supports. Referred to as the Three Boxes (figure 18), these (now expired but still functioning) categories—amber, blue, and green—set limits on agricultural supports depending on how much they distort trade. Amber box subsidies, which fund cheap exports or encourage overproduction, are the most limited at 5 percent of total production (either on a specific crop basis or across all agricultural output) for developed countries and 10 percent for developing countries. Current US amber box payments include crop insurance subsidies, dairy price supports, marketing loan benefits, and renewable energy programs. Blue box subsidies are direct payments to farmers when production falls below 85 percent according to area, yield, or number of livestock. The United States has not made any blue box payments since the first round of negotiations in 1995 and ended deficiency payments in 1996. Blue box payments have per-nation ceilings. Green box payments are "minimally trade-distorting" and are currently unlimited under WTO rules. Green box payments support conservation, rural development, renewable energy, and other investment programs. The United States' former direct payments and current disaster relief payments are exceptions under the green box, along with our numerous conservation supports. This category also includes domestic food aid, which rose from $46 billion in 1995 to $125 billion in 2011.

Over the lives of the last three Farm Bills, commodity support has been well within amber box compliance as commodity payments fell in response to rising prices. A few reasons explain the price surge: greater demand for meat and animal protein in emerging economies, an expanding use of biofuels, and crop failures due to extreme weather events. At the same time, the US commodity supports are shifting to crop and revenue insurance rather than subsidies. In its first report to the WTO on subsidy spending since 2014, the United States reported in early 2017 that US amber box payments are a mere $4 billion, well below the $19.1 billion limit. That is because increased domestic support has fallen under the green box category, consisting primarily of nutrition support as well as crop insurance schemes that are considered exceptions.[8] Thus, we remain compliant even though prices are now falling.

The US Farm Bill's counterpart across the Atlantic, the European Union's Common Agricultural Policy (CAP), has committed to shifting trade-distorting export subsidies into the WTO's green box. Under the Decoupling 2013 plan developed when the CAP was released, all tariffs and export refunds on agricultural goods were to be eliminated by 2013. Ninety-five percent of subsidies remain direct payments, however. Other reforms sought to more evenly distribute decoupled direct payments and tie 30 percent to environmental practices.[9] Similarly, the United Kingdom's Environmental Stewardship program phased out trade-distorting subsidies and began paying farmers for the public services they provide, such as wildflower meadows and bird habitats, the restoration of traditional hedgerows, enhanced animal welfare, food safety, and food quality. As mentioned above, supports that promote conservation and rural development fall under the WTO's green box category and are unrestricted. Although highly unlikely, the United States could follow this lead and promise to phase out amber box

Figure 18

WTO's Three Boxes

Box	Status	Payment Type	US Spending Limits
Amber	Trade-distorting	• Marketing loan benefits • Product-specific supports • Crop and revenue insurance subsidies • Irrigation subsidies • Renewable energy programs	$19.1 billion
Blue	Market-distorting and production-limiting	• Deficiency payments	NA
Green	Non-trade-distorting	• Environmental payments • Natural disaster relief • Decoupled income support • Farm credit programs	NA

Source: Schnepf, Randy. "Agriculture in the WTO: Rules and Limits on Domestic Support," Congressional Research Service, September 18, 2014.

subsidies altogether by transferring supports to its already established green payments plan, the Conservation Stewardship Program.

Since its decision to exit the European Union, the United Kingdom has been in the process of forming its own agricultural policy before current CAP subsidies end in 2020. While the National Farmers Union is advocating for maintaining these large subsidies that cost 3 billion euros annually, many others would like to see more spending tied to environmental practices or income restrictions.[10]

LABELING

At times, WTO rulings can work against efforts to protect US consumers. The 2002 Farm Bill, for instance, established Country of Origin Labeling (COOL) to inform consumers about the origins of perishable foods. Where does your meat come from? Are those mangoes from Mexico? Is that garlic from China? But meat-packers immediately put up a fuss. Ground beef often contains varying grades and cuts commingled from different countries, and all those sources would have to be listed on the label. Meat products remained immune from COOL through the 2002 Farm Bill, but COOL was reauthorized and put into effect in 2009.

Canada and Mexico immediately filed a challenge within the WTO. Both countries export live animals across the US border for fattening, processing, and distribution, and they argued that COOL stigmatized their products as being of foreign origin, even if they were processed in the United States. In an initial ruling in May 2011, the WTO found the US COOL program in violation of international fair trade rules.

The US Beef Cattlemen's Association, which opposed the program from its inception, immediately applauded the provisional decision. Other groups objected that the WTO was overruling the national desire to know information as fundamental as where food comes from. Ultimately, this labeling requirement for pork and beef through COOL was repealed through the 2015 omnibus stimulus bill (although a few western states have unsuccessfully proposed their own labeling bills since 2017).

TRANS-PACIFIC PARTNERSHIP

In the last several years, the potential formation of the Trans-Pacific Partnership (TPP) has dominated global trade discussion. This regional free trade agreement would have increased international markets for US agricultural exports by lowering tariffs and increasing quotas, as well as making other changes such as reducing sanitation measures that impeded trade. The US International Trade Commission believed the partnership would have greatly benefited our system, and the Congressional Research Service estimated it would have increased US exports by 2.6 percent, US imports by 1.5 percent, and US agricultural employment by 0.5 percent. Yet opposition came from union workers who believed the deal would transfer jobs to lower-cost producers in other countries. Others criticized the TPP for neglecting to address currency manipulation.[11] Many NGOs and prominent politicians, including the leading presidential candidates in 2016, similarly believed it would hurt our own economy, farm workers, and rural environments.

Shortly after taking office in 2017, President Donald Trump withdrew the United States from the TPP. Many representatives of the food and agriculture industries were upset by the decision because they lost opportunities to expand exports. Other participating countries are continuing to move forward with their own free trade agreements, which may edge the United States out of potential trade relationships. Former US Trade Representative Ron Kirk said, "This is going to be devastating for American farmers and ranchers and businesses."[12] Meanwhile, the US government plans to pursue alternative bilateral agreements, such as with China, which was left out of the TPP. The impact on production and farmers' income in the United States remains to be measured.

LEVELING THE PLAYING FIELD

The effects of America's food policies and subsidies absolutely spill over international borders, and at the same time, international trade rules have profound ramifications on the domestic front. As demands on the world's productive agricultural regions intensify due to rising populations, changing climate conditions, and increasingly scarce resources, these interactions and stresses will intensify. In fact, the need for closer collaboration between countries may become more important than ever. Although these rules can lead to international games of chicken over trade, there is a more direct path. The Farm Bill can begin to more closely align with trade goals established in 1995 by supporting rural development, conservation, public health and nutrition, energy security, and other related public benefits. Reduced farm subsidies could open new international markets for other sectors of the economy. They could also lead to job creation here and abroad and a more level playing field for all farmers.

Corporate Agricultural Dumping: Growing the Wealth Gap

Sophia Murphy and Karen Hansen-Kuhn

The Institute for Agriculture and Trade Policy (IATP) has used World Trade Organization formulas to document the systematic dumping of US-grown agricultural commodities (specifically wheat, soybeans, corn, cotton, and rice) for two decades. We found that in the wake of the volatile commodity markets that dominated in the period from 2007 to 2013, export prices largely exceeded production costs. In recent years, however, US agricultural commodity dumping has started again. According to IATP's calculations, in 2015 US wheat was exported at 32 percent less than the cost of production, soybeans at 10 percent less, corn at 12 percent less, and rice at 2 percent less.

Dumping clearly increases inequality between farmers in the global North and South. Less visibly, dumping also worsens incomes and increases inequality within rural America.

For the farmers who grow the same (or substitutable) crops in the importing countries, agricultural dumping makes it nearly impossible to make a profit. It is especially devastating for such farmers in low-income countries, where governments have no means to provide compensation, nor the economic power to use trade rules to defend their markets.

Dumping creates unfair competition for producers in other exporting countries, too. And by encouraging overproduction in the United States, dumping traps US producers as well, forcing them to engage in a never-ending push for higher yields or bigger farms, or both.

The biggest winners from dumping are the handful of agricultural commodity trading corporations that dominate the markets (four corporations control an estimated 75 to 90 percent of the global grain trade). Their enormous market power allows these agribusinesses to squeeze small farmers and consumers, keeping the vast majority of profits for themselves. Farmers typically earn just a few pennies out of each dollar of food their grain goes into making.

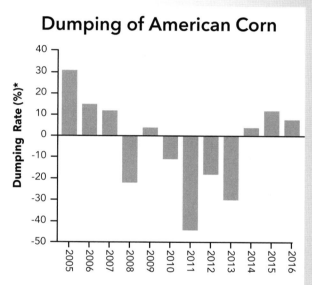

Dumping of American Corn

*Using corn as an example, the dumping rate is calculated based on the difference between production and export price. In years when export prices exceed costs, dumping does not occur.

Source: Murphy, Sophia, and Karen Hansen-Kuhn. "The True Costs of U.S. Agricultural Dumping." February 2018. Under review for publication by Renewable Agriculture and Food System.

Farmers do make a profit some years. But many other years, farmers work at a loss, while agribusinesses make money much more consistently. When we look at the cost of production and the movement to ports and then to export, there are profits and losses at various stages but much of it is hidden behind vertically integrated supply chains, for example when grain traders own feedlots or when poultry producers contract with farmers to control the breeding and raising of chickens while also controlling the processing and marketing.

Corporate concentration in nearly every sector of agricultural inputs, production, processing, and distribution has increased substantially over the last twenty years. The system is structured in a way that allows, even encourages, farmers to operate at a loss, which maximizes profits further downstream for agribusiness and leaves the public covering the farmers' losses.

The current US Farm Bill includes revenue insurance programs that respond to price drops, but they are not designed to resolve them. They compensate

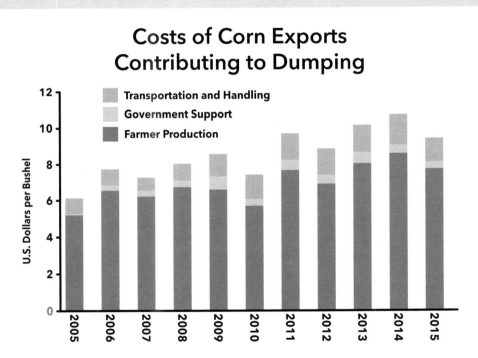

Costs of Corn Exports Contributing to Dumping

Again using corn as an example, this figure shows the costs of various factors involved in the calculation of dumping rates. When the export price falls below the full cost of production and distribution, American corn farmers dump corn on international markets to make up for lost revenue.

Source: Murphy, Sophia, and Karen Hansen-Kuhn. "Counting the Costs of Agricultural Dumping." June 26, 2017. Institute for Agriculture and Trade Policy.

farmers to some degree for the catastrophic drop in farm prices, even as costs have continued to rise. They do nothing to slow or lessen production. Farm incomes have plummeted for the last four years, and the level of farm debt as a share of farm income is the highest since the 1980s.

The US government's answer has been to encourage even more exports to compensate for low prices. The value of revenue insurance will also diminish over time as its value is calculated by a moving average of prices that are now, once again, decreasing. The fall in revenue will increase the political pressure on Congress to introduce "emergency measures," as has happened often in the past. Such financial bailouts, while providing much needed relief, do nothing to redress the market inequalities between producers on the one hand and farm input companies, grain traders, and processors on the other.

One of the countries hardest hit by unfair competition with US agricultural exports is Mexico. Corn holds an important place in Mexico's economy, diet, and culture. Under the 1994 North American Free Trade Agreement (NAFTA), US corn exports to Mexico increased more than 400 percent in the first few years, disrupting local markets. Based on Mexican Census data, Tim Wise estimates that more than two million Mexicans left agriculture in the wake of NAFTA's flood of imports, or as many as one-quarter of the farming population. Even when dumping rates decreased during the period of high prices, existing public support programs for agriculture in Mexico, as in the United States, tended to support the largest farmers and agribusiness interests rather than the smaller producers who had been the backbones of their rural economies.

The Mexican government has responded to the Trump administration's calls to renegotiate—or abandon—NAFTA by seeking to diversify its sources of corn imports. One proposal in the Mexican Senate calls for the government to cease corn imports from the United States and instead purchase from Brazil, in effect substituting imports from one set of agribusinesses to another.

The big grain traders have also profited from new technologies, such as the computer-driven high-frequency trading that now dominates financial markets and has amplified commodity price swings. These firms are in the business of adding value to primary commodities, whether they are fattening animals or turning corn into ethanol. Cheap grain then becomes an input, and the companies are happy to keep those prices low. The structure of those supply chains, as well as the rules that govern them, favor agribusinesses with global reach.

There is an urgent need for a new approach to global trade rules—an approach that respects the obligation on governments to protect food security at home, the complex relationship of food systems to economic development, and the importance of accountability in domestic politics in rich and poor countries alike. Prices must incorporate environmental costs as well and allow for sustainable resource use. It is time for strong, clear rules that value more equitable returns to food production and distribution throughout the supply chain, as well as stable and predictable food prices.

Sophia Murphy is a PhD candidate at the University of British Columbia and an advisor on trade at the Institute for Agriculture and Trade Policy. Karen Hansen-Kuhn is director of trade and global governance at the Institute for Agriculture and Trade Policy.

Source: Sophia Murphy and Karen Hansen-Kuhn, "Corporate Agricultural Dumping: Growing the Wealth Gap," *Institute for Policy Studies*, July 12, 2017.

14. An Alternative System

New Zealand's farm leaders brought national attention to the urgent need for subsidy reform.

IN 1984, THE GOVERNMENT OF NEW ZEALAND ANNOUNCED THE UNTHINKABLE. Faced with mounting deficits and spiraling inflation, the country abandoned the extensive programs that had been cushioning farmers with as much as 40 percent of their total income through the 1970s and early 1980s.

At the time, New Zealand's farmers faced a crisis not radically different from the shocks that hit US agriculture during the 1970s and 1980s. Rising oil prices had triggered inflation, and farmers were finding it difficult to recoup fair prices on the open market. Great Britain, historically New Zealand's most secure trading partner, had joined the European Union and was realigning its trading relationships. No longer privy to special status as a Commonwealth nation, New Zealand's agricultural exports were cast into the already overflowing basket of the global economy.

The New Zealand government initially responded the way most developed countries do: by shoveling cash and incentives at the farm sector in the hope that boosting production would also boost farm income. Tax breaks, fertilizer subsidies, price supports, low-interest loans, disaster relief, weed-eradication payments, special training programs, and other farmer-friendly incentives unfortunately all funneled toward the same disappointing result. They generated oversupply, which, in turn, depressed commodity prices.

New Zealand farmers were quick to catch on to the flawed logic. They dubbed the "livestock incentive scheme"—a direct payment program to help farmers increase the size of their herds—the "skinny sheep scheme."[1] Alas, even a pasture-rich country falls victim to such fundamental laws as carrying capacity: there are practical limits to the number of sheep that can be productively placed on the land. One farmer sarcastically named his newly purchased boat the *SMP* after the "supplementary minimum prices" subsidy, the backbone of the country's farm supports.[2] Apparently, the country's subsidy programs helped pay for it.

It was New Zealand's farm leaders who brought national attention to the urgent need for subsidy reform. It had become obvious to them that farm support programs weren't boosting prices, but instead were overburdening the national treasury. In 1982, the country's leading farm organization, the Federated Farmers of New Zealand, advocated a partial overhaul of the subsidy system. Its argument that subsidies were at least partially responsible for high inflation caught the attention of economists across the country.[3] Then, in 1984, the country's Labour Party won a landslide victory, and included in its sweeping economic restructuring was the elimination of nearly all agricultural programs. Although certain safety net programs remained in place to support this transition, New Zealand's farm sector was forced to go it alone.

By most accounts, the six-year transition was rocky, especially for farmers paying off loans for equipment and improvements. Farm income plummeted. Land and livestock prices fell. Some farmers committed suicide. An estimated 800 farmers, or 1 percent, were forced to leave their land, but that toll was far lower than the 8,000 farmers, or 10 percent, that had been anticipated. Sheep farmers, who were the most heavily subsidized before the reforms, bore the brunt of the hardships. By the early 1990s, however, land values, commodity prices, farm profitability, and other indices had stabilized or even begun to show steady improvement.

According to most reports, rather than a collapse of agriculture, New Zealand's shift led to an

Why New Zealanders Don't Like Subsidies

1. Resentment among farmers, some of whom will inevitably feel that subsidies are applied unfairly.
2. Resentment among nonfarmers, who pay for the system once in the form of taxes and a second time in the form of higher food prices.
3. The encouragement of overproduction, which then drives down prices and requires more subsidization of farmers' incomes.
4. The related encouragement to farm marginal lands, with resulting environmental degradation.
5. The fact that most subsidy money passes quickly from farmers to farm suppliers, processors, and other related sectors, again negating the intended effect of supporting farmers.
6. Additional market distortions, such as the inflation of land values based on production incentives or cheap loans.
7. Various bureaucratic blunders, such as paying farmers to install conservation measures like hedgerows and wetlands—after having paid them to rip them out a generation ago, while those farmers who have maintained such landscape and wildlife features all along get nothing.

Removing subsidies, on the other hand, forces farmers and farm-related industries to become more efficient, to diversify, to follow and anticipate the market. It gives farmers more independence and gains them more respect. It leaves more government money to pay for other types of social services, like education and healthcare.

Source: Excerpted with permission from Laura Sayre, "Farming without Subsidies? Some Lessons from New Zealand," New Farm, March 2003.

New Zealand Ministry of Agriculture and Forestry

A subsidy-free view. More than thirty years after New Zealand's Labour Party shut down an extensive agricultural support program, the farm sector is overachieving. Sheep stocking numbers have declined but have been replaced with a diversity of activities. Agricultural productivity, which averaged 1 percent growth per year in the subsidy era, has reportedly grown 5.9 percent per year since 1986 when farm supports were abandoned.

energizing transformation of the country's food and farming sectors. Although approximately 90 percent of New Zealand's total farm output is exported, most of the food consumed inside the country is grown domestically. The total number of sheep has fallen by half, but weight gain and lambing productivity have increased while exports remain constant.[4] Similar efficiencies emerged in other areas. New Zealand's dairy industry was earning more foreign exchange than sheep farming by 2000. Its dairy production costs were among the lowest in the world, partly the result of an export strategy to supply milk to developing and oil-exporting countries.[5] Barely in its infancy in the pre-1984 era, New Zealand's wine industry is now thriving. It is on track to export $2 billion worth of wine by 2020.[6]

Abandoning the old system of commodity supports made such diversification possible and nec-

essary. A new generation of New Zealanders has entered the farming industry with little knowledge or expectation of subsidies. In a 2001 *BBC News* interview, Alistair Polson, chairman of the Federated Farmers of New Zealand, offered this advice to farmers in the developed world: "Get off the subsidy gravy train as soon as possible."[7]

Current government support for farmers in New Zealand is less than 1 percent of average farm income, down from 40 percent in the 1980s.[8] Production and income are on the rise. Agriculture contributes slightly more to the overall economy than it did during the subsidy era and has taken on a culture of creativity and entrepreneurship.[9] The chief architect of New Zealand's free market initiative and minister of finance from 1984 until 1988, Roger Douglas, was initially vilified, but has been knighted for his implementation of successful economic reform.

This market-based approach has not come without serious challenges. China and New Zealand signed a free trade agreement in 2008, and since then, trade between the countries has tripled.[10] New Zealand's milk and meat products, in particular, are helping to feed rising demand among China's industrializing and growing population. Milk powder accounts for 40 percent of the export value to China.[11] With the intensification of its dairy sector, New Zealand has become the world's third largest exporter of dairy products. There are increasing concerns, however, about the ecological impacts of the country's industrial dairy production, such as water and air pollution, chemical use, loss of native biodiversity, soil erosion, greenhouse gas emissions, and animal welfare issues.[12] Demand is expected to expand dramatically, with predictions of an additional 3 million acres required to be brought into production by 2050. Unless curtailed, greenhouse gas emissions, soil nitrogen losses, and other production impacts will only intensify.[13] Some citizens now question whether there might be a role for revived government policies to incentivize farming practices that encourage better outcomes, including conservation efforts and shifting away from dairy toward other crops.[14]

One might argue that New Zealand represents a unique case because of its abundant resources, relatively small population, and geographic diversity. Another sound case can be made for the country's social safety net, which includes public healthcare, education, and other services. As the country moves into its fourth decade without subsidies, however, it's clear that the policy is no longer experimental. Although New Zealand's size and isolation distinguish it from the United States, this experience shows that a gradual transition away from federal farm supports is possible.

What could agriculture look like with far fewer subsidies and direct payments? What could agriculture look like if subsidies were primarily used as a tool to incentivize diversification and the adoption of landscape-scale conservation practices? New Zealand presents a thirty-year case study that policy makers should carefully examine for insights about the opportunities and challenges of subsidy reform.

Is the United Kingdom on an Unwise Path Towards Adopting Crop Insurance?

Honor Eldridge

In June 2016, the United Kingdom (UK) voted in a referendum to leave the European Union, a separation nicknamed Brexit. While the decision remains controversial, the process of divorcing the UK's legal and judicial system from Brussels and returning it to Westminster has begun. After over forty years of integration, the process is challenging. The withdrawal impacts every aspect of British life, from security and pharmaceutical regulation, to air travel and university funding.

The return of powers from Brussels also provides an opportunity to rethink the UK's approach to agricultural supports. While often portrayed as such, providing financial support to farmers is not about subsidizing production. Taxpayer money is not being dished out to farmers to encourage them to increase their yields. Nor is it being handed out to artificially prop up a failing industry that would otherwise falter without direct government intervention.

When implemented in a holistic and visionary way, farm payments can support the positive contributions that farmers make to the environment, to rural economies, and to society. Farm supports can encourage farmers to adopt practices that promote healthy soils, filter runoff, reduce chemical use, and expand natural habitats within and around farms. They can maintain levels of employment to promote rural communities and preserve the heritage of the countryside. They can increase the affordability and availability of locally produced food in nearby cities, promoting economic resilience and improving public health.

Currently, UK farmers benefit from the European Union's Common Agricultural Policy (CAP) that divides payments into area-based basic payments (known as Pillar1) and environmental payments for ecosystem services, such as cover-cropping, hedgerow maintenance, and forest conservation (known as Pillar2). The UK government announced its intention to end Pillar1 payments and to transfer the majority of the money into Pillar2 payments with the goal of promoting a greener vision of agriculture post-Brexit.

Such a shift from production to stewardship subsidies would signal fundamental changes in the system in which UK farmers operate. Risks come from the potentially damaging economic impacts of Brexit, as well as from increasing extreme weather events caused by climate change. The combination of uncertain economic and growing conditions means farmers could face increased production pressures. However, supporting the establishment of programs to help landowners increase deep-rooted groundcover and expand habitats within farms and rural landscapes could help to mitigate the effects of extreme storm events. Even so, the UK government is considering introducing crop insurance into post-Brexit UK agricultural policy.

Crop insurance (CI) programs are often cited as a key tool for managing risk. CI is a financial method by which an agricultural crop can be insured against potential future harvest loss. While the goal of reducing volatility in the food system is essential, most of the CI schemes that have been implemented around the world have been shown to be both environmentally damaging and financially irresponsible.

The United States and Canada have the world's largest and most well-established models of CI. With the UK now considering developing its own insurance programs, it's important to take stock of the impacts of CI on farming globally and study its ecological consequences. Blindly walking down the path of CI without fully considering the long-term impacts would be shortsighted.

Studies show that CI has significant negative environmental impacts due to the resulting adoption of riskier farming practices, more intensive methods, and the expansion of monoculture crop cultivation. Study after study has found that CI programs directly correlate with land-use change. Their function is to transfer risk, so farmers have more incentive to plant on marginally productive and environmentally sensitive lands to the detriment of the local ecosystem. If crops fail, subsidized insurance programs will compensate.

The wholehearted adoption of CI has already had significant repercussions in the United States and contributed to the loss of more than 23 million acres of grassland, shrubland, and wetlands between 2008 and 2011. In the Midwest, researchers have observed higher rates of fertilizer and pesticide use on corn farms that had greater program participation. These increases resulted from farmers feeling wealthier due to the financial security provided by CI and were therefore willing to spend more on agrichemicals, a phenomenon known as the "psychological wealth effect." The studies determined that ending federal CI programs would reduce nitrogen fertilizer use by 7 to 10 percent.

At a national economic level, crop insurance is, simply, fiscally irresponsible. The public, rather than farmers, bears the majority of the financial burden of CI since it's a government-funded program. Farmers pay only a minor share of the premium, meaning they are likely to financially benefit, regardless of yield loss or mismanagement, creating a classic moral hazard. In the United States, the average rate of return on crop insurance for all farmers in all states between 2000 and 2014 was 120 percent per year. This means that the average US farmers who held a federal crop insurance policy got back more money from the government than they paid into the policy in the first place.

The UK government would do well to explore other options that can support both farmers and the environment. The existing models of crop insurance have done little to support a more sustainable vision of agriculture and have been a drain on government coffers. The desire to help farmers mitigate the economic gap caused by dissolving Pillar1 funding and reduce the risk caused by a changing climate is noble. However, crop insurance is not the answer and the UK government must strive to find another solution.

In the United States, farmers face another important impact caused by crop insurance programs: they encourage increased production and higher farmgate yields. By driving up supply, the prices often fall as the market becomes saturated, which often leads to lower prices and ultimately does not work in the producer's favor since the profitability of his crop per acre would drop. That means that the US government is subsidizing poor farming practices and oversaturated markets through its support of CI.

Honor Eldridge is a policy officer at the Soil Association.

References

Babcock, Bruce. "Crop Insurance: A Lottery That's a Sure Bet." Environmental Working Group. 2016.

Eagle, Alison J., James Rude, and Peter C. Boxali. "Agricultural Support Policy in Canada: What Are the Environmental Consequences?" *NRC Research Press* 24, no. 1 (2016): 13–24.

Faber, Scott, Soren Rundquist, and Tim Male. "Ploughed Under: How Crop Subsidies Contribute to Massive Habitat Losses." Environmental Working Group. 2012.

Hennessy, David A. "The Production Effects of Agricultural Income Support Policies under Uncertainty." *American Journal of Agricultural Economics* 80, no. 1 (1998): 46–57.

Horowitz, John K. "Insurance, Moral Hazard, and Chemical Use in Agriculture." *American Journal of Agricultural Economics* 75, no. 4 (1993): 926–35.

PART IV

REFORMING THE FARM BILL

15. Opportunities for Change

IT WOULD BE NAIVE TO IMAGINE THAT THE FARM BILL could be radically overhauled during any single negotiation cycle (i.e., New Zealand-style). Considering everything at stake—our health, food, and environment—one might think that the forces opposing corporate industrial food and farming (conservationists, family farm advocates, and anti-hunger groups) could constitute a united front for change. More often than not, however, reform groups have remained divided, winning important concessions for their own special interests only to make an unsatisfactory system slightly less bad. At the same time, the agribusiness and food industry lobbies are unconstrained, farm states wield too much power, and entitlement programs are too entrenched. It is easy to see Farm Bill negotiations as a fully-rigged game.

At least three times since its inception, however, the Farm Bill has undergone true seismic changes (figure 19). In 1961, the food stamp program was reinstated in the early days of the Kennedy administration. Commodity growers and an emerging congressional anti-hunger caucus eventually made common cause, tying agricultural output to a food safety net for the poor. In the mid-1980s, conservation resurfaced as an important Farm Bill priority. Environmental and wildlife advocates successfully lobbied for stewardship incentives that went beyond simple erosion control. In the 1980s and 1990s, a wave of deregulation reforms dismantled a long-standing federally run supply management system and replaced it with the subsidy supports so favorable to corporate agribusinesses and industrial food processors that we have today.

Figure 19

Turning Points in

Nutrition

1939 In the wake of the Great Depression, millions struggle for food and the nation launches an experimental food stamp program.

1943 The experimental food stamp program ends.

1946 The National School Lunch Program is launched amidst concerns for the security of a malnourished nation.

1943-1961 After the experimental food stamp program ends, food stamps cease to exist for nearly 20 years.

1961 Inspired by his encounters with poverty on the campaign trail, President John F. Kennedy begins a new experimental food stamp program on his first day in office.

1964 President Lyndon Johnson establishes a national food stamp program.

Conservation

1936 The Soil Conservation and Domestic Allotment Act promotes soil conservation and profitable use of agricultural resources.

1947 The Federal Insecticide, Fungicide and Rodenticide Act requires all pesticides to be registered and labeled but does not address environmental or human safety concerns.

1950 Agriculture begins to shift toward industrialization.

1950 Farmers rapidly increase their use of synthetic fertilizers. Misapplication leads to major pollution problems.

1965 The Food and Agricultural Act of 1965 authorizes a long-term plan to retire some farmland from crop production.

On the Farm

1933 The first Farm Bill, officially titled The Agricultural Adjustment Act of 1933, establishes minimum commodity prices and acreage reduction incentives.

1942 To assuage fears of economic hardship, Congress guarantees price supports for 20 farm commodities at 90 percent.

1954 The Agricultural Act of 1954 establishes a government-run grain reserve program.

1954 Earl Butz is appointed Assistant Secretary of Agriculture and promotes industrial farming.

1961 The Kennedy Administration revives acreage controls, sets price supports close to market prices, and pays farmers for significant land retirement, helping to reduce subsidies.

1930s	1940s	1950s	1960s

Historical Context

1930 21.5 percent of the employed population works in agriculture.

1931 The Dust Bowl begins.

1939-1943 Approximately four million people rely on food stamps.

1947 International Harvester begins commercial production of cotton-picking machines.

1950 Sixteen hours of human labor are required to produce 100 bushels of corn, down from 147 hours of labor for 100 bushels in 1900.

1960-1969 Output per worker on American farms increases by 82 percent.

1965 More than half the corn in the US is shelled mechanically.

Food and Farm Policy

1972 An amendment to the Child Nutrition Act of 1966 establishes the Special Supplemental Nutrition Program for Women, Infants, and Children (WIC).

1977 President Jimmy Carter eliminates the requirement of purchasing food stamps in order to receive benefits.

1981 In an effort to reduce reliance on public support for survival, President Ronald Reagan makes significant cuts to food stamp benefits.

1996-2001 A series of congressional and local government actions restrict food stamp eligibility and the ability of those who are eligible to claim their benefits.

2004 Food stamp benefits shift to electronic benefit transfer (EBT) cards.

2008 The food stamp program is renamed the Supplemental Nutrition Assistance Program (SNAP).

2017 About 43 million Americans rely on SNAP benefits to eat.

1972 The use of DDT, a powerful insecticide, is banned in the US after publicity about the threats to human health and wildlife.

1985 Congress begins requiring farmers to implement approved soil conservation systems in order to receive certain USDA benefits.

1996 The Federal Agriculture Improvement and Reform Act of 1996 eliminates acreage reduction programs.

2002 The Farm Bill includes provisions for organic and local food.

2005 The Energy Policy Act adds the Renewable Fuel Standard, mandating inclusion of ethanol, mostly from corn, in gasoline.

2014 The USDA cuts funding to conservation Farm Bill programs for the first time since 1985, with a $6.1 billion reduction over the subsequent 10 years.

1971 The Nixon administration limits land diversion payments to $55,000 per farm operator, but many farmers find loopholes.

1972 A major grain deal with the Soviet Union absorbs accumulated surpluses and wheat prices skyrocket.

1985 The Food Security Act of 1985 effectively ends the minimum-price program for commodities and eliminates the government-run grain reserve program.

1998 The US government makes emergency payments to farmers because of low market prices.

2011 Crop insurance premium subsidies pay a new peak of $7.7 billion to support 2.1 million policies.

2014 The 2014 Farm Bill removes direct and counter-cyclical payments, instead focusing on crop insurance premium subsidies.

1970s	1980s	1990s	2000s	2010s

1970 Five percent of the employed population works in agriculture.

1970 Japanese food scientists develop high-fructose corn syrup as a sweetener.

1980 Food stamp enrollment reaches 20 million.

1980 Routine dosing of antibiotics becomes standard practice in livestock production.

1990 A mere three hours of labor are required to produce 100 bushels of corn.

1994 Food stamp enrollment reaches 27 million.

2000 1.9 percent of the employed population works in agriculture.

2007–2009 The Great Recession hits North America and Europe the hardest.

2012 The number of farms in the US falls to 2.1 million, the lowest number since the 1800s.

2012 Minority farmers increase by 15 percent over five years.

It remains to be seen which, if any, current or ongoing issues might truly rattle the next round of negotiations, including:

- Need to significantly reduce the national debt burden;
- Mounting healthcare costs due to adult and childhood obesity;
- Fluctuating costs and eventual limited availability of fossil fuels;
- Diminishing sources of clean, fresh water;
- Major push for income limitations on farm program eligibility and caps on total subsidies per recipient;
- Extreme weather events due to climate change;
- Emerging local food movements;
- International trade negotiations and growth in developing countries.

As an old saying goes, cultural shifts usually precede policy changes, which come slowly and idiosyncratically. It often takes years and multiple Farm Bill cycles for even a single issue or new program to take root. Successful wedge interests become pilots and later programs with mandatory budgets and perhaps titles, over time demanding more money and sometimes raiding the till from other programs. Revoking them becomes difficult, even long after they have stopped being relevant, appropriate, or effective. Sometimes agribusiness simply co-opts programs, keeping the language of public benefit but funneling money to corporate agribusinesses and mega-farms. (Using conservation money to finance pollution compliance on concentrated animal feeding operations and giving renewable energy subsidies to capital-wealthy corn ethanol plants come to mind.) The most recent major change in subsidies replaced direct payments with federally funded crop insurance that guarantees income based on historic crop prices and can provide seemingly unlimited premium subsidies to the country's wealthiest farmers. Still, a food and farm policy earthquake could start along any one of multiple rumbling fault lines in the coming years.

GOVERNMENT DEFICITS

With the implications of a trillion-dollar deficit looming on the nation, conservatives and liberals alike are looking at ways to trim the fat. The US Department of Agriculture's food and farm programs, while making up just a small percentage of total government spending, are always targets of discontent about government pork. Decades of taxpayer giveaways to millionaire landowners have made farm programs enormously unpopular. Despite their value as a social safety net for low-income Americans and their children, food assistance programs are also under constant attack. Yet the need for investments in conservation, research, regional food production, nutrition programs, renewable energy, and other priority areas makes supporting food and agriculture more important than ever. It might be time to look to other agencies that also have a stake in a healthy food system—such as public health, defense, or energy—to contribute a fair share.

ENERGY

Energy issues will dominate Farm Bill debates well into the future. The corn-based ethanol industry has enjoyed enormous growth thanks to three decades of generous tax credits, federal mandates, and other subsidies, sometimes totaling as much as $6 billion per year. These supports are more of a corn policy than a responsible energy policy. Public opinion is slowly turning against support for corn-based ethanol despite continued government support. In 2011, the federal tax credit and import tariff for corn ethanol was retired, although the renewable fuel standard still mandates certain volumes of biofuels (most of which come from corn). And although the mandated percentage of cellulosic ethanol (see chapter 18) will increase and surpass corn-based fuel by 2022, energy efficiency measures need to take the place of growing crops to replace liquid fuels. Efforts to reduce energy-intensive and polluting nitrogen fertilizer must become national priorities.

HEALTHCARE

Perhaps the most influential lobbying force poised to weigh in on Farm Bill discussions is the healthcare community. With the annual medical costs of the obesity crisis estimated at almost $150 billion,[1] the healthcare community is a sleeping giant about to awaken and throw significant resources behind food and farm policies. Will the healthcare community demand an agricultural policy that promotes healthier diets? Will it join forces with other movements calling for regional food production, nontoxic farming methods, grass-fed livestock, and closer links between farmers and consumers? It is about time we focus on preventing so many of the chronic diseases that burden this country by supporting healthier diets as opposed to ignoring the causes and treating the symptoms.

FOOD WASTE

Food waste is an increasing global concern. An estimated 40 percent of all food produced in the United States is never eaten, with food waste occurring at every level of production and consumption.[2] The economic costs of food waste have been reported to exceed $200 billion annually in the United States alone.[3] More than 60 million tons of food end up in landfills or decaying on farms at great environmental costs.[4] As food slowly breaks down in landfills, it emits methane, a greenhouse gas twenty-five times as potent as carbon dioxide. Food waste reduction could become a galvanizing issue in future Farm Bills with programs focusing on prevention, recovery, public awareness, public participation, research, and education (see chapter 19).

CLIMATE CHANGE

Scientists have warned for decades that the planet's climate is changing, in part due to human activity. These changes appear to have a direct bearing on farming: heavy storms, searing droughts, and unpredictable weather patterns are becoming common challenges to modern agriculture in the United States and around the world. In addition, because long-term patterns are so difficult to predict, estimates of the impact on agriculture through longer growing seasons, heat stress, and other factors vary widely.[5] At the same time, agriculture contributes an estimated 9 percent of America's greenhouse gas emissions.[6] Worldwide, the food system's contributions are much higher. Methane emissions from concentrated livestock production, nitrous oxide from fertilizer use, and carbon dioxide from livestock and equipment all contribute to agriculture's influence on global climate change. Agriculture could greatly contribute to reducing atmospheric greenhouse gases through farming systems that consume less fossil fuel energy, use organic no-till methods, raise fewer grain-fed animals, offer resilience against flooding and drought, and sequester carbon in perennial landscapes.[7]

LOCAL FOOD SYSTEMS

A movement has long been afoot to increase access to locally produced foods. As the US population becomes increasingly urban and food deserts severely restrict access to healthy food, initiatives to reconnect Americans with the sources of their food are increasingly important. Farmers markets, community-supported agriculture, farm-to-school and farm-to-institution programs, and many other innovative developments are connecting local farmers to consumers now more than ever. Healthcare providers are beginning to write fruit and vegetable prescriptions for overweight patients, farmers market vendors are accepting Supplemental Nutrition Assistance Program electronic benefits, and consumers are seeking out regional produce. Local food production is being expanded to promote regional food security, create jobs, and give schoolchildren an understanding of where their food comes from. City governments and regional food policy councils are even weighing in with their own platforms and principles that they hope can shape future Farm Bill funding priorities.[8]

The more citizens learn what is at stake—and, to an even greater extent, have a clear picture of the kind agriculture and food system they want their elected officials to support—the better the chances for national reform. But reformers must also learn to build bridges to integrated solutions that address deep systemic problems, such as the loss of diversity in the farming system and overreliance on fossil fuels to produce food. Only when the United States creates a food and farming system that is fully healthy—economically, ecologically, and socially—will citizens also be able to gain full health. It is essential to keep in mind that implementation and revision of the Farm Bill is an ongoing process. It will require our ongoing attention long after each of the next versions becomes law.

16. Public Health

The obesity epidemic may have been the catalyst, but now pesticide exposure, antibiotic-resistant bacteria in livestock, and air and water contamination are all coming to be seen as public health priorities.

IN RECENT YEARS, the public health community has tuned in to the importance of agriculture and the Farm Bill. The American Public Health Association, the Centers for Disease Control and Prevention (CDC), the Academy of Nutrition and Dietetics, the Johns Hopkins Center for a Livable Future, and hundreds of other organizations all view crop choices, farming practices, animal welfare, and regional food security as key issues in promoting good health. The obesity epidemic may have been the catalyst, but the skyrocketing cost of healthcare has created a new national focus on reducing the need for medical treatment. In 2014, the top five most expensive and yet preventable chronic diseases cost the United States almost $495 billion, or more than 15 percent of healthcare expenditures.[1] Many experts are looking to the Farm Bill for solutions to obesity and other debilitating but preventable diseases.

Today, many Americans do not consume a healthy diet, despite benefiting from one of the world's most technologically intensive food and farming systems. We spend a smaller percentage of income on food than most other nations, yet we spend the most on healthcare per person in the world. Here are just a few of the symptoms of our unhealthy national farm and food policy:

- Almost 13 percent of Americans are food-insecure, meaning that they sometimes lack access to adequate, healthy food.[2]
- About one in three American children and teens is overweight or obese.[3] More than 70 percent of American adults are overweight or obese.[4]
- At least one-half of Americans suffer from a chronic disease, such as heart disease or type 2 diabetes, that is frequently preventable by following a healthy diet and lifestyle.[5]

- More than 60 percent of Americans consume too much added sugar, sodium, and saturated fat while not consuming enough vegetables and fruits.[6]

- The average American consumes 38 gallons of soft drinks annually.[7] Sweetened drinks provide the largest source of added sugar and about 5 percent of calories in the average diet.[8]

- The food industry spends $1.79 billion per year marketing to children, with almost three-fourths spent on breakfast cereal, fast food, and carbonated drinks.[9]

OBESITY

In 2001, Surgeon General Richard Carmona sounded a public health alarm, declaring that US obesity rates—double those of the early 1970s—had reached "epidemic" dimensions.[10] One year later, researchers tallied that two out of every three adult Americans were clinically overweight. That included 31 percent of adults between the ages of twenty and seventy-four who were medically obese, with higher susceptibility to chronic ailments such as heart disease and diabetes. Perhaps most troubling is that about 20 percent of children and adolescents are now obese, triple the number of the early 1970s (figure 20).[11,12] A systematic review of the medical costs of being overweight or obese concluded that this condition costs approximately $113.9 billion nationally and up to $1,723 per person.[13]

It would be convenient to pinpoint a single bad actor in this unfolding public health tragedy. Unfortunately, a smorgasbord of influences is driving the country's excessive weight gain: insufficient exercise; meals more frequently eaten on the run or outside the home; ubiquitous snacks; high-calorie processed foods in school cafeterias; stress and lack of money; underconsumption of fruits and vegetables; supersized portions; and addictiveness of foods that are high in sugar, fat, and sodium. Add in a "thrifty gene" condition that predisposes some to deposit more fat[14] or exposure to endocrine-disrupting chemicals dubbed *obesogens*, which alter our ability to control body weight by changing metabolism and increasing fat cell development.

Mostly, it is just more food. According to the US Department of Agriculture (USDA) Center for Nutrition Policy and Promotion, the aggregate food supply in 2010 provided 4,000 calories per person per day.[15] Adjusting for spoilage, waste, and other losses, the USDA estimated actual daily caloric intake at just under 2,600 calories per person per day, up about 25 percent from 1970.[16,17] The study reported that almost 90 percent of these additional food calories come from added fats and oils, refined grain products, and added sugars and sweeteners. On average, for example, each American consumes 77.3 pounds of caloric sweeteners every year or 22.9 teaspoons per person per day (half of which comes from corn).[18]

Saturated fats can also pose a risk to heart health if eaten in large quantity. These fats are found in meats and dairy products as well as in coconut, vegetable, and palm oils frequently added to processed foods. Although some scientists now question the link between saturated fat consumption and heart health, the 2015 Dietary Guidelines for Americans still recommend limiting them to 10 percent of caloric intake.[19] All these factors get in the way of adopting a health-promoting lifestyle (figure 21).

FROM THE FOOD PYRAMID TO MYPLATE

What is the Farm Bill's role in the obesity crisis? Some critics give it primary blame because of its hefty emphasis on subsidizing commodities—used

Figure 20

Overweight and Obesity on the Rise

Age-Adjusted Prevalence Among Adults, Ages 20–74, 1976–2012

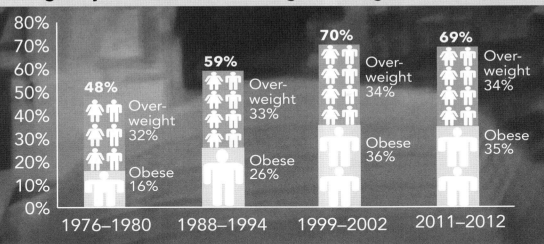

48%
Over-weight 32%
Obese 16%

59%
Over-weight 33%
Obese 26%

70%
Over-weight 34%
Obese 36%

69%
Over-weight 34%
Obese 35%

1976–1980   1988–1994   1999–2002   2011–2012

Prevalence Among Children and Adolescents, Ages 2-19 Years, 1976–2012

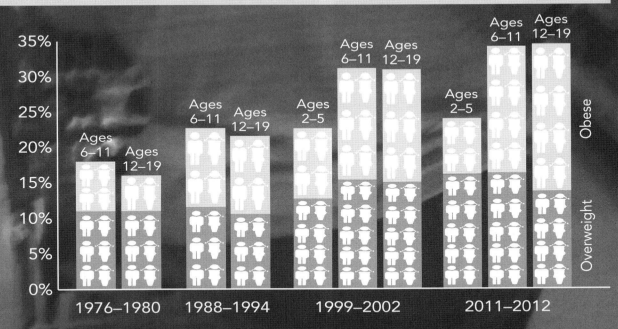

Ages 6–11   Ages 12–19

Ages 6–11   Ages 12–19

Ages 2–5   Ages 6–11   Ages 12–19

Ages 2–5   Ages 6–11   Ages 12–19

Obese

Overweight

1976–1980   1988–1994   1999–2002   2011–2012

Source: Child overweight and obesity data from: "Overweight Children and Youth." Published August 2014. Child Trends Data Bank. Adult overweight and obesity data from 1976—2002 from: "Prevalence of Overweight, Obesity and Extreme Obesity among Adults: United States, Trends 1960-62 through 2005-2006." Updated December 23, 2009. Centers for Disease Control and Prevention. Adult overweight and obesity data from 2011–2012 from: Ogden, Cynthia L., Margaret D. Carroll, and Katherine M. Flegal. "Prevalence of Childhood and Adult Obesity in the United States, 2011–2012." *Journal of the American Medical Association* 311, no. 8 (2014): 806–814.

Figure 21

Daily Health Prescription

5	**2**	**1**	**0**
servings of fruits and vegetables	hours of "screen time"	hour of physical activity	sodas or sugar-sweetened drinks

Body Mass Index (BMI) = $\frac{\text{weight (lbs)}}{\text{height (in)}^2} \times 703$ Overweight (BMI > 25)   Obese (BMI > 30)

to primarily produce animal feeds, high-fructose corn syrup, and soybean oil—rather than fruits, nuts, and vegetables. Others are quick to point out that there is no causal connection between crop subsidies and obesity; even the most recent evidence proves an association rather than causation.[20] If commodity supports were eliminated, the cost of processed foods would only increase marginally, and farmers would continue to grow corn and soybeans.[21] Rather, they would argue that it is the food processing and distribution system—influenced by convenience, packaging, and marketing—that has spurred a cultural shift toward unhealthy eating habits.

Still, we cannot be too quick to dismiss how badly USDA agriculture policies are out of alignment with its nutritional recommendations. It is not a minor disconnect. It's more like two trains on separate tracks running in completely different directions.

In 2011, the USDA replaced its ever-evolving Food Pyramid with MyPlate, an easy-to-use graphic representation of the food groups recommended in the Dietary Guidelines for Americans that it codevelops with the Department of Health and Human Services. MyPlate's message is clear: a healthy plate should be at least half full of fruits and vegetables, and another fourth should be whole grains. If there were a matching USDA Subsidy Plate, however, its message would be to fill your plate with animal proteins and processed foods. Nearly two-thirds of the corn, more than half of the soybeans, a great deal of the cottonseed and cottonseed meal, and even some of the wheat produced in the United States are fed to livestock. According to the Physicians Committee for Responsible Medicine, the meat, egg, and dairy sectors were the beneficiaries of the majority of the $246 billion in subsidies provided to US food producers between 1996 and 2009[22] (figure 22). Until the

Figure 22

MyPlate

Source: Food and Nutrition Service. "MyPlate." Updated June 21, 2017. US Department of Agriculture.

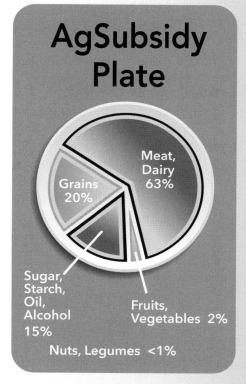

AgSubsidy Plate

Source: "Agriculture and Health Policies in Conflict: How Food Subsidies Tax Our Health." 2011. Physicians Committee for Responsible Medicine.

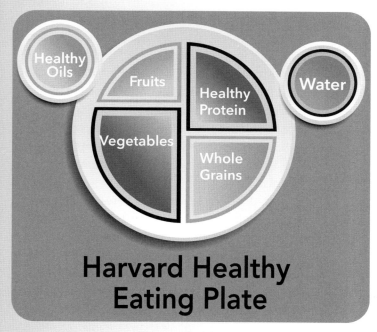

Harvard Healthy Eating Plate

Source: "Healthy Eating Plate." Updated June 5, 2017. Harvard Medical School.

ethanol industry began gobbling up more than one-third of the corn crop in 2007, an oversupply of corn and soybeans was a boon to animal feeding operations. Feed is one of the largest costs of these factory farm operations, and when it's cheap and abundant, so are meat, high-fat dairy, and eggs—the same foods the USDA instructs us to eat in moderation.

On one hand, the USDA has been encouraging a switch to low-fat dairy products since the 1970s. On the other, its commodity subsidy programs have steadily supported an oversupply of milk. Although milk consumption has decreased over the same time span, cheese has proven to be a profitable outlet for surplus milk fat.[23] In fact, cheese is now the top source of saturated fat in the US diet, contributing almost 9 percent.[24] The average American eats more than 35 pounds of cheese every year, more than a threefold increase from the 1970s (figure 23). It's layered on burgers, sandwiches, and pizzas, sometimes with cheese in the crust or cheese sauce on top. And it's included as a "meat alternate" in school lunches, providing a low-cost option to larger portions of meat. A single ounce of many cheeses can pack as much saturated fat as a glass of whole milk and doesn't provide nearly the micronutrient or protein content of other dairy foods.[25] Poultry and sugar consumption have also drastically increased in recent decades (figures 24 and 25).

During the 2008 Farm Bill reauthorization, numerous reports surfaced about how much the cost of fruits and vegetables had risen relative to processed foods, particularly sweetened beverages, over the previous three decades.[26] The need to improve the affordability of fruits and vegetables dominated reform discussions in 2008, resulting in numerous USDA programs to educate consumers, broaden access to produce, fund healthy snack programs for public schools, and dedicate nearly $1 billion to support specialty crop growers. The 2014 Farm Bill authorized funding for pilot programs to provide entitlement funding to help schools purchase local produce, both fresh and processed, as well as pulse crops—such as dried beans, chickpeas, and lentils—as an additional protein source for school lunches.

The different cost ranges between highly processed foods and nutrient-dense fruits and vegetables may have more to do with the nature of their production chains than with Farm Bill subsidies per se. Fruits and vegetables can be expensive, especially when eaten out of season or shipped great distances. In general, produce is perishable and requires far more handling than storable commodity crops. Consumers are also increasingly turning to

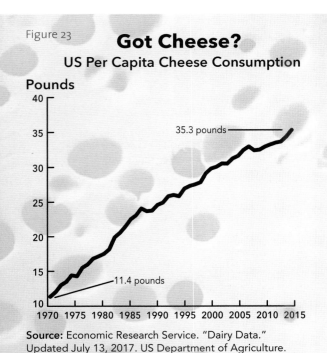

Figure 23

Got Cheese?
US Per Capita Cheese Consumption

Pounds

35.3 pounds

11.4 pounds

1970 1975 1980 1985 1990 1995 2000 2005 2010 2015

Source: Economic Research Service. "Dairy Data."
Updated July 13, 2017. US Department of Agriculture.

Figure 24

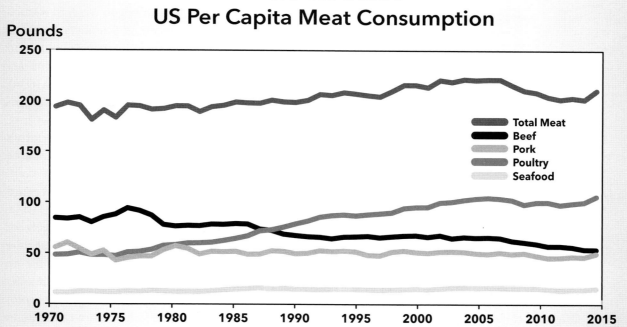

Eat Meat?
US Per Capita Meat Consumption

Pounds

Legend:
- Total Meat
- Beef
- Pork
- Poultry
- Seafood

Source: "Per Capita Consumption of Poultry and Livestock, 1965 to Estimated 2016, in Pounds." Updated April 13, 2017. National Chicken Council.

preprocessed produce—bagged spinach, baby carrots, and salad mixes, for example—that add value and cost to items. Although Farm Bill subsidies may have no tangible direct bearing on the high costs of fresh produce, current and future Farm Bill programs could markedly improve the conditions for growers of specialty crops. Some key barriers to expanded production of fruits and vegetables include specialized equipment and labor, higher production costs, lack of proximity to processing plants or markets for fresh produce, difficulty accessing credit,

and insufficient public demand for fruits and vegetables. Removing such barriers would mean tilting the balance of subsidies more in the direction of the Dietary Guidelines for Americans to encourage all sectors of society to eat more fruits, vegetables, whole grains, and nuts.

ENVIRONMENTAL HEALTH
Public health concerns don't begin on the store shelves, but, rather, in farm fields and livestock production facilities. Industrial agriculture can make

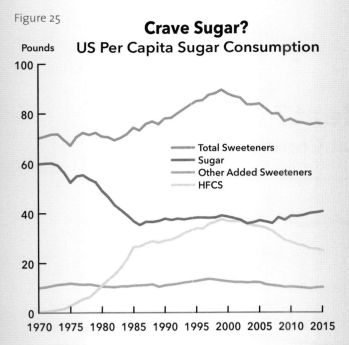

Figure 25

Crave Sugar?
US Per Capita Sugar Consumption

Pounds

- Total Sweeteners
- Sugar
- Other Added Sweeteners
- HFCS

Source: "Sugar and Sweeteners Yearbook Tables." Updated July 6, 2017. USDA Economic Research Service.

living in a rural community a health hazard given water and air contamination, exposure to pesticides and antibiotic-resistant bacteria, and high rates of occupational injuries in farm and food processing jobs. And the damage doesn't just stay on the farm. Harmful chemicals, hormones, and other substances make their way into the food system. Some of these are persistent and accumulate inside the food chain as well as inside our bodies.

Conventional meat production is a big contributor to environmental health problems, both because of the monoculture farming of feed crops and because large concentrations of animals are packed tightly into crowded facilities. Animals are routinely

given antibiotics to promote growth and to protect against infections that are easily spread in unsanitary conditions. This practice has been widely criticized by organizations such as the American Public Health Association, the American Medical Association, the Union of Concerned Scientists, the CDC, the Pew Commission on Industrial Animal Food Production, and dozens of other organizations. According to the Food and Drug Administration (FDA), nearly 35 million pounds of medically important antibiotics were used by the livestock industry in 2015, representing more than 70 percent of the country's total annual consumption of these drugs.[27] Despite increasing outcry from the public health community, sales have increased by 26 percent since 2009.[28]

When these drugs are used excessively or inappropriately, bacterial populations can become resistant as strains that are not susceptible to the drug's effects survive and spread. Antibiotic-resistant bacteria can then spread from food production facilities to the public through human contact with infected animals, consumption of contaminated foods, or animal wastes that are spewed across the landscape. Partially due to the overuse of antibiotics in animal production, many bacteria are now resistant to important human medicines such as tetracycline, penicillin, and vancomycin.[29,30] The CDC estimates that 23,000 Americans die each year from bacteria that have become resistant to our existing antibiotic drugs.[31]

During the 2008 Farm Bill cycle, the FDA issued recommendations for limiting antibiotic use in food animals. States (most notably California) have also made incremental progress in mandating reductions in usage. And after many years of failed attempts to pass federal legislation, the FDA finally implemented a rule to make it illegal to use antibiotics to promote growth in early 2017. The rule also requires a veterinarian prescription (as opposed to buying over-the-counter) for antibiotics used to prevent disease. Despite these victories, drug resistance will continue to be a problem as long as the Farm Bill supports meat production in unsanitary, confined conditions.

Exposure to agricultural chemicals creates another serious health issue. Fertilizers and pesticides are used heavily on the vast monocultures of commodities as well as many specialty crop operations. Although low doses of pesticides may not be immediately dangerous, the long-term cumulative effects of these chemicals may include elevated cancer risk; blood disorders; birth defects; and disruption of the body's reproductive, immune, endocrine, and nervous systems. The risk is even greater for farm workers and their families, who experience a higher and more frequent exposure in their fields and rural homes.

Until recently, arsenic, a known carcinogen, was regularly added to poultry feed to increase growth and prevent disease in chickens and turkeys. Although the FDA began banning the primary arsenic-based drug in 2014, it will take time to completely remove it from the market.[32] Some has wound up in the meat, although there is much less or none in organic chicken.[33] Poultry waste also poses serious health concerns. Many tons of poultry litter—a mixture of feces, feathers, feed pellets, heavy metals, and pharmaceuticals—are dumped on farmland as fertilizer. Untreated poultry waste is also routinely fed to livestock. This untreated waste can harbor dangerous bacteria and concentrated chemicals that were present in the feed.

Although arsenic is being phased out, nitrogen is still very much in use. In fact, it is essentially the backbone of industrial agriculture. Every year, farmers apply millions of tons of nitrogen fertilizer to their land to increase yields, with much of it leaking into the environment (figure 26). For example, corn plants take up roughly 35 percent of the nitrogen applied to the soil. Most crops utilize less than 50 percent of fertilizer that is applied.[34] Much of the remainder becomes airborne, contributing to greenhouse gases, or leaks into waterways. This excess nitrogen generates algal blooms, which can poison drinking water. The problem has gained national attention in recent years as algal blooms in Lake Erie have contaminated water supplies in Toledo, Ohio. They can also create dead zones where animals can no longer survive; in fact, the depleted area in the Gulf of Mexico reached a record 8,776 square miles (i.e., the size of New Jersey) in the summer of 2017 (figure 27).[35]

The Farm Bill includes a limited number of programs dedicated to addressing these environmental health risks. Some initiatives attempt to reduce dependence on nitrogen and decrease the use of drugs in livestock production. Other beneficial programs prevent animal waste from entering waterways and mitigate respiratory diseases very common among workers who raise livestock. Pilot programs also have funded the retiring of polluting diesel engines to improve air quality. Sustainable Agriculture Research and Education programs,

Figure 26

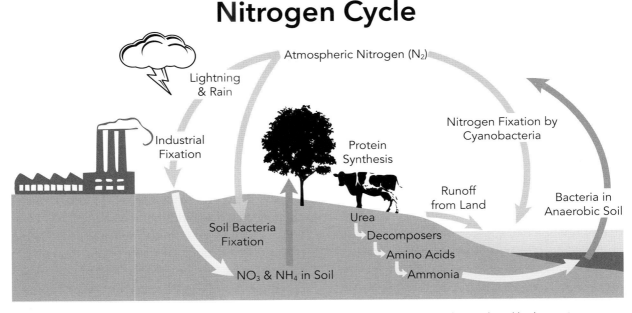

Nitrogen Cycle

Atmospheric Nitrogen (N₂)

Lightning & Rain

Industrial Fixation

Protein Synthesis

Nitrogen Fixation by Cyanobacteria

Runoff from Land

Bacteria in Anaerobic Soil

Soil Bacteria Fixation

Urea

Decomposers

Amino Acids

Ammonia

NO₃ & NH₄ in Soil

Fertilizers and animal agriculture add nitrogen into the cycle that is otherwise largely regulated by bacteria.

Source: Adapted from Vitousek, Peter M., John Aber, Robert W. Howarth, Gene E. Likens, Pamela A. Matson, David W. Schindler, William H. Schlesinger, and G. David Tilman. "Human Alteration of the Global Nitrogen Cycle: Causes and Consequences." *Issues in Ecology* 1 (1997): 3.

funded by the USDA's National Institute of Food and Agriculture, introduce farmers to innovative techniques to reduce the amount of chemicals they use. As discussed earlier, the Farm Bill also provides a small amount of support to increase organic production, which prohibits the application of synthetic chemicals.

Of course, programs can backfire. The Environmental Quality Incentive Program (EQIP) was originally designed to help small landowners improve soil and water quality by reducing fertilizer and waste runoff into waterways. As discussed in chapter 8, hundreds of millions of EQIP dollars have been directed toward managing waste at concentrated animal feeding operations (CAFOs) since 2002. Using taxpayer dollars to enable the livestock industry to expand and concentrate livestock production into even fewer hands has only perpetuated an already serious health contagion. CAFOs are regularly linked to the leakage of manure from containment lagoons into groundwater and surface waters that kill fish and contaminate drinking water. Dairy cows alone

Figure 27

Dead Zone Through the Years

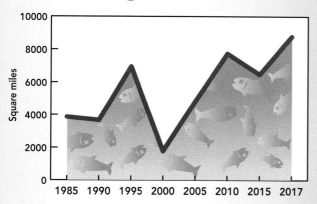

Continuing its long-term trend, the size of the dead zone in 2017 hit a new record. To achieve the recommendations of the intergovernmental Mississippi River/Gulf of Mexico Watershed Nutrient Task Force, nitrogen pollution in the Mississippi River would need to decrease by 59 percent.

Sources: National Centers for Coastal Ocean Science. "Gulf of Mexico 'Dead Zone' Largest Ever Measured." Published August 8, 2017. National Oceanic and Atmospheric Administration; Scaviaa, Donald, Isabella Bertania, Daniel R. Obenourc, R. Eugene Turnerd, David R. Forreste, and Alexey Katinc. "Ensemble Modeling Informs Hypoxia Management in the Northern Gulf of Mexico." *Proceedings of the National Academy of Sciences of the United States of America* 114, no. 33 (2017): 8823–28.

produce more than 2 billion pounds of manure each year.[36] The United States has experienced a record number of manure spills in recent years, reaching 1 million gallons in the state of Wisconsin in 2013 alone (one-third of which came from CAFOs).[37]

In addition, Farm Bill programs can do a better job of supporting sustainable farming practices. In row crop agriculture, practices such as cover cropping and crop rotation help optimize soil health and restore essential nutrients. These practices are currently supported by programs like EQIP and the Conservation Security Program but at levels far below what they deserve, given their economic and ecological benefits. Unfortunately, many farmers have more trouble proving eligibility for crop insurance when they adopt such measures—which is nonsensical given that improving soil resilience can reduce variability in cash crop production. Farm Bill programs should reduce red tape for farmers to qualify for support when they take holistic measures to limit erosion, increase soil organic matter, and improve the health of their farms. A 2016 survey conducted by the USDA's Sustainable Agriculture Research and Education program found that two-thirds of farmers nationwide would be encouraged to plant more cover crops (which protect and enhance soil health) if their premiums were discounted, suggesting that financial incentives could also significantly impact such decisions.[38]

A HEALTHIER FARM BILL?
If the Farm Bill is to achieve its purpose—to create a secure, healthy food system from field to plate—it must support fundamentally healthy agriculture: fair prices for farmers, resilient rural environments,

a diversity of crops, a conservation ethic that values wildlife, respectable conditions for food animals, and citizens who appreciate the importance of food and farming. The Farm Bill will also need more programs that promote healthier forms of agriculture, including crop diversification, pasture-raised animals, habitat protection, and "know your farmer" programs that educate consumers.

With refocused priorities, the Farm Bill's billions of dollars could jump-start a transformation of the food system. Sea changes in public behavior around health are not unprecedented. In the mid-1960s, Surgeon General Luther Terry's warning against cigarette smoking changed attitudes about the long-term health effects of tobacco use. The President's Council on Physical Fitness established new protocols and standards for physical education in public schools in the 1970s. There is no reason a healthy food movement could not radiate through all levels of society. Farmers markets and school lunchrooms could serve as hubs of nutrition education and healthy food distribution.

Michael Pollan and colleagues wrote a widely circulated article in the *Washington Post* in 2015 that called for the creation of a national food policy. Such a policy would "lay the foundation for a food system in which healthful choices are accessible to all and in which it becomes possible to nourish ourselves without exploiting other people or nature" by incorporating all these related issues and externalities.[39] Replacing our current high-calorie and high-cost bill with a robust Food and Farm Bill that invests in healthy citizens, healthy lands, and healthy urban and rural economies requires voters to demand a diet that meets the nutritional and environmental challenges of the twenty-first century. Public health just might deliver the political bridge that unites us around those fundamental connections.

17. Food Security

ALTHOUGH THE UNITED STATES IS AWASH IN RELATIVELY CHEAP FOOD, too many Americans suffer from malnutrition and hunger. In fact, the most affordable and accessible food is often the least nutritious. Since its early years, the Farm Bill has tried to address this issue, and federal nutrition support has grown to be by far its largest expenditure.

The Farm Bill's Nutrition title has evolved from an effort to distribute surplus crops during the Great Depression into the largest food assistance program in the country (figure 28). In 2016, more than 44 million people, or almost 1 in 7 Americans, relied on the Supplemental Nutrition Assistance Program (SNAP) to avoid going to bed hungry. Women, Infants, and Children (WIC) vouchers and subsidized school meals are particularly important for improving the well-being of low-income Americans. Benefits range from increasing the availability of healthy food to promoting better performance in school. SNAP participation has even been shown to reduce poverty rates.[1,2,3]

To its great credit, the anti-hunger lobby has heroically defended the country's hunger safety net in Farm Bill after Farm Bill, getting the necessary votes to "do no harm" to food assistance programs that counter an entrenched national commitment to low minimum wages. The anti-hunger lobby has also worked to destigmatize food assistance. An innovative debit card–style electronic benefit transfer (EBT) system has replaced paper SNAP vouchers and could be used in approximately 40 percent of the country's 8,000-plus farmers markets. It will soon be used for all WIC benefits as well.

The biggest challenge may be that the Thrifty Food Plan, which caps the SNAP allotment at just above $2 per person per meal (for the highest-earning single person), makes it nearly impossible for

Figure 28

Total SNAP Outlays

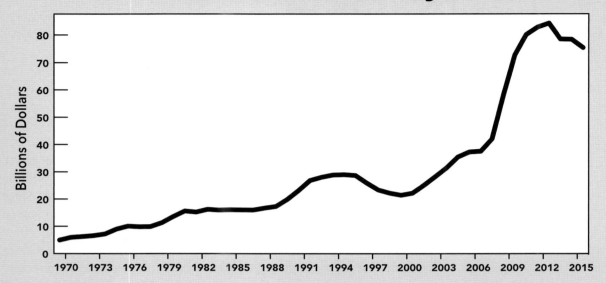

SNAP outlays have increased drastically since the program began, but have dropped since the Great Recession.

Source: US Department of Agriculture. Food and Nutrition Service. "Supplemental Nutrition Assistance Program." Updated September 8, 2017.

recipients to afford a balanced diet. Likewise, low-income populations disproportionately rely on foods that are loaded with added sugars, refined carbohydrates, and other calorie-dense foods.[4] The easiest-to-prepare products in supermarket aisles often turn out to be those that are mass-produced and made from heavily subsidized crops: frozen prepared foods, dairy products, and baked goods. And when grocery stores aren't available, many instead rely on fast food or whatever corner stores are accessible. According to Adam Drenowski, professor of epidemiology at the University of Washington, the poor in particular are gaining weight and getting sick because unhealthy food is cheaper and often more available than healthy food.[5]

Evaluations of the SNAP program's effect on health have not consistently yielded positive results. A 2015 study commissioned by the US Department of Agriculture (USDA) found that participants had poorer diets, including more empty calories and fewer fresh fruits and vegetables, than income-eligible nonparticipants.[6] A 2017 prospective study also found that participants had an increased risk of mortality associated with heart disease and diabetes than income-eligible nonparticipants and noneligible nonparticipants.[7] Data regarding the types of foods purchased with SNAP benefits have historically been restricted, preventing thorough analyses. A recent study of Americans across the country, however, revealed concerns. Foods purchased using SNAP benefits included more total calories and nutrients that should be avoided (such as sweeteners, processed meat, and salty snacks) than foods purchased by income-eligible nonparticipants.[8]

Admirable efforts were made in the 2014 Farm Bill to shift the mission of nutrition programs from simple hunger relief to making healthier foods available to the public and sustaining socioeconomic advancement. SNAP retailers were required to offer a greater diversity of fresh foods. The Food Insecurity Nutrition Incentive Grants cover half of the cost of incentives to purchase fruits and vegetables with SNAP benefits. The Fresh Fruit and Vegetable Program, which funded an increase in the volume of healthy snacks in public schools, was reauthorized and included a pilot for using canned, frozen, and dried produce. A Healthy Food Financing Initiative supports food retailers in underserved communities to sell healthier food. Benefits may also be used to pay for community-supported agriculture shares to increase access to local produce in food deserts. The list of eligible recipients for the Community Food Projects Competitive Grant Program, which supports innovative food resources and nutrition education efforts in low-income communities, increased as funding grew to $9 million per year.

In upcoming Farm Bills, legislators must find ways to realign subsidy programs with public health outcomes. Public health demands more federal attention to nutrient-rich foods and less to feed crops and commodities. Many health professionals, including leaders of the Physicians Committee for Responsible Medicine, have developed a model "Healthy Staples" program that would supply nutritionally adequate vegetarian diets for $26 billion less than current spending. It would likely promote better health than the food currently bought on SNAP.[9] While professionals debate whether SNAP should involve stricter regulations about the types of food that may be purchased, a survey of participants and another of general citizens suggests they would prefer support for healthy foods and limits on unhealthy choices.[10] Similarly, the American Medical Association recently took the stance that SNAP should incentivize healthy purchases and discourage unhealthy ones, better aligning the program with WIC standards.[11]

Recipients continue to need more education about how to afford a simple and balanced diet on a very limited budget. The two existing programs—SNAP-Ed, which reaches recipients through local implementing agencies, and the Expanded Food and Nutrition Education Program, which trains educators through land-grant universities—were reauthorized in 2014, and, in fact, SNAP-Ed expanded to include physical activity education. Given the current expenditures in the SNAP program and the resulting health of recipients, however, it's clear that programming must be made more effective or accessible so that the positive effects measured on local scales can be realized nationally.[12,13]

The good news is that improving diets on SNAP can be a very powerful tool for creating jobs—thus engaging young farmers, supporting regional food hubs, and bringing up a new generation of chefs and food entrepreneurs. As a starting point, we can make proper nutrition and deliciousness the top priority of the school lunch programs that feed more than 30 million children every day and are so important in the development of lifelong eating habits.

FOOD DESERTS

The lack of substantial Farm Bill support for fruit and vegetable crops makes growing healthier foods a risky proposition for farmers. Even if they want to diversify, farmers often face rural economic infrastructures tailored to commodity production and lacking in necessary equipment, supplies, technical expertise, cold storage warehouses, and slaughter and processing facilities. Regional food distribution chains that once accommodated a diversity of crops and livestock have been entirely eliminated in many traditional farming areas.

While our farmers grow predominantly feed grains, cotton, and oil seed crops, we are shipping fruits and vegetables across the country or even around the world. Since the mid-1990s, our imports of fresh and processed produce have increased more rapidly than exports to the point at which we now have a trade deficit of more than $11 billion and Mexico alone supplies almost half of our imported produce.[14] So, even in farm country, much of the cash that residents spend on their weekly food bills leaves the region and the state. Dinner tables remain disconnected from the fields that surround them. Across the Midwest, the result is a paradox: so much agriculture, so little food.

Food deserts—low-income areas where fresh produce is in limited supply—are by no means just an urban problem. The USDA defines a food desert as a "low-income and low-access tract," meaning "a Census tract where 33 percent or 500 people,

whichever is less, live more than a mile from a grocery store in an urban area or more than 10 miles away in a rural area. At least 20 percent of the residents must live below the Federal Poverty Level, currently $24,600 for a family of four."[15] The 2008 Farm Bill funded a $500,000 study to map food deserts across the country to find out where access to healthy foods is most urgently needed (figure 29). This Food Desert Locator later became the Food Access Research Atlas, which provides maps and data to use for program and policy development. A related Food Environment Atlas also provides data related to food access and health, such as SNAP benefit redemptions and fast-food restaurant distribution.

In so-called food swamps, which are often in low-income, inner-city neighborhoods, it is easier to find a fast-food restaurant or a convenience store than a basic grocery store. Estimates show, for example, that 16 percent of New York City's 8.5 million residents lack access to healthy, affordable food outlets, and this fraction reaches one-fifth in Brooklyn.[16] Rural food deserts, even in farming areas, are also common, particularly across the Great Plains. Within five Plains states (Iowa, Kansas, Missouri, Nebraska, and South Dakota), 188 counties include areas that lack an adequate grocery store.[17] This critical element of rural infrastructure has been vanishing as populations plummet, businesses shutter, and access to healthy food means driving ever-longer distances.[18,19] Items purchased in a gas station or small convenience store, whether in a rural or urban area, are rarely a worthy substitute for the wholesome foods that a full grocer may offer.

If expanding access to healthy foods throughout the country becomes a Farm Bill goal, spending

Food Deserts

Low-Income Areas Where Access to Healthy Food Is Limited

The problem of food deserts—low-income areas with limited access to healthy food—affects rural regions and inner-city neighborhoods alike. For example, residents of California's Central Valley, many of them farm workers, have trouble accessing fresh produce. Yet the region produces more than half of the fruits, vegetables, and nuts grown in the United States. In urban areas, food deserts exist primarily in poor neighborhoods, where access to healthy food is limited by both availability and purchasing power. To reverse these trends, many communities are establishing partnerships, with the support of NGOs and local government agencies, to improve the quality and/or affordability of food sold. These may include corner stores that don't traditionally sell fresh produce, farmers markets that typically charge higher prices, and alternative food delivery methods—ranging from mobile produce trucks to weekly drop-offs at churches or libraries.

Source: Economic Research Service. "Food Access Research Atlas." Updated May 18, 2017. US Department of Agriculture.

Figure 29

priorities must be drastically altered. Consider, for example, that over the life of the 2014 Farm Bill, an average of almost $9 billion has been spent each year on commodity programs.[20,21] Just $175 million per year has been directed toward specialty crops during the same time period, even though fruits, vegetables, and nuts make up one-fourth of the economic output of all US cropland production.[22,23]

Changes may eventually mean removing long-standing restrictions that currently prevent commodity producers who receive crop subsidies from growing fruits and vegetables. They may also include support for programs that bring healthy food into food deserts, such as mobile markets and food incubator programs. These types of initiatives will be vital if we want our nation to be food-secure.

Farmers Markets Reaching More Consumers Who Get Nutritional Benefits

Mercy Mena arrived at Heart of the City Farmers Market in the shadow of San Francisco's City Hall on a crowded Wednesday.

Before she meandered the stalls for fresh herbs, broccoli and nuts, she stopped at the main tent. After a swipe of her electronic benefits card on a wireless machine, she was handed bright yellow tokens in exchange for her federal Supplemental Nutrition Assistance Program benefits—formerly known as food stamps.

Mena, the mother of a 4-year-old, lives in the nearby Tenderloin, where poverty rates are high, there are no supermarkets, and life expectancy is 20 years lower than in surrounding neighborhoods largely because of preventable diet-related disease.

A grower-run nonprofit since 1981, Heart of the City knows those statistics well: It has made the most successful push of any farmers market state-wide to let local residents know their federal benefits are welcome, processing more than $230,000 in electronic benefits last year.

"Where we live there are so many corner stores with bad food, just bad," said Mena, 25, who recently lost her cafe job. "This is just amazing to have."

Other California farmers markets have also begun to reach more consumers who receive nutritional benefits, thanks in part to a subsidy from private and public sources that stretches their buying power.

The Market Match program has been modest—and Heart of the City has simply been too successful to qualify. (It would burn through the available incentive in one market day.)

But now, thanks to $100 million set aside in the 2014 federal Farm Bill for precisely such incentives over the next five years, the program is poised to expand.

Lee Romney, *Los Angeles Times*

Heart of the City Executive Director Kate Creps estimates that access to the incentives could help her market triple its already hefty electronic benefit sales, reaching more at-risk customers while supporting small growers.

An outside evaluation of Market Match and three similar incentive programs in other states—which collectively serve 518 farmers markets—showed that consumers in "food deserts" were buying fresh fruits and vegetables with their benefits.

The research helped persuade federal lawmakers to act, said Martin Bourque, executive director of the Berkeley-based Ecology Center, which manages Market Match.

The catch: the Farm Bill dollars must be matched by state or private funding, and many market organizations lack the time and capacity to pool those resources.

A bill sponsored by Assemblyman Phil Ting (D-San Francisco) would have brought the Market Match program under the control of the California Department of Food and Agriculture. The agency ultimately would have provided the matching funds, applied for the federal dollars on behalf of California's farmers markets, and ensured that even those operating on a shoestring had technical support.

The appropriations committee last month placed the bill in "suspense" because of cost concerns after unanimous passage in the agriculture committee. Ting plans to reintroduce it.

"The beauty of this thing is that it works," said Michael Dimock, president of Oakland-based Roots of Change, which in 2009 created Market Match and recently handed the management reins to Bourque's group. "We're going to go back. We have support on the Democratic side and on the Republican side, and I think it's just a matter of timing."

California has already seen a huge uptick in the purchasing power of benefit recipients at farmers markets, with or without the match.

Mena, who receives $230 per month, greeted a nut farmer by name in Spanish before getting an informal lesson from a sprout grower on his offerings—along with some tastings. The bounty at Heart of the City, she said, is "a blessing, really."

Farmers market vendors once liberally accepted federal nutritional benefits—when they were paper documents. But when the federal government in 2003 switched over to the electronic benefit, or EBT, swipe card, the markets were caught off guard.

"They don't have hard-wired phones and power, which you needed for swipe devices," Bourque said.

The Ecology Center helped devise a wireless, battery-powered point-of-sale swipe card device that satisfied the security concerns of federal officials, and launched a campaign to get them into markets.

According to the California Department of Social Services, which has provided free EBT machines to markets, the number accepting electronic benefits grew from 50 in 2008 to 428 as of last month.

Market Match, generally capped at $10 a week per shopper, served 38,000 families last year who, using just $237,000 in incentives, spent more than $1.5 million at 150 California markets, according to Roots of Change.

Last month, the early-childhood support organization First 5 LA funded the largest expansion of Market Match to date, with a $2.5-million grant to the Ecology Center that will help 37 Los Angeles-area farmers markets.

James Haydu, executive director of Sustainable Economic Enterprises of Los Angeles, which operates eight markets set to benefit from the grant, said Market Match has driven "overwhelming" customer growth at its Watts and Central Avenue locations. "We're gleaning new customers weekly."

Lee Romney originally published this article on June 8, 2014, in the Los Angeles Times.

18. Ethanol

For politicians and lobbyists, ethanol became a sacred cow, but the high costs of these policies are now being viewed in a more critical light.

ENERGY IS THE LIFEBLOOD OF MODERN SOCIETY, and industrial nations are largely dependent on oil to maintain global trade and economic activity. Highly mechanized agriculture is no exception. Without transformative changes, we will eventually reach the age of "peak oil," the point at which the volume of global oil production begins to decline. In response, federal programs have promoted a shift to liquid biofuels and biomass energy derived from farms. The Renewable Fuel Standard created by the Energy Policy Act of 2005 and expanded by the Energy Independence and Security Act of 2007, for instance, boosted production by mandating that up to 36 billion gallons of ethanol be blended into gasoline by 2022. This figure includes allocations for cellulosic ethanol, biomass-based diesel, and advanced biofuel.[1] But through various Farm Bills, taxpayers have been investing in this industry for decades via corn subsidies, import tariffs, tax credits for every gallon of ethanol blended with gasoline, loan guarantees, construction cost shares, and gas pump upgrades. This excess of cheap agricultural products has driven much of the increase in ethanol production. And for politicians and lobbyists, ethanol became a sacred cow, untouchable, because of beliefs that these public investments would (1) support farmers, (2) reduce dependence on foreign oil (currently about 25 percent of US petroleum consumption—a record low in recent decades[2]), (3) cut greenhouse gas emissions, and (4) strengthen national defense.

The high costs of these policies—$17 billion between 2005 and 2009 alone—are now being viewed in a more critical light.[3] Voters and politicians can no longer ignore certain facts. For example:

- In 2016, 38 percent of the US corn crop was turned into ethanol, but that only constituted 10 percent of the nation's gasoline.[4,5]
- A 1.1 mile per gallon increase in passenger vehicle fuel efficiency would save as many gallons of oil as all the ethanol produced in the United States today, according to a 2010 analysis.[6]

FEED CROP VERSUS CELLULOSIC ETHANOL

Ethanol can be made from feed crops such as corn or from cellulosic sources such as grasses, leftover corn stalks, and other woody materials that contain so much cellulose fiber that they have no food value. Today, most corn ethanol is produced in dry-grind factories, which consume less energy than earlier-generation wet-mill plants. The corn is dried, milled, and then fermented and later distilled into ethanol. The leftover coproducts are called distiller's dried grains with solubles (DDGS). After a major expansion of dry-grind facilities over the course of the 2002 and 2008 Farm Bills, the United States has become the world's largest ethanol producer—even selling its surplus to Brazil, whose sugar-based biofuel industry has recently increased after a temporary decline. The two countries together produce about 85 percent of the world's supply.[7]

Making ethanol from stalks and grass is a bit more challenging. It takes an additional step to separate the plant's lignin from the cellulose. Extra energy is also required during distilling. On the plus side, the lignin can be used instead of fossil fuels as an energy source for distillation.

Creation of a cellulosic ethanol industry is predicated on a massive shift from annual crops like corn, sorghum, and soybeans to perennial native plants such as switchgrass, forest thinnings, or high-biomass perennial crops like Chinese myscanthus, which are sources that theoretically won't require excessive plowing or chemicals to pump up yields. It's a compelling notion, but it's still years from providing a significant proportion (currently at 3 percent) of our production.[8] After years of government mandates, two cellulosic ethanol plants operate commercially,[9] which cumulatively produced 18.2 million gallons in 2014, surpassing the Environmental Protection Agency's volume standards. One of these plants was opened by DuPont after the company invested more than $200 million, none of which came from federal subsidies.[10]

The United States continues to invest hundreds of millions of dollars in the effort to improve production efficiency. Cellulose cost more than $10 per gallon to produce as recently as 2005, but extensive research at the National Renewable Energy Lab has decreased that cost to below $2 per gallon, indicating it may soon become a cost-competitive alternative.[11]

Cellulosic crops don't even have to be made into ethanol to displace fossil fuels. They can also be converted directly into electricity, a process that can be much more efficient, be achieved more readily with existing technology, and could replace coal and natural gas. Reports show, for example, that an electric car can go twice as far on wood or switchgrass as an equivalent vehicle powered by ethanol.[12]

IS CORN ETHANOL SUSTAINABLE?

By early 2011, drums were finally beating inside the nation's capital for a repeal of ethanol subsidies and tax breaks that were sucking up $7 billion per year or more from American taxpayers. Some Iowa counties were reportedly receiving up to $26,800 per rural household in ethanol subsidies despite evidence that using corn to help fill gas tanks might not be the best use of crops, technology, and scarce taxpayer dollars.[13] The existing Volumetric Ethanol Excise Tax Credit, which benefited gasoline blenders, and the Small Ethanol Producer Tax Credit, which benefited small producers, both expired in 2011. The remaining Renewable Fuel Standard supports production by mandating blending at a certain level. In the last few years, many crop farmers and the ethanol industry have advocated for increasing the mandated blend of ethanol to 15 or even 30 percent—called "intermediate blends."

Whether or not ethanol is a good alternative fuel depends on a simple "energy in, energy out" equation. In other words, the amount of power derived from ethanol should be greater than what is required to grow and refine it. Recent analyses reveal that when all the "well to wheel" inputs of growing, fertilizing, irrigating, harvesting, drying, and processing are tallied, the in/out energy ratio is about one to two, meaning that just over 1 gallon of oil is required to produce 1 gallon of ethanol.[14] The bulk of energy used to make ethanol currently comes from coal-fired or natural gas-fired power plants. That makes you wonder: how renewable can the fuel be if you need nonrenewable energy to produce it?

Depending on which life cycle assessment you read (and there are dozens to ponder), the shift from hydrocarbon- to carbohydrate-based fuels could either ease particulate greenhouse emissions significantly or make things far worse. In 2006, researchers from the University of California, Berkeley's Energy and Resources Group reported a roughly 13 percent per mile reduction in greenhouse gas emissions from switching to corn-based ethanol.[15] On the same campus, Tad Patzek argued that in its present form, ethanol produces 42 percent more carbon dioxide and sulfur emissions (along with lung and eye irritants) than fossil fuels.[16] According to Michael Bomford of Kentucky State University, the differences between studies almost entirely depend on how researchers assess the value of DDGS, which are fed to livestock. In short, the jury is still out on ethanol, but it is certainly not a panacea for sustainable energy and likely brings with it new ecological and economic woes (figure 30).

THE CASE FOR CONSERVATION

Even the most ardent proponents admit that, at best, biofuels can be only a part of a diversified energy future. There is simply not enough french fry grease to satisfy the world's diesel addiction and only so much arable land to grow feedstock. Already more than 31 million acres (the equivalent of all the cropland in Iowa and then some) are dedicated to ethanol corn, but the output is displacing less than 8 percent of gasoline (figure 31). The same amount of gasoline could have been saved simply by increasing fleet-wide fuel economy just 1.1 miles per gallon.[17] (And that would have saved US taxpayers nearly $20 billion between 2005 and 2011 alone.)

Clearly, increasing fuel efficiency is a more effective way to reduce gasoline use than switching

Figure 30

Bio-Based Energy: Pros and Cons

Purported Benefits	Challenges
Strengthens national security by displacing foreign oil. As oil supplies contract, a transition beyond a petroleum-based economy is necessary.	Replacing 8 percent of the US gas consumption required 36 million acres of corn in 2010. Improving fuel efficiency standards by 1.1 mpg would have done the same.
Helps in the transition to new generations of more efficient types of biofuels, such as cellulosic ethanol.	After many years and billions of dollars in government and industry supports, there are only two commercially viable cellulosic ethanol plants on line.
Could eventually shift away from corn-based agriculture to perennial crops like switchgrass, myscanthus, perennial sorghum, and others that have less impact.	Challenges still remain in terms of crop storage and transport, prices required to make farming profitable, and the agricultural impacts of next-generation fuel crops.
Reduces greenhouse gas (GHG) emissions.	Studies show that ethanol from Brazil has lower GHG emissions than U.S. corn-based ethanol. Currently, tariffs prevent the import of foreign ethanol.
Becomes an economic engine for rural development.	Almost 80 percent of ethanol plants are now absentee-owned operations that have profited mightily from state and federal supports.
Helps with future development of crop "residues" such as straw, stalks, and other by-products for primary fuel source.	The use of biofuels to produce energy that charges batteries may be far more practical than running cars with liquid biofuels.
Biotechnology can overcome obstacles with specifically designed energy crops, innovative enzymes, and other breakthroughs.	Biotechnology's impacts include uncontrollable cross-pollination, the creation of resistant weeds and organisms, human health allergies, and concentration of wealth and seed supply.
Biofuels are just part of a larger integrated future energy strategy.	It takes at least 1/2 of a gallon of fossil fuel to make 1 gallon of corn ethanol. This diverts us from the real need for energy conservation and fuel reduction.
Provides farmers with new markets and opportunities for farmer-owned multinational cooperatives.	There are far more effective ways to compensate farmers fairly than to support an industry now dominated by large corporations.
Ethanol is a clean-burning fuel.	Making ethanol with coal power emits more GHGs than gasoline. Making ethanol with natural gas and biomass power emits less than gas.

Source: US Department of Agriculture. Natural Resources Conservation Service. "Summary Report: 2012 National Resources Inventory." August 2015.

Figure 31

The Grain Ethanol Gold Rush
US Corn-Based Ethanol Production

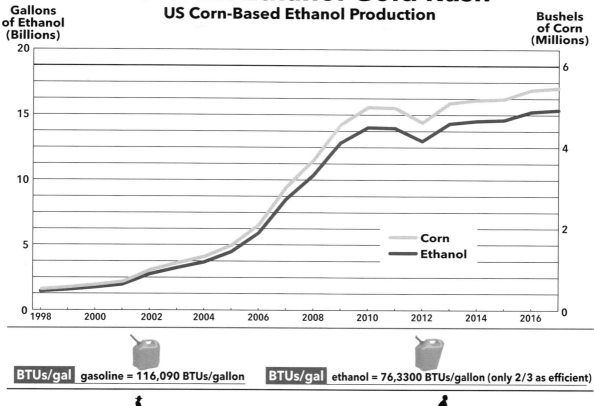

Gallons of Ethanol (Billions)

Bushels of Corn (Millions)

Corn
Ethanol

(x-axis: 1998, 2000, 2002, 2004, 2006, 2008, 2010, 2012, 2014, 2016)

BTUs/gal gasoline = 116,090 BTUs/gallon

BTUs/gal ethanol = 76,3300 BTUs/gallon (only 2/3 as efficient)

2003 50% of refineries majority farmer-owned

2010 19% of refineries farmer-owned

7.5% of gas consumption displaced by ethanol in 2016

36% of the US corn crop used for ethanol in 2016 (31.3m acres)

Sources: Alternative Fuels Data Center. "Alternative Fuels Data Center—Fuel Properties Comparison." US Department of Energy. October 29, 2014. Economic Research Service. "Feed Grains Customer Query." Updated August 11, 2017. US Department of Agriculture. CropWatch. "Bioenergy Corn." University of Nebraska, Lincoln Institute of Agriculture and Natural Resources. Accessed August 21, 2017. "Why Is Ethanol Important?" Accessed August 21, 2017. Renewable Fuels Association. National Agricultural Statistics Service. "Corn and Soybean Production Up in 2016, USDA Reports Winter Wheat Seedings and Grain Stocks Also Reported." January 12, 2017. US Department of Agriculture. Korth, Shelia. "Will the Real Ethanol Beneficiaries Please Stand Up?" Environmental Working Group. 2010.

to corn ethanol. Changing driver habits can also improve gas mileage without a costly ethanol industry. Simple things—such as avoiding excessive speeding and acceleration and performing regular car maintenance, including oil changes, proper tire inflation, and filter replacements—can make a difference (figure 32).

If helping small farmers diversify their economic portfolios were another goal of federal policy makers, ethanol has failed to deliver. What began as a movement of farmer-owned-and-operated small-scale plants has given way to facilities dominated by global agribusiness giants like Archer Daniels Midland, one of the most vocal ethanol advocates and most prolific beneficiaries of farmer ethanol subsidies.[18] Spurred on by mandates and incentives from the Energy Independence and Security Act of 2007, the federal Renewable Fuel Standard, and the California Low-Carbon Fuel Standard, numerous corporations and engineering firms joined the grain-based ethanol gold rush.[19] Dozens of relatively small dry-grind plants (producing 15 million to 30 million gallons per year) have been erected in proximity to large grain supplies, thanks in no small part to former government subsidies and continuing standards.

ETHANOL'S STEWARDSHIP LEGACY?

Food prices are on the rise around the globe. Land values and crop prices throughout the Corn Belt skyrocketed until 2013 and are only now beginning to fall.[20] Along with ethanol, drought has also driven up prices. One estimate suggested that reducing the Renewable Fuel Standard by 20 percent could have offset the crop loss due to drought in 2012 by saving it for other uses.[21] The grim reality is sinking

Figure 32

How to Boost US Fuel Economy

With an average fuel economy of the US fleet at 24.8 miles per gallon in 2009, the following actions could be adopted to further increase efficiency:

Action to Boost Fuel Economy	Low Est. +MPG	High Est. +MPG
Sensible driving	1.0	6.6
Observing the speed limit	1.4	4.6
Regular engine tune-ups	0.8	0.8
Proper tire inflation	0.6	0.6
Recommended motor oil	0.2	0.4
Replacing clogged air filters	0.4	1.2

Sources: "Light-Duty Automotive Technology, Carbon Dioxide Emissions, and Fuel Economy Trends Report Overview." Updated November 2016. Environmental Protection Agency; Cox, Craig, and Andrew Hug. "Driving Under the Influence: Corn Ethanol and Energy Security." June 2016. Environmental Working Group.

in that even if the entire US corn crop were distilled into liquid fuel, it would still supply about 25 percent of domestic demand.[22] Conservationists worry about transforming every potentially productive acre—including land set aside for conservation and protected grasslands and parklands—into some form of biofuel monoculture feedstock.

Any benefits of the ethanol boom—increased farm revenue, lower greenhouse gas emissions, and a more diversified fuel supply—come with a high environmental price tag. As the demand for fuel corn pushes farmers to intensify their land use, studies suggest that soil and water quality, human health, and bee health may suffer.[23,24,25]

Some optimists hope that farming standards can prevent the worst damage. In 2011, countries in the European Union (EU) agreed on standards for sustainable cultivating and harvesting of biofuel crops. In 2016, the EU proposed updates for both transport fuels and biomass fuels for heat and electricity. Similar efforts have stalled, however, in the United States, where there is no consensus on what constitutes "sustainable" farming practices. If not done properly, harvesting crop residues like wheat straw and corn stalks could eventually impoverish the soil. Sir Albert Howard, the early twentieth-century pioneer of the organic and sustainable farming movements, called it the "Law of Return," which states that what comes from the soil must return to the soil.[26] Organic matter must be added back into soil for it to stay productive. Cover cropping, crop rotations, and other natural methods are critical not just for biofuel production, but also for all agriculture.

In addition, harvesting cellulose from lands now set aside to protect wildlife could have devastating consequences to biodiversity and could reverse decades of gains made by Farm Bill conservation programs. Here are some guiding questions:

- Will federal mandates for biofuel production continue to drive idled lands into production?
- Will parks, forests, and other public lands become vulnerable to energy exploitation and food production?
- How will biorefineries manage the challenges of seasonality, storage, and transport of crops?
- Will food and energy shortages feed on each other?
- Can subsidies be structured to protect farmers during price falls, yet still protect taxpayers from huge payouts to biofuel producers that no longer need them?
- What about other sources of cellulose, such as the municipal waste stream, that could prevent immense agricultural expansion?
- What about the prospect of producing biofuels from algae, which could prevent additional land being used for production?

Perhaps a long-term benefit will emerge—once ethanol ceases to be a way for huge corporations to profitably dump excess corn and a more logical energy order arises. A sensible biofuel movement, embracing a diversification of fuel and nonfuel crops on landscapes, could evolve. To be ecologically sustainable, any production, whether for ethanol or food, must include crop rotations, streamside protection, the maintenance of healthy soils, and abundant wildlife habitat and wild areas.

GMO Designer Fuels: In a Station Near You

Fuel produced from genetically modified organisms (GMO)—plants that have been altered through the gene-splicing techniques of biotechnology—is already in your gas tank. Currently, about 92 percent of the US corn crop and 94 percent of soybeans are genetically modified varieties, primarily approved for animal feed rather than for human consumption. With consumers in Europe, Japan, Mexico, and Africa increasingly reluctant to allow GMO crops inside their borders, the rapidly expanding North American biofuels industry has become a convenient outlet.

In addition, because many of our major trade partners are wary of importing GMO products, our opportunities to trade these commodities are limited. China rejected an entire shipment of GMO-contaminated conventional corn in 2014, costing the companies who developed the technology millions of dollars. This situation has created a complicated and unreliable basis for international trade.

Rival seed giants Monsanto (recently purchased by Bayer Pharmaceuticals) and DuPont have been jockeying for market share with conventionally bred corn varieties that boast higher starch content to maximize ethanol production. But most experts acknowledge that corn has its limitations (and negative ecological implications) as a fuel source. So some are turning to biotechnology for alternatives.

Who's Growing GMOs

Percent of Global Land Area Planted in Biotechnology Varieties by Country
(2016 Total Global Land Area: 457.4 Million Acres)

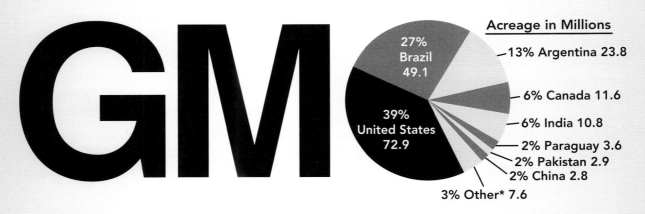

Acreage in Millions

- 27% Brazil 49.1
- 39% United States 72.9
- 13% Argentina 23.8
- 6% Canada 11.6
- 6% India 10.8
- 2% Paraguay 3.6
- 2% Pakistan 2.9
- 2% China 2.8
- 3% Other* 7.6

*Considered "biotech mega-countries," other countries that grow at least 50,000 hectares include: South Africa, Uruguay, Bolivia, Australia, Philippines, Myanmar, Spain, Sudan, Mexico, and Colombia.

Source: International Service for the Acquisition of Agri-Biotech Applications. "Brief 52—Global Status of Commercialized Biotech/GM Crops: 2016." Ithaca, NY.

"More miles to the acre" may be the new mantra of biotech agribusiness firms eager to cash in on the biofuel craze in at least two different ways: (1) modifying the genetic structure of plants to make fermentation easier and (2) boosting yields of both annual and perennial crops.

Syngenta, for example, was approved in 2011 to sell a "self-processing" corn. Each transgenic kernel would carry an amylase enzyme otherwise added separately to starch at the ethanol plant. To achieve that, engineers inserted a gene from a thermophilic microbe that lives near hot-water vents on the ocean floor. Meanwhile, DuPont and Bunge launched a joint venture to genetically engineer soybeans for biodiesel and other uses.[a]

Researchers are also branching out into perennial plants such as fast-growing poplar trees and dense grasses such as the Chinese myscanthus, which promoters tout can grow 20 tons of biomass per acre with little fertilizer or irrigation. California-based Ceres Corporation has been breeding switchgrass, native to prairie states, so that it would need even less fertilizer and irrigation and require infrequent replanting.

Another goal of biotech firms is to reduce the amount of lignin that holds plant cells together. Removing lignin presently complicates converting cellulose into ethanol. But it's also nature's way of endowing plants with the stiffness to grow upright. Researchers at the US Department of Energy's Oak Ridge National Laboratory and others have demonstrated that substituting a genetically modified lignin molecule can increase the amount of biofuel that can be recovered without impairing the plant's growth. Studies continue to investigate this prospect in various types of plants.

Even the conventional agriculture community is cautioning against a massive increase in intensive corn farming. Many fear that the abandonment of crop rotations could strain the soil, diminish water resources, and lead to vulnerability to pests and disease. The emergence of "superweeds" resistant to the herbicide Roundup is causing a return to even more toxic herbicides such as dicamba or 2, 4-D.

At the same time, the spread of new and GMO energy crops that have undergone few safety tests holds its own set of complications. The transfer of exotic genes and enzymes from energy crops to the human food supply or to the wild is entirely possible. Pollen transfer in open fields between the same types of crops or their wild plant relatives is a naturally occurring and uncontrollable phenomenon.

The intermingling of seed is also almost impossible to prevent. This fact was soundly proven with StarLink corn (approved only for animal consumption, it has surfaced in tortilla chips). In 2006, herbicide-resistant Liberty Link rice contaminated conventional supplies and resulted in plummeting sales for US farmers. Genetically engineered, Roundup-Ready alfalfa has proven particularly problematic. A 2015 US Department of Agriculture study showed that the modified strains have contaminated conventional ones, costing millions of dollars to farmers and exporters and disproving the idea that genetically modified crops could coexist without contaminating adjacent crops. Such contaminations—of plants and seed banks—are essentially irreversible.

There are health implications as well. Bill Freese from the Center for Food Safety in Washington, DC, reported that some amylase added to GMO corn can induce allergies and requires further study.[b] While many fear potential toxicity, gene transfer, or reduced nutritional content, studies over multiple generations in mice have so far proven them false.[c] Concerns remain, however, about negative impacts to human health due to cumulative, lifelong exposure.

The biotech industry is poised to go to great lengths to produce fuel from agriculture. The question we all need to ask is whether our national addiction to liquid fuels and automobiles could possibly be worth such risks.

The concentration of plant gene patents in the hands of just a few global corporations most concerns Dave Henson, an expert on genetically modified crops. "GMO biofuel conglomerates have the potential to become the next OPEC," cautioned Henson.[d] "Controlling patents and the seed supply means these giants are no longer just grain brokers and dealers, but will have the power to exercise control over growers and communities all over the world."

NOTES

a. Andrew Pollack, "Redesigning Crops to Harvest Fuel," *New York Times*, Friday, September 8, 2006, C1–C4.

b. Pollack, "Redesigning Crops."

c. Megan L. Norris, "Will GMOs Hurt My Body? The Public's Concerns and How Scientists Have Addressed Them," *Science in the News*, August 2015.

d. OPEC, the Organization of Petroleum Exporting Countries, has had profound influence over the flow of trade and price of oil around the world.

19. Energy and Climate Change

> We now expend twice as much energy processing, packaging, storing, transporting, and preparing something after it leaves the farm as we use to grow it in the first place.

ENERGY IS THE DRIVING FORCE behind all contemporary economic activities, and food production and farming operations are no exception. From natural gas-rich nitrogen fertilizers, to power for irrigation and processing, to fossil fuels for cars, ships, trucks, tractors, and laser-guided farm equipment, to the gas and electricity we use at home to cook and refrigerate, energy is gobbled up in every stage along the way (figure 33).

When it comes to measuring how much energy it takes to put food on our tables, however, some surprising results surface. The energy required to grow food, although significant, has been declining for decades as farmers switch to diesel power and adopt other more efficient technologies and practices. In fact, we now expend twice as much energy processing, packaging, storing, transporting, and preparing something after it leaves the farm as we use to grow it in the first place. But as energy and climate concerns converge, attention turns to farms to offer solutions and improve. The twenty-first-century farm is viewed as an energy generator: raising crops for biofuels, installing industrial-scale wind turbines, and capturing methane gas from liquid manure pits. Pastures, woodlots, and permanent ground cover act as carbon sinks, removing carbon dioxide from the atmosphere and storing it in organic matter in the soil.

THE OIL WE EAT

As late as 1910, 27 percent of all US farmland was still devoted to growing feed for horses used in transportation and cultivation.[1] Modern agriculture is so dependent on fossil fuel energy that some critics say

Figure 33

How US Agriculture Uses Energy

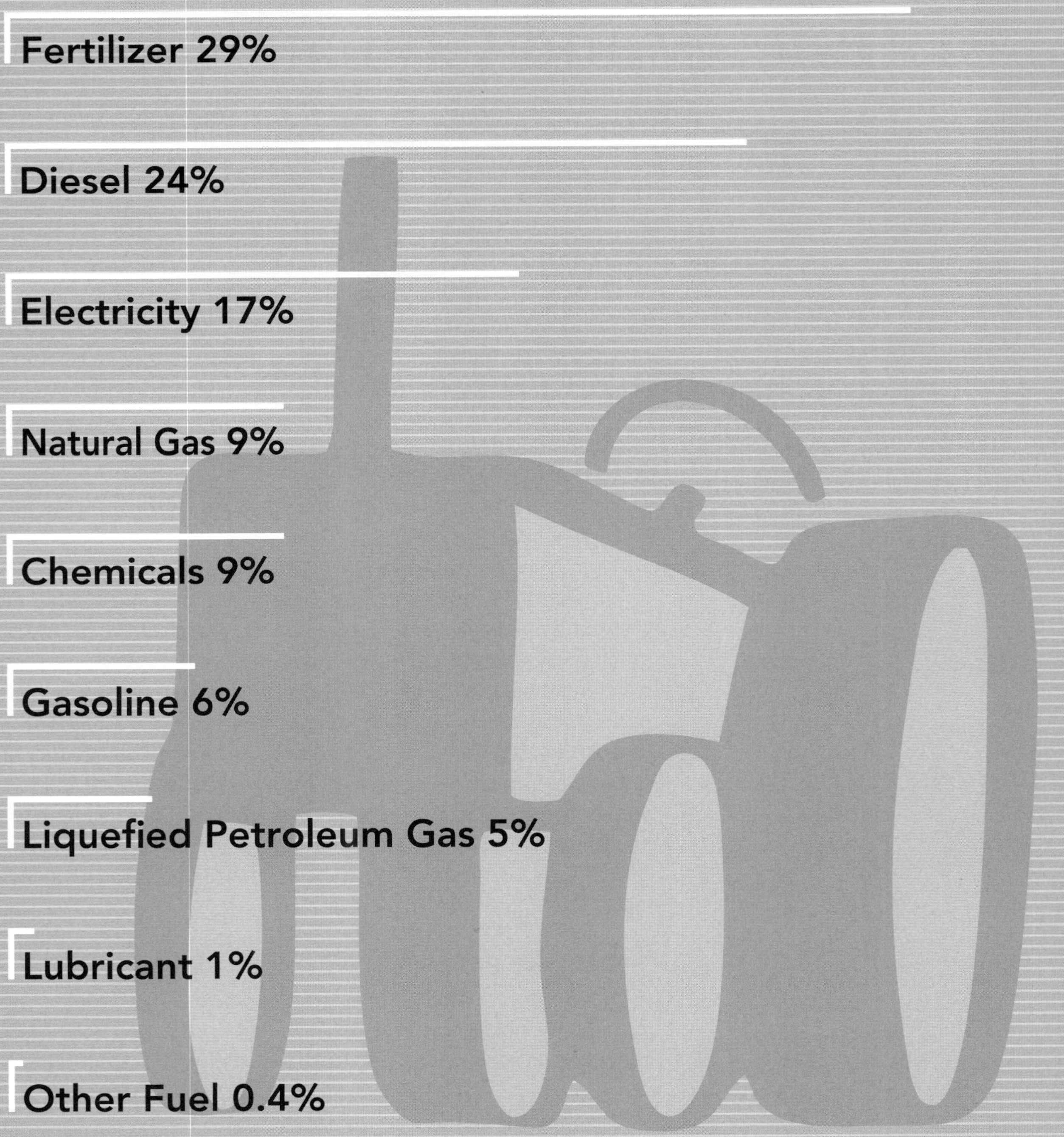

Fertilizer 29%

Diesel 24%

Electricity 17%

Natural Gas 9%

Chemicals 9%

Gasoline 6%

Liquefied Petroleum Gas 5%

Lubricant 1%

Other Fuel 0.4%

Source: Hitaj, Claudia, and Shellye Suttles. "Trends in U.S. Agriculture's Consumption and Production of Energy: Renewable Power, Shale Energy, and Cellulosic Biomass." EIB 159. USDA Economic Research Service. August 2016.

we are now literally "eating oil" (figure 34). Just a casual look at the facts demonstrates how intricately food and energy are interrelated:

- An estimated 12.5 percent of energy consumption in the United States in 2012 was food-related.[2]

- On average, at least 10 calories of fossil fuel are used for every 1 calorie of industrial food eaten.[3]

- Harvesting a single bushel of corn requires the energy equivalent of one-third of a gallon of gasoline.[4]

- The average 1,200-pound steer consumes the energy equivalent of 130 gallons (three barrels) of oil over its short lifetime from cow-calf operation to conventional midwestern feedlot.[5]

- Nitrogen fertilizers, synthesized from natural gas, are the backbone of high-yield industrial farming, consuming almost one-third of the energy used in US agriculture.[6]

THE ENERGY-EFFICIENT FARM

One of the Farm Bill's greatest strengths has been its capacity to serve as an economic catalyst. In 2002, the Renewable Energy and Energy Efficiency Improvements Program was launched to jump-start a "clean energy" initiative within Farm Bill programs. Known as Section 9006 grants, these funds provided cost-share and loan guarantees to invest in on-farm renewable energy systems, promote energy auditing and conservation, and diversify energy sources in rural areas. These investments in renewable energy have been recognized as green box payments by World Trade Organization rules—unlike corn subsidies that support ethanol production—and are not limited by payment restrictions.

The 2008 Farm Bill's Energy title (see the "Farm Bill Titles" feature in chapter 3 for a listing of the various titles) quadrupled the 2002 Farm Bill's previous energy budget, adding nearly $1 billion in supports, including a number of programs geared toward making US farms more energy efficient.[7] The ethanol industry still emerged the real winner from these increases, accounting for nearly two-thirds of the funding boost: $320 million to the Biorefinery Assistance Program and $300 million to the Bioenergy Program for Advanced Biofuels.[8] The Rural Energy for America Program (REAP) superseded the Section 9006 program with an allotment of $255 million for on-farm energy improvements.[9] These grants have helped landowners install renewable energy sources (wind, solar, geothermal, biomass, etc.) and make energy efficiency improvements (retrofitting existing buildings, upgrading to a more efficient heating system, or replacing equipment).[10]

The 2014 Farm Bill reauthorized most programs but eliminated the requirement to fund feasibility studies. Funding was set at a $50 million annual baseline through the life of the Farm Bill.[11] In 2015, $63 million was awarded for grants and loans.[12]

Like many Farm Bill program categories, renewable energy funding has not been guaranteed. The Chicago-based Environmental Law and Policy Center and other groups have waged hard-fought campaigns every year to defend the annual appropriations of the REAP budgets. Between 2008 and 2013, the US Department of Agriculture (USDA) awarded

Figure 34

How the US Food System Uses Energy

Home Refrigeration
& Preparation 28%

Processing 20%

Wholesale/Retail 16%

Agricultural Production 14%

Food Service 12%

Packaging 6%

Transportation 4%

Source: Canning Patrick, Ainsley Charles, Sonya Huang, Karen R. Polenske, and Arnold Waters. "Energy Use in the U.S. Food System." USDA Economic Research Service. 2010.

$57 million in grants and loan guarantees, but it also turned away more than half of all funding requests[13] (figure 35). Meanwhile, ethanol profits and subsidies soared.

Outside of the Energy title, on-farm energy conservation incentives have also been integrated into the Farm Bill's Conservation title. The Environmental Quality Incentives Program (EQIP) allocates cost-share funds to perform energy audits, reduce energy consumption, and build methane digesters that are placed on top of liquid manure lagoons to capture gas emissions. Under the Conservation Stewardship Program (CSP), farmers can receive financial incentives for (1) energy auditing; (2) decreasing tillage and the use of fertilizers and other fossil fuel inputs; (3) recycling used motor oil; (4) purchasing ethanol and biodiesel; and (5) generating renewable solar, wind, hydroelectric, geothermal, or methane power.

Methane digesters (also known as anaerobic digesters) have become more common in recent years. In 2016, there were 242 digesters operating on livestock farms, with more than 80 percent of those on dairy farms.[14] The AgSTAR program of the Environmental Protection Agency (EPA) estimates that methane digesters could possibly produce up to 1,670 megawatts of energy across the country.[15]

Public financing for methane digesters has a lot in common with taxpayer support for corn ethanol. As with an ethanol plant, it is extremely expensive to build contraptions that capture the potent methane greenhouse gas vapors rising off cesspools on dairies or hog farms. And like those in the ethanol industry, operators of concentrated animal feeding operations have been increasingly relying on large infusions of taxpayer subsidies to help them build this type of infrastructure. Methane produced from animal waste is not extremely efficient. Most of the energy consumed in feed is used to fuel an animal's metabolism. The manure contains far less energy as a result. Producing any large quantity of energy in a methane digester requires additional biomass. In the end, government funding for industrial-scale methane digesters does more to make the concentrated animal feeding industry look responsible (a questionable goal) than it does to promote sensible energy production. Farm Bill funds should be used for methane digester production, but only on small- and medium-scale, highly efficient operations, where the numbers of animals are in balance with the amounts of waste generated.

There are other ways to produce animals for food while reducing greenhouse gas emissions. Animals kept on pasture spread wastes naturally over the soil, allowing for greater penetration and nutrient retention without heavy concentrations of methane. Hogs raised in deep straw bedding generate significantly lower methane emissions than those in industrial confinement systems as well.

STOPPING FOOD WASTE AT THE SOURCE

The United States currently throws away about 40 percent of the food it produces, meaning that about $218 billion is spent to bring food to consumers that ends up in the trash.[16,17] That is not just a tremendous waste of food, but also a waste of all the energy and resources that went into producing it. Overall, food waste accounts for 21 percent of freshwater usage, 19 percent of fertilizer usage,

Figure 35

Demand Outpaces Supply
REAP Popularity & Funding

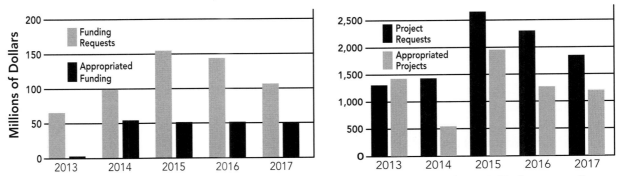

REAP project funding requests have fallen since peaking in 2011, and appropriations are consistently less than 50% of funding requests. Since passage of the 2014 Farm Bill, appropriations have been roughly consistent, though the number of projects have declined. The proportion of rewards for energy efficiency projects has decreased under the 2014 Farm Bill, while the proportion for solar and wind energy has increased.

Renewable Priorities
REAP Funding Totals by Technology

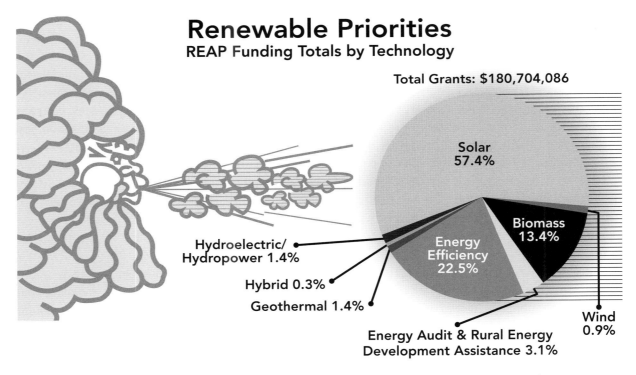

Total Grants: $180,704,086

Solar 57.4%

Biomass 13.4%

Energy Efficiency 22.5%

Hydroelectric/ Hydropower 1.4%

Hybrid 0.3%

Geothermal 1.4%

Energy Audit & Rural Energy Development Assistance 3.1%

Wind 0.9%

Source: Data for REAP awards came from personal communication with Andy Olsen, Senior Policy Advocate for Environmental Law and Policy Center, on October 27, 2017. Office of Rural Development. "Rural Energy Savings Program: Questions and Answers." US Department of Agriculture. Published 2016.

and 18 percent of cropland usage nationwide,[18] and the food waste that ends up in landfills produces methane, releasing this potent greenhouse gas as it decomposes. Although retail businesses account for the majority of this waste, approximately 10 percent of the waste occurring on farms can and should be more directly addressed by innovative Farm Bill programs.[19]

Food may be wasted on farms for many reasons, including overproduction and lack of labor to harvest crops. Consumers also have notoriously high cosmetic standards for their produce, so most grocery stores or markets will only accept blemish-free foods. Perishable foods may be lost in storage, particularly for small or isolated farmers who must transport produce over long distances. Some of this loss is inevitable, but farmers can divert some of this unwanted feedstock into compost, creating a valuable source of fertilizer or material for anaerobic digestion, yielding a source of biofuels. Unfortunately, many small farmers cannot afford the cost of constructing these facilities.

In 2015, the USDA and EPA set a national goal to reduce food waste by 50 percent by 2030. Initiatives to reduce waste on the farm have yet to appear beyond a few isolated sections of the Farm Bill and should be greatly expanded in the future.[20] In 2017, experts at Harvard University's Food Law and Policy Clinic compiled a list of top recommendations. As one example, programs such as EQIP and CSP could support composting or small-scale anaerobic digestion by setting aside a portion of funding or by broadening the definition of "conservation practice."[21] Support could come from the Value-Added Producer Grants within the Rural Development title or the Farmers Market and Local Food Promotion Program within the Horticulture title to help farmers repurpose their unattractive produce as new products or sell their surplus food at a lower cost.[22] The Farm Bill's Miscellaneous title could revise the Bill Emerson Good Samaritan Food Donation Act (Emerson Act) to allow producers to donate their surplus directly to those in need rather than working through nonprofit organizations, and to receive liability protection. It could also rank the applications for Specialty Crop Research Initiative grants under the Research title to give preference to those seeking to preserve crops and reduce post-harvest loss. These and other measures would demonstrate our country's commitment to reducing the waste of both food and energy.

NITROGEN FERTILIZERS

Since the middle of the twentieth century, nitrogen fertilizers have formed the backbone of industrial agriculture. Each year, US farmers apply more than 22 million tons of nitrogen fertilizers to increase crop yields as the soil's nutrients become exhausted.[23] As long as fossil fuels have been cheap and abundant, nitrogen fertilizers have also been relatively inexpensive. Farmers heap nitrogen on fields in increasing quantities even as gains in productivity decline. Nitrogen fertilizers have been extremely effective in maintaining yields, even functioning as a form of relatively cheap crop insurance to boost harvests.

Any gains in yield have come at considerable environmental and health costs, however. Overdependence on synthetic nitrogen fertilizers represents one of the most important challenges facing modern agriculture. Fertilizers are responsible for almost one-third of all energy expended in modern farming. Much of that is used during the fertilizer manufacturing process, in which nitrogen and hydrogen gas are combined to make ammonia under extremely high pressure. The energy sources that create those manufacturing conditions are frequently powered by coal or natural gas.

Nitrogen fertilizers are also extremely "leaky"; that is, they are very difficult to contain after application. Unlike wastes contained in a natural ecosystem that can provide food and nutrients for other species, high concentrations of this fixed nitrogen become toxic pollution that takes a long time to break down. Less than one-half of the fertilizers actually reach the crops they are intended to fortify. The rest end up in groundwater as nitrates and in surface water as ammonia, where they fertilize algal blooms that die off and create dead zones. Nitrous oxide is released in the atmosphere with three hundred times the heat-trapping capacity of carbon dioxide. According to one USDA report based on data from 2006, 108 million acres of US cropland—two-thirds of the fields that receive synthetic nitrogen—need improved management to prevent leakage. Corn was the crop managed most poorly.[24] Given that the Gulf of Mexico's dead zone reached a record size in 2017 (see chapter 16), that proportion has probably increased.

Intentionally growing plants that absorb nitrogen out of the atmosphere—a traditional farming practice known as cover cropping—is one logical shift away from overloading ecosystems with synthetic nitrogen. Unfortunately, present regulations and incentives are not sufficient to sway farmers away from nitrogen fertilizers and toward cover cropping. Until 2014, the USDA's Risk Management Agency required that cover crops could only be applied after crops that were covered by insurance had reached maturity, which dissuaded many farmers from growing them at all to avoid risking any complications. Farmers can now plant cover crops earlier as long as they don't impact the yield of the insured crop. But cover crops must still be terminated by a certain time and in a certain manner, leaving many farmers wary.

The benefits of planting cover crops could be considerable. In addition to pollution prevention and energy savings from reduced manufacture of synthetic fertilizers, the National Wildlife Federation estimated in 2011 that planting cover crops on all suitable acreage (182 million acres) could eliminate 5 percent of annual US greenhouse gas emissions by increasing storage.[25] Bolstering USDA budgets to support biological rather than chemical solutions to maintaining soil fertility represents one of the most urgent and underfunded priorities of all future Farm Bills.

ADAPTING TO CLIMATE CHANGE

Energy issues are inextricably linked with climate change and its effect on food security. Recent years have brought rising temperatures, radical fluctuations in precipitation patterns, extreme flooding, and drought in agricultural areas across the world. Worldwide, agriculture contributes an estimated 24 percent of total greenhouse gas emissions, (9 percent in the United States).[26,27] This figure includes almost one-fourth of the carbon dioxide, two-thirds of the methane, and nearly all of the nitrous oxide emissions.[28] More than half of the world's food system emissions come directly from crop and livestock production, including nitrous oxide released through soil disturbance and methane emissions generated by livestock.[29] Although production accounts for a smaller proportion of energy use, farming still has a bigger impact on climate than the energy-intensive activities that take place after foods leave the fields. Even the emissions associated with the ever-lengthening "food mile," the distance an item travels from farm to fork (1,500 to 4,200 miles), are dwarfed by the climate-altering impacts of clearing land, soil tillage, and the global production of more than 50 billion food animals.[30,31]

Agriculture can conserve energy and reduce climate change by increasing the food system's ability to capture carbon. That is the natural process by which living plants and some bacteria take carbon dioxide out of the air, convert it to carbohydrates through photosynthesis, and trap it in the soil in the form of organic matter. It's one way of offsetting the tremendous amounts of carbon dioxide that humans have pumped into the atmosphere by burning fossil fuels, raising food animals, and plowing soils. Farming practices such as grass-pastured livestock production and organic agriculture are increasingly proving to be excellent ways to both produce healthy food and decrease carbon emissions related to agriculture.

A 2011 USDA report entitled "Putting Dairy Cows Out to Pasture: An Environmental Plus" demonstrated that in terms of energy use, negative climate impacts, and air quality, raising dairy cows outside on pastures year-round results in a much smaller ecological "hoofprint" than raising cows in confinement facilities.[32] This peer-reviewed study found that total emissions of greenhouse gases in year-round, grass-based systems were 10 percent lower than comparably sized confinement oper-

ations. More dramatically, ammonia emissions, a major source of air pollutants, were reduced by 30 percent.

Keeping cows on pastures also reduced fuel consumption and cut carbon dioxide emissions from farm equipment. Researcher Al Rotz concluded, "When farmland is transitioned from rotated crops to perennial grassland, you can build up lots of carbon in the soil and substantially reduce your carbon footprint for 20 to 30 years."[33] Although the volume of milk produced by grass-fed cows dropped substantially compared to grain-fed, confined dairy cows, the total quantity of nutrients, such as milk protein and fat, was found to be the same.

THE ORGANIC ADVANTAGE

USDA studies also show that scaling up organic grain production could significantly reduce greenhouse gas emissions. The benefits come from organic farmers replacing synthetic nitrogen fertilizers with compost, manure, and cover crops that naturally accumulate atmospheric nitrogen in the soil. Overall, organic agriculture requires 60 percent less energy to fuel production than does nonorganic agriculture.[34]

Organic systems also typically increase the amount of carbon contained in the soil. Storing carbon in organic matter supports many critical functions in building healthy soil: acting as a reservoir of plant nutrients, binding soil particles together, maintaining soil temperature, providing a food source for microbes, tying up heavy metals and pesticides, and increasing water retention capacity and aeration.[35] A United Kingdom Soil Association review of thirty-nine studies covering one hundred comparisons of organic and nonorganic farming showed that, on average, organic systems yield 20 to 28 percent more soil organic carbon (SOC) in topsoil than do nonorganic systems.[36] Studies show that organic production also often leads to further increases of SOC deeper in the subsoil.

CHANGING ENERGY AND CLIMATE POLICY

The Farm Bill has no climate change title. Programs that help landowners adapt to climate change and improve energy efficiency currently reside in the Conservation and Energy titles. Few, if any, programs are tailored to changes in rainfall cycles, sea levels, air and water temperatures, and vegetation patterns, which will inevitably reshape agriculture and life as we know it. The Farm Bill needs to both address climate change's impact on agriculture and agriculture's impact on climate change.

Agriculture differs from almost every other sector of the economy in that most of its greenhouse gas emissions are not caused by energy use. Soil disturbance, land clearing, and livestock release more than three times as much greenhouse gas as total farm energy use. Nevertheless, it is important to keep in mind how the Farm Bill can shape our energy future. Programs and financial support in the bill can do more than simply profit corporations already thriving in the marketplace. Instead, initiatives can support energy conservation and a move away from fossil fuels.

Tough choices will be made in the decades ahead. Regional production of diverse renewable energy sources should be aggressively scaled up.

At the same time, energy is not renewable if essential resources such as soil and water are despoiled in its production. Simply increasing the supply of renewable energy without a national strategy to make the United States carbon neutral may only succeed in providing yet more power to consumers. Options for integrated energy solutions are found in figure 36.

Progress in wind energy expansion is one such example. Across the world, and particularly in agricultural areas, large wind farms are gaining traction as alternative electricity producers. Indeed, many analyses suggest that our capacity to generate wind power is expected to double from 2015 to 2021 now that its cost has dropped 61 percent since 2009.[37,38]

The latest generation of turbines has been criticized as noisy, visually polluting, and ultimately beneficial primarily to investors outside of the communities where they are installed. However, it should be possible to identify appropriate areas to locate utility-scale wind farms, with exceptions such as the following, proposed by conservationist and author John Davis:

- No energy production in roadless areas
- No windmills or energy production in wildlife migration corridors
- No windmills in parks or protected areas
- Keep windmills away from water bodies
- Complement renewable energy funding with a national energy conservation platform

Figure 36

The Answer Is . . .
Components of an Integrated Energy Solution

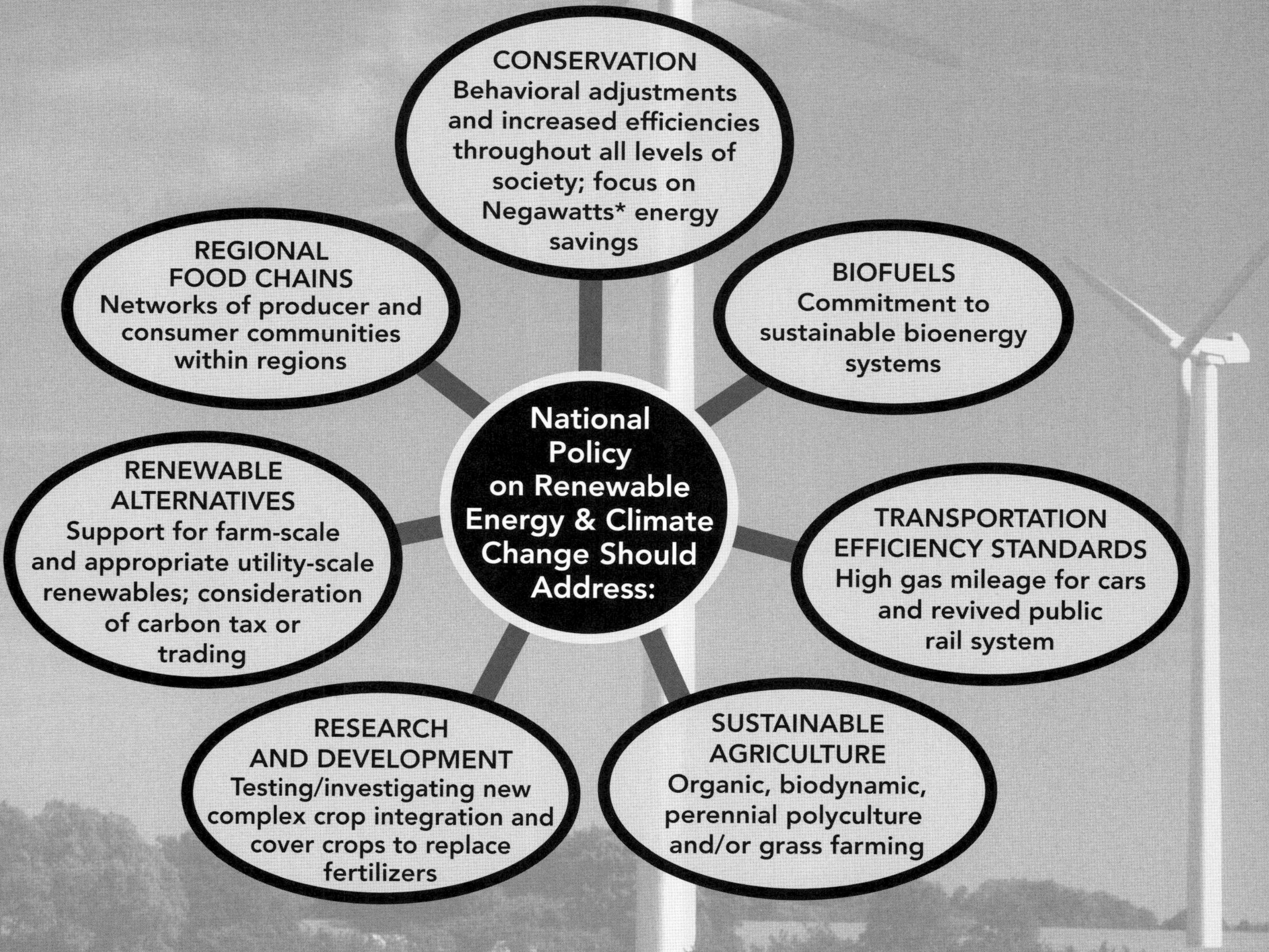

CONSERVATION
Behavioral adjustments and increased efficiencies throughout all levels of society; focus on Negawatts* energy savings

REGIONAL FOOD CHAINS
Networks of producer and consumer communities within regions

BIOFUELS
Commitment to sustainable bioenergy systems

National Policy on Renewable Energy & Climate Change Should Address:

RENEWABLE ALTERNATIVES
Support for farm-scale and appropriate utility-scale renewables; consideration of carbon tax or trading

TRANSPORTATION EFFICIENCY STANDARDS
High gas mileage for cars and revived public rail system

RESEARCH AND DEVELOPMENT
Testing/investigating new complex crop integration and cover crops to replace fertilizers

SUSTAINABLE AGRICULTURE
Organic, biodynamic, perennial polyculture and/or grass farming

*Negawatt, a term first used by Amory Lovins at the Rocky Mountain Institute in 1985, refers to a theoretical megawatt saved through improved energy conservation or efficiency.

20. Conservation

FEDERAL FARM PROGRAMS ARE DESIGNED TO SUPPORT THE GROWTH of production agriculture as well as help conserve biodiversity on the landscape. When out of balance, however, these two functions can work at cross-purposes. As commodity prices have continued to decrease since years of record harvests caused them to crash in 2013, one might think that interest in idling land for conservation purposes would make a comeback.

According to a 2011 US Department of Agriculture (USDA) report, the same tools—subsidized crop insurance, disaster assistance, and marketing loans—that farmers insist are essential to their viability are eroding decades of conservation gains by encouraging agricultural expansion into grasslands.[1] Between 2008 and 2012, 1.6 million acres of long-term grasslands were converted to crop production. Land that formerly served as important habitats and soil carbon sinks was plowed as farmers weighed the economic rewards of crop insurance over conservation benefits.[2]

Across the Corn Belt, too, grassland bird populations, important indicator species, have experienced a precipitous decline. Breeding grounds have disappeared for once-common species such as the bobolink, Savannah sparrow, Baird's sparrow, northern harrier, horned lark, loggerhead shrike, and eastern and western meadowlark as grasslands are converted to subsidized row crops and subdivisions. Although some farmers and ranchers have adopted stewardship practices to accommodate these declining species, the critical mass needed to stem the losses has not materialized. Grasses can be reseeded, but once land is cultivated, it is extremely difficult to reestablish the full range of habitat diversity. Ornithologists warn that we have only a decade to restore perennial ground cover across what is now the corn and soybean landscape before many grassland birds disappear from their traditional ranges altogether.

PAYING FARMERS NOT TO FARM

Why pay farmers not to farm? It's a natural enough question. The answer partly lies in the value of healthy rural landscapes that are not compensated by the almighty marketplace. Water filtration and flood prevention, open spaces, wildlife habitat, carbon storage, scenery, and species protection are just a few of the benefits of well-protected private lands. But farmers motivated to maximize profits through intensive production often work directly against these benefits by: diminishing biodiversity with genetically identical monocultures, mining the soil, overdrawing groundwater reserves, physically concentrating livestock in huge numbers, or continually applying agrochemicals. Without financial compensation, farmers have little incentive to minimize their production at any given time.

All citizens have a stake in what happens on farmlands. Here are a few compelling reasons why:

- Just over half of the 2.3 billion acres in the United States is made up of crop, pasture, range, and forest land—almost 70 percent of which is privately owned (figure 37).[3]

- Only one-tenth of the contiguous forty-eight states falls under some form of state or federal habitat protection, and these areas have become increasingly fragmented.

- Public lands are being exploited for natural resources, grazing, timbering, off-road recreation, mining, and other harmful activities.

- As of 2016, 62 percent of all plants and animal species listed globally as threatened or near-threatened were at risk solely due to agricultural activities.[4]

- A 2016 Environmental Protection Agency report on national use of pesticides found that at least 79 percent of the species protected by the Endangered Species Act are threatened by three common pesticides.[5]

With the US population now more than 320 million and showing no signs of a plateau, agricultural lands face constant development pressure. Nationwide, more than 350,000 acres of farmland are lost to development every year, yet an estimated 400 million acres of agricultural land will transfer to owners by 2026. Without a new generation of farmers and ranchers willing to take over, the probability that some of this land will be converted to nonagricultural uses remains high.[6,7]

The outright purchase of all the land necessary to safeguard our natural heritage is simply not economically or politically feasible. (Even if purchased, many landscapes would require ongoing management.) Government agencies and land trust organizations have effectively used easements to acquire rural lands (or their development rights) to fight sprawl and protect biodiversity, but these measures aren't enough. Conservation incentives for private landowners remain essential for maintaining a network of healthy habitat. And the Farm

Figure 37

Land Cover/Use
Surface Area of the Contiguous United States in 2012

	Public	Range	Forest	Crops	Pasture	Developed	Water	Conservation Reserve Program	Other Rural Land*
US land base	21%	21%	21%	19%	6%	6%	3%	3%	2%
Millions of acres	405.3 (± 0.0)	405.8 (± 1.8)	413.3 (± 1.5)	362.7 (± 1.2)	121.1 (± 0.9)	114.1 (± 0.7)	52.1 (± 0.1)	24.2 (± 0.2)	45.4 (± 0.8)

*Other rural land includes farmsteads, barren land, marshland, and permanent snow/ice.

Source: Natural Resources Conservation Service. "Summary Report: 2012 National Resources Inventory." August 2015. US Department of Agriculture.

Bill's Conservation title potentially provides not just millions, but billions of dollars—when properly appropriated—to accomplish just that (see the "Conservation Program Landscape" feature for descriptions).

The best programs, said wildlife biologist and retired USDA National Resource Conservation Service (NRCS) biologist Randy Gray, encompass a habitat large enough to permit the recovery of a species in that area. For example, Environmental Quality Incentives Program (EQIP) payments to ranchers and landowners in midwestern and northern plains states helped protect food availability for honeybees on 35,000 acres in the area where they pollinate crops plans during their summer months in an important effort to counter their population declines in recent years.[8] In addition, funding from both EQIP and wetland easements through the Agricultural Conservation Easement Program (ACEP) supports the Sage Grouse Initiative, which conserved 5.6 million acres of prime habitat from 2010 to 2015. Studies showed that the initiative also increased populations of other local species, such as the green-tailed towhee and Brewer's sparrow.[9]

THE CONSERVATION RESERVE PROGRAM AND THE WETLANDS RESERVE PROGRAM: A MODERN NEW DEAL

During the Dust Bowl, the displacement of our continent's soil and farm population—driven by drought and economic depression—spurred the early Farm

Conservation Program Landscape

Agricultural Conservation Easement Program (ACEP—2014). This program helps conserve agricultural lands and wetlands by enrolling land through easements into cooperative agreements with the Natural Resources Conservation Service. Agricultural Land Easements maintain productive land, and Wetlands Reserve Easements maintain habitat and water quality. ACEP incorporated the now-defunct Wetlands Reserve Program, Grasslands Reserve Program, and Farm and Ranchlands Protection Program. Although more than 240,000 acres have been preserved since 2014, the new program receives just a fraction of what the disparate programs formerly utilized.

Agricultural Management Assistance (AMA—2000). AMA provides cost-share assistance for agricultural producers in sixteen states (most northeastern states plus Hawaii, Utah, Nevada, and Wyoming) to construct or improve water management structures or irrigation structures; plant trees for windbreaks or improve water quality; and mitigate risk through production diversification or resource conservation practices, including soil erosion control, crop rotation, integrated pest management, or transition to organic farming.

Conservation compliance. Conservation compliance refers broadly to disincentive programs (Sodbuster, Highly Erodible Land Conservation and Wetland Conservation provisions, and Swampbuster) created by the 1985 Farm Bill to decrease destructive practices on highly erodible cropland without adequate erosion protection and to prevent the draining of wetlands on agricultural land. Violation of these provisions can result in denial of commodity subsidies and conservation payments, although enforcement has been lax and succeeding Farm Bills have weakened the rules. Swampbuster rules are key to achieving the national wetlands no-net-loss policy. Proposals to strengthen Sodbuster rules are getting renewed attention as limited remaining native prairie gets converted to cropland.

Conservation Innovation Grants (CIG—2002). Under CIG, EQIP funds award competitive grants to nonfederal governmental or nongovernmental organizations, tribes, or individuals to accelerate technology transfer and adoption of promising technologies and approaches to pressing natural resource concerns.

Conservation Reserve Program (CRP—1985). In this voluntary land retirement program, landowners sign up for ten- or fifteen-year contracts and receive annual rental payments and cost-share assistance to establish resource-conserving ground covers on eligible, mostly highly erodible, farmland. Total land enrollments will be gradually reduced by 25 percent over five years, and biofuels advocates are eyeing CRP land for grain and cellulosic ethanol production.

Conservation Stewardship Program (CSP—2008). CSP was derived from the Conservation Security Program, which was the first comprehensive green payments approach to subsidizing agriculture that began in 2002. It was also the first conservation program enacted as an entitlement program, with a budget set by the number of farmers deciding to apply and able to meet the rigorous environmental standards required. Although the 2014 reauthorization decreased total enrollment from 12.8 million acres to 10 million acres, it did increase minimum stewardship requirements for eligibility.

Conservation Technical Assistance (CTA—2008). CTA provides the technical capability, including direct conservation planning, design, and implementation assistance, that helps people plan and apply conservation programs on the land. It is a key part of the basic infrastructure for all conservation programs.

Environmental Quality Incentives Program (EQIP—1996). EQIP provides cost-sharing and incentive payments to install or implement structural and management practices. From 1996 to 2002, EQIP was prohibited by law from subsidizing large-scale, regulated industrial livestock confinement operations, and payments were capped at $10,000 per farm per year. In fiscal year 2015, EQIP funded more than $100 million for management of large concentrated animal feeding operations, accounting for 12 percent of all assistance.

Regional Conservation Partnerships Program (RCPP—2016). The USDA uses this program to designate special projects and enter into stewardship agreements with nonfederal entities, including state and local agencies and nongovernmental organizations, to provide enhanced technical and financial assistance through the integrated application of all the Farm Bill conservation programs. The partnerships help organize landowners in particular watersheds or defined constituencies and energize them through special incentives to create flexible and efficient solutions to complex resource conservation challenges.

Bill conservation programs. In the following decades, a new ethic of soil protection gave rise to sensible practices, such as cover crops that protect soil between harvests, field rotations that discourage pest and weed buildup, contour strips that prevent erosion on hilly lands, and windbreaks or hedgerows that guard against damaging weather. Federal subsidies to implement these new practices, however, came with strings attached. Farmers who got the money had to idle a portion of their land to avoid price-crushing overproduction of crops. During the 1970s "Get Big or Get Out" era, however, Farm Bill conservation programs took a U-turn. Farmers were encouraged to plant fencerow to fencerow, eliminating former habitat linkages and any wild areas that might get in the way of industrial farm equipment. Drainage tiles and open ditches, used to remove water and make low-lying areas plantable, became standard management practices of the USDA's conservation and farm extension outreach. Every year from the mid-1950s to the mid-1970s, more than 500,000 acres of wetlands were lost due to agriculture.[10]

Conservation took a more positive turn during the early 1980s. Concern among biologists about declining North American waterfowl populations, whose breeding grounds fell within farmed areas of the northern prairie states (or the Prairie Pothole Region), generated a new wave of reforms. Three provisions in the 1985 Farm Bill charted a new course for wildlife management on private lands.

The Conservation Reserve Program (CRP) paid yearly rental fees to farmers to idle up to 40 million total acres of critical waterfowl breeding habitat and highly erodible cropland.[11] Two "disincentive" policies—Swampbuster and Sodbuster—revoked subsidy payments to any farmers who drained wetlands or converted prairies into cropland. Congress strengthened stewardship incentives with the Wetlands Reserve Program (WRP) in the 1990 Farm Bill. This program contracted with landowners to restore and protect formerly converted wetlands through permanent easements.

Idling and restoring these millions of acres kept the landscape from turning into an ecological sacrifice zone for the production of feed, food, fiber, and fuel. Although far from perfect, the CRP and the WRP placed nearly 10 percent of all croplands and more than 2 million acres of wetlands under some form of protection. Among the quantifiable outcomes:

- Annual soil erosion on croplands fell from 3.1 billion tons per year in the pre-CRP era to 1.7 billion tons in 2007 (figure 38).[12]
- More than 26 million ducks were estimated to have hatched between 1992 and 2003 as a direct result of CRP enrollments.[13]

- Nearly 70,000 acres of wetlands were restored each year between 1997 and 2003.[14]

Unfortunately, those and other stewardship gains are in clear retreat now. Commodity crop prices are expected to stay roughly flat in coming years.[15] However, the expansion of the biofuels industry and generous Farm Bill safety net programs, such as crop insurance, disaster assistance, and marketing loans, are drawing idled acreage back into production. Overall, public discourse about the future of agriculture is often focused on growing more food for an ever-increasing human population rather than promoting farming practices that respect basic ecological limits.

CRP acreage actually declined by 30 percent during the 2008 Farm Bill, a decline that constituted a 10 percent loss in conservation lands despite a 10 percent increase in CRP rental payments.[16] After record flooding and droughts, farmers wanted out of their CRP contracts (without penalty) so that they could put the protected acreage into crop production. The mounting loss of soils and productive farmland to drought, flooding, and wildfire should signal that more, not fewer, conservation programs are needed to make the landscape more resilient to weather extremes, but that message hasn't gotten through. As shown in figure 39, enrollment in the CRP is lower than it has been in a long time mainly due to a surge in the number of expiring contracts and strong demand for feed and fuel crops. Most significantly, the acreage cap was cut by 25 percent in the 2014 Farm Bill, reducing coverage further. The WRP was also cut by the 2014 Farm Bill and put under the jurisdiction of ACEP to maintain the

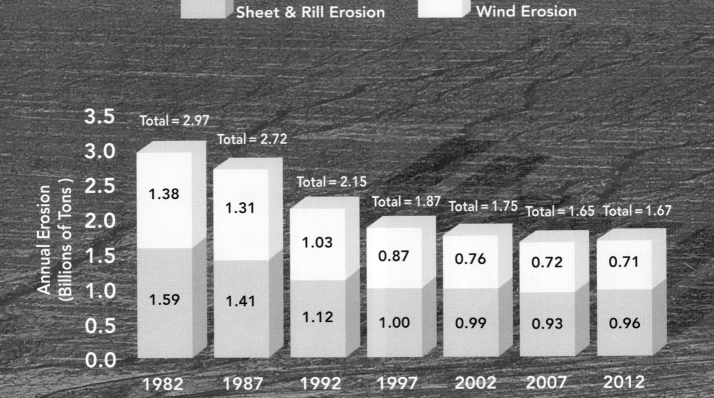

Figure 38

Erosion on Cropland

Conservation programs have reduced but not eliminated erosion on farmland

Sheet & Rill Erosion   Wind Erosion

Annual Erosion (Billions of Tons)

Year	Wind	Sheet & Rill	Total
1982	1.38	1.59	Total = 2.97
1987	1.31	1.41	Total = 2.72
1992	1.03	1.12	Total = 2.15
1997	0.87	1.00	Total = 1.87
2002	0.76	0.99	Total = 1.75
2007	0.72	0.93	Total = 1.65
2012	0.71	0.96	Total = 1.67

Source: US Department of Agriculture. Natural Resources Conservation Service. "Summary Report: 2012 National Resources Inventory." August 2015.

Figure 39

What Will Become of CRP Contracts?
Millions of conservation acres may go under the plow 2016–2030

The Conservation Reserve Program is at a critical junction with over 24 million acres scheduled to expire between 2016 and 2030. The USDA has undertaken an initiative to re-enroll and extend some of these contracts on a short-term basis. But it remains unclear whether millions of CRP acres will remain idled and protected in the coming years.

Number of acres due to expire (Thousands)

Source: Farm Service Agency. "Conservation Reserve Program Statistics." Updated 2016. US Department of Agriculture.

existing conservation contracts with landowners. The decline of both these conservation and stewardship programs could bode poorly for many species.

CROP INSURANCE AND CONSERVATION COMPLIANCE

Crop insurance has become the largest and most popular form of federal farm support. Unlike traditional subsidies, however, there are no conservation compliance requirements for crop insurance and risk management programs. And the numbers of recipients of disaster-related insurance claims is on the rise.

Meanwhile, many other nonprofit organizations, including the Isaac Walton Foundation, Environmental Working Group, Center for a Livable Future, Sustainable Agriculture Coalition, and Wild Farm Alliance, are calling for all federal risk management programs to be linked to conservation compliance. In other words, those who receive taxpayer support for crop insurance would agree not to drain wetlands, plow highly erodible lands, or plant crops with a low chance of successful harvest. The 1996 Farm Bill had removed compliance requirements from insurance subsidies, but the 2014 Farm Bill reestablished them. Specifically, farmers may not convert or harm a wetland or produce agricultural commodities on highly erodible land without a conservation plan. How well these obligations are enforced or actually promote conservation remains to be seen.

GETTING CONSERVATION PROGRAMS ON TRACK

Beginning in 1985 and continuing with each successive Farm Bill, legislators pushed more and more money at landowners to achieve conservation goals, but other shortcomings undercut progress. Budgets for on-the-ground technical assistance have not kept pace with conservation funds. In the words of one former top official, "NRCS staff have been turned into money obligators, pushing money out the door, frequently to the largest landowners, so that allocations aren't lost by the end of the fiscal year, without always being able to do the conservation planning they have been trained to do."

More recently, the dearth of qualified USDA NRCS field biologists has led to an increasing number of partnerships with conservation organizations. Groups such as Pheasants Forever, Ducks Unlimited, Trout Unlimited, and the California Waterfowl Association—typically hunting, fishing, and wildlife associations—are working with USDA NRCS offices to help determine the best uses of valuable Farm Bill conservation dollars. Although it is important to have their input, this process requires a new level of communication and integration to address the competing viewpoints.

Who receives the money is a second critical problem. Paradoxically, some of the country's worst stewards have been rewarded with the most money under the premise that landowners with egregious problems deliver the highest benefit per dollar spent. Good stewards, for the most part, have been left out of this process. In the most unfortunate cases, opportunistic landowners plow up and erode intact prairie remnants, or remove functional terraces and shelterbelts that protected fields and slopes, to apply for set-aside payments. In the case of the defunct WRP—arguably the Farm Bill's most successful conservation effort to date—only wetlands previously impacted by agricultural development were eligible for funding; the money couldn't be used to save pristine ecosystems. EQIP has doled out more than $100 million per year since 2002 to help concentrated animal feeding operations comply with the Clean Water Act, even though EQIP was originally established to target small producers. Meanwhile, conservation programs generally have far more applicants than available funds.

The Senate and House Appropriations Committees also deserve a heaping share of criticism. Their budgets are delivered months late and double-digit percentage points short of the cash promised. Even as the popularity of conservation programs among farmers has soared, Congressional appropriations committees have slashed allocations during annual budget negotiations and cyclical reconciliation battles.

Conservation efforts have also suffered from years of poor regional planning. Efforts become hit-or-miss without strategic watershed-wide, habitat-specific, or larger regional and statewide plans. Conservation biologist Gray has criticized such approaches as "random acts of environmental kindness."[17] As environmental threats become more dire and conservation dollars more scarce, strategies are evolving. The USDA's scattershot funding is slowly being replaced by goal-oriented conservation plans to restore habitat across agricultural regions rather than just at the individual farm or ranch level. Efforts such as the Sage Grouse Initiative, the Mississippi River Basin Healthy Watersheds Initiative, and the Bay Delta Initiative demonstrate a shift toward investments in landscape-scale conservation.

Yet nothing—nothing—continues to be more counterproductive than the complete disconnect between commodity crop subsidies and conservation programs. On the one hand, subsidies encourage farmers to maximize acreage, insurance programs eliminate economic risks, and disaster bailouts encourage plowing of even marginally productive and erodable lands. Meanwhile, the USDA directs about 6 percent of its overall spending toward conservation, much of that to right past wrongs and to clean up problems stemming from overfarming. Consider, for example, that more than 1.3 million acres of grassland from expired CRP enrollment were converted to corn and soy crops between 2007 and 2011,[18] over a period when the CRP consistently included more than 30 million acres.[19, 20] Grassland conversion has only accelerated during the last two Farm Bills as hay and pasture acreage was transformed into commodity monocultures. Such a dichotomy makes Farm Bill conservation programs seem more like a distraction than a coordinated national stewardship strategy (figure 40).

In Jonathan Foley's publication "The Other Inconvenient Truth: The Crisis in Global Land Use," the former director of University of Minnesota's Institute on the Environment said the following:

> We are demanding more and more from our global agricultural systems, pushing them to their very limits. Continued population growth (adding more than 70 million people to the world every year), changing dietary preferences (including more meat and dairy consumption), rising energy prices, and increasing needs for bioenergy sources are putting tremendous pressure on the world's resources. And, if we want any hope of keeping up with these demands, we'll need to double, perhaps triple, the agricultural production of the planet in the next 30 to 40 years.

Figure 40

The Conservation Challenge

Ongoing Concerns	Critical Programs and Ideas
Conservation efforts are too isolated to have far-reaching effects.	Initiatives should be undertaken at the landscape scale and augmented with more on-the-ground technical staff.
Conservation programs continue to be flat-funded or ChIMPed.	Conservation budgets should not be cut disproportionately compared to other Farm Bill titles.
Conservation Reserve Program contracts expire and millions of acres may become intensively cropped for biofuel grains.	CRP contracts protect erodible land, provide wildlife habitat, and decrease overproduction; energy crops should be produced from diverse perennial crops under sound conservation guidelines.
The Conservation Stewardship Program remains slow to roll out across the country.	Conservation Stewardship Program has the potential to transform the farm support system and at the same time achieve far-reaching conservation and trade goals.

Meeting these huge new agricultural demands will be one of the greatest challenges of the 21st century. At present, it is completely unclear how (and if) we can do it.[21]

REWARDING STEWARDSHIP RATHER THAN YIELD

One initiative has shown that farm subsidies and conservation do not have to be at odds. Backed by Iowa Senator Tom Harkin and referred to inside the Beltway as "the Harkin Program," it was pilot-tested in 2002 and adopted as the Conservation Stewardship Program (CSP) in the 2008 Farm Bill. Rather than offering subsidies to maximize commodity output or take land out of production, the CSP rewards landowners for sound stewardship, including soil protection, clean water, energy efficiency, and pesticide reduction. It is crafted to support a whole new era of agriculture, allowing farmers to transition away from commodity crop production, increasing the equity of subsidy payments, and conforming to World Trade Organization rules of acceptable agricultural supports. Today, almost 60 million acres of land are enrolled in the program, which account for almost 7 percent of our national farm and ranch land.[22]

Designed as a full entitlement program, the Conservation Stewardship Program is available to all landowners who meet a set of environmental standards.

Designed as a full entitlement program, the CSP is available to all landowners who meet a set of environmental standards. Successful applicants must demonstrate that they are preventing manure or other fertilizer from running into streams and that they are conserving soil and minimizing pesticide use, among other requirements. Extra points—and higher payments—are available for those who provide habitat for wildlife or protect streams and groundwater, including reducing fertilizer or pesticide use, converting cropland into permanent pasture, or installing farm-scale windmills or solar photovoltaic arrays to supply the farm with energy.

Advocates of healthy agriculture agree, hands down, that the CSP is the most inventive idea to grace a Farm Bill in decades. Rather than encouraging damaging high-output commodity agriculture with one title and funding remedial conservation with another, this program embodies a holistic approach for the first time since the New Deal. Organic farmers—who represent the fastest-growing segment of the food sector and have been long ignored by Farm Bill spending—finally have an advantage in program eligibility. The CSP also holds the promise of serving as a safety net for farmers interested in transitioning from commodity row crops toward perennial grass pastures for livestock, an urgent reform required of the food and farming system.

The National Sustainable Agriculture Coalition reports that the USDA has encouraged increased participation among beginning and disadvantaged farmers through the program since 2016 and also set a minimum payment to encourage smaller farms to enroll and engage in conservation.[23] Despite these directives, the total acreage covered by the CSP decreased under the 2014 Farm Bill. The number of new acres to be enrolled each year fell from 12.8 million acres to 10 million acres, threatening the potential future impact of the program. And its fate in upcoming Farm Bills is uncertain.

HEALTHY LANDS, HEALTHY HABITATS, HEALTHY ECONOMIES

From a taxpayer perspective, it's hard to argue against the benefits of efforts to protect natural habitat and native wildlife species. The things humans depend on for survival—food production, a stable climate, clean air and water, and vibrant biodiversity—are directly a function of healthy ecosystems. Recent scientific reviews show that biodiversity is particularly critical; it is the wide variety of species in an area that gives an ecosystem the resilience to adapt to ever-changing conditions.[24] In fact, signs show that the more species that live in the places where we live and farm, the more successful our agricultural operations become.

Consider, for example, that one out of every three mouthfuls of the foods and beverages we consume depends on pollination.[25] Farmers grow more than one hundred crop plants—ranging from apples and cherries to squashes and blueberries—that rely on pollinators, such as bees, butterflies, moths, hummingbirds, and bats. According to researchers at Cornell University, insect-pollinated crops contributed an estimated $29 billion to farm income, both directly through products such as berries and almonds and indirectly through products such as alfalfa and onions, in 2009.[26]

Due to a number of environmental factors, the number of European honeybees, the world's most important agricultural pollinator, has declined by more than 25 percent each winter since 2006, reflecting an ongoing downward trend.[27] Likewise, North America's thousands of native pollinators have suffered from the fragmentation of habitats and the extensive use of pesticides. A growing body of evidence supports the idea of restoring habitats in and around farmlands to allow native pollinator populations to rebound, if only as an insurance policy against predicted catastrophic losses of honeybees. Native habitats in and around farms can support dozens of resident pollinating species (as well as other beneficial insects) that eagerly go to work in farm fields and orchards.

Bats, too, provide invaluable services to farmers, but are under threat. A colony of just 150 big brown bats, for example, can eat more than one million insect pests in a year.[28] Today, though, bats are dying en masse from a mysterious fungus that causes a disease known as white-nose syndrome. These losses are compounded by the proliferation of windmills across the Midwest. With windmill blades towering above tree lines, bats are frequently struck and killed or have their lungs crushed by sudden pressure changes. Although bat mortalities due to wind energy are not officially tracked nationwide, estimates from 2012 ranged from 600,000 to 888,000 bat deaths, and this number is increasing annually.[29] Wildlife researchers estimated the economic impact of bat loss to be at least $3.7 billion per year (based on the cost of pest control that farmers would not need to spend with healthy bat populations), but could reach $53 billion.[30] Just as honeybee colony collapse has become a research priority in recent years, the USDA should also pay careful attention to this impending crisis.

One might also think that clean water would be a Farm Bill priority because agriculture is responsible for 70 percent of US water contamination, primarily through nutrient leaching and animal waste.[31] A report from the USDA showed that farmers can reduce nitrogen leaching at lower costs than sewage plants can remove it from water.[32] A study in the Pacific Northwest showed that every dollar invested in riparian vegetation (which helps filter water and recharge groundwater) could save $7.50 to $200 in municipal water treatment.[33]

Clearly, a nationwide campaign to improve habitats throughout all the nation's waterways could have positive impacts on public health, wildlife, and regional economies. Farm Bill dollars are already at work to revegetate thousands of miles of farmland waterways throughout Pennsylvania's and Maryland's tributaries to the Chesapeake Bay. Another important regional focus is the Upper Mississippi River watershed, where fertilizer runoff is linked to the dead zone in the Gulf of Mexico, more than 1,000 miles away.

The most fundamental reason to bolster and refine conservation spending is simple: species, once lost, are gone forever, and once they're gone, the fibers of the continent's distinct biological fabric begin to unravel. The health of the land and people will always be deeply interconnected. There can be no agriculture on completely degraded habitats. And the loss of one element in an ecosystem, no matter how large or small, is often a precursor to a cascading effect of further landscape degradation.

Converting Farm to Wetlands

Ned Gerber, Director of Chesapeake Wildlife Heritage, and Pickering Creek Audubon Center Director Mark Scallion began planning and implementing the construction of Pickering's wetlands in 2002.

Happily for birds and plants and other wildlife, this first wetland of 24 acres along the Center's entry drive was such a success that, over the next five years, 50 more acres were transformed into vibrant wetlands. Now, every spring and autumn, the resulting pools and adjacent seed-rich meadows have become a haven for migrating birds, sustaining them on their journeys.

"The place is a birder's delight," commented David Bent, a member of the Talbot County Bird Club who performs bird-counts almost every week at Pickering and who joined the morning's expedition. The newest wetland is shallower than the others and, Bent explains, will attract shorebirds such as sandpipers and yellowlegs that benefit from being able to wade along the shore and snatch their meal along the water's edge.

As we stood atop the Center's existing 10-foot-tall viewing platform (a virtual skyscraper within the flat characteristic landscape of Maryland's Eastern Shore), we saw avenues of clay—pushed into berms that will surround the new wetland. In other places stood piles of topsoil, scraped from the earth before the deeper digging began. The topsoil will cover the berms, which then will be planted with native grasses.

Mark and Ned see the completed project in their minds' eyes: boardwalks around the wetland to cover muddy areas, spaces here and there between trees for visitors to peek through, a new viewing station with equipment for Pickering's educators to use with visiting classes.

Photo by Susanna Scallion

Indeed this will be a haven for students and wildlife. Students from Caroline County and Wicomico County will visit the new wetland this fall to learn about how wetlands affect wildlife and water quality, with their trip culminating with the installation of wildlife friendly shrubs in the newest wetland that will provide food and cover for birds, insects, reptiles, amphibians, and mammals. In the spring both middle and high school students from Talbot County will conduct their hands-on investigations of the wetlands.

Of course, early concerns about the feasibility of creating wetlands had justification. Not all lands can be converted. Most of the historic wetlands on Maryland's Eastern Shore have been drained to make them viable agricultural fields. Soil maps provide a guide to the part of a farm containing so-called hydric soils, indicative of historic wetland sites. Pickering, like many Eastern Shore Maryland farms, has extensive hydric soils that were ditched and drained for farming long ago. Heavy machinery was brought in to help restore the field's original hydrology. To prepare for the present digging, Ned and his team from Chesapeake Wildlife Heritage studied the soil composition of the area of the new site and created a map from which to work.

Ned is adamant about the importance of wetland preservation: "Without it, there would be no wildlife left on the Eastern Shore, on its lands and in its waters." Teresa Kampmeyer of the United States Department of Agriculture's Natural Resource Conservation Service was quoted in *Winging It*: "Wetlands help to improve water quality, reduce erosion, and aid in flood prevention while providing a wildlife habitat for wetland and upland bird species. They store water after it rains, allowing water to percolate slowly in the ground, evaporate, or be absorbed by the roots of wetland plants. This temporary storage reduces the peak water flows after a storm event."

Pickering Creek is unique in offering the general public an opportunity to observe wetlands in action. Landowners too can take advantage of the same programs that helped build Pickering's wetlands, the USDA's Conservation Reserve Enhancement Program (CREP) and Conservation Reserve Program (CRP), which offer a sum (per acre) to replace marginal farmland with conservation practices that improve water quality and provide wildlife habitat.

The project is supported through the USDA CREP program and a grant from the Chesapeake Bay Trust.

Source: "Converting Farmland to Wetlands," Pickering Creek Audubon Center, 2014.

21. National Security

ALTHOUGH "AGRICULTURE" AND THE "WAR ON TERROR" rarely appear in the same sentence, Americans have long recognized the critical role that agriculture plays in keeping the nation safe. Until the Organic Act of 1862 established the US Department of Agriculture (USDA), the Department of State handled agriculture policy. Today, food and farm policies are on the front lines of national security debates in issues as varied as military preparedness, the vulnerability of food production systems, and soldiers' relationships with rural citizens in foreign war zones.

During World War II, malnourishment plagued the military, contributing to the rejection of 40 percent of draftees due to poor health.[1] Today, the opposite problem limits our draftees: obesity has become the top medical basis for refusing young Americans for military service.[2]

In both cases, the nation has looked to school lunches as at least a partial solution. Right after World War II, Congress passed the National School Lunch Act of 1946. In creating this federally subsidized school meal program, Congress declared it "a measure of national security, to safeguard the health and well-being of the Nation's children." More than half a century later, in 2010, a group of more than one hundred retired generals and admirals issued a letter to Congress, under the banner "Mission Readiness," urging bigger budgets to improve children's access to healthy foods like fruits and vegetables.[3]

The Child Nutrition Act mandates the spending of more than $12 billion per year to provide lunches for more than 30 million American children in public schools and serves as a companion to the Farm Bill's nutrition programs. It was reauthorized as the Healthy, Hunger-

Free Kids Act of 2010, with only a modest budget increase, and is now overdue for reauthorization. Many nutrition experts argue that this program came about because farmers needed to find an outlet for excess commodity crops. Unfortunately, that has meant that children are often receiving low-quality food. Today, all schools are entitled to receive free commodities from the federal government to supplement the ingredients they purchase.

In their report titled "Too Fat to Fight: Retired Military Leaders Want Junk Food Out of America's Schools," the retired generals and admirals stated that between 1995 and 2008, 140,000 candidates nationwide failed their physical exams due to weight problems. At the time, more than one in every four Americans age seventeen to twenty-four was too overweight to enlist.[4] Colonel Gaston Bathalon, an army nutrition expert, said that the problem "is quickly becoming a national security issue for us. The pool of recruits is becoming smaller" (figure 41).[5] Active troops are also struggling with their diets. More than five thousand men and women were relieved of service in 2012 alone because they couldn't control their weight.[6]

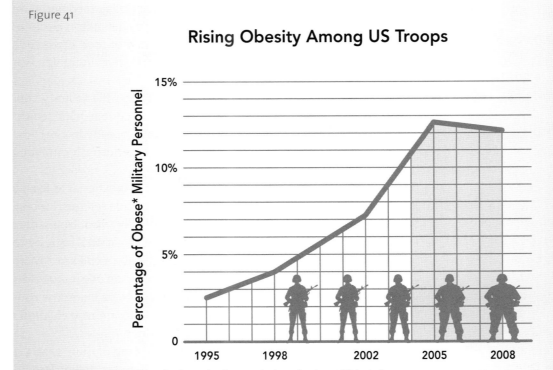

Figure 41

Rising Obesity Among US Troops

*Obesity is here defined as having a body mass index of at least 30 kg/m².

Source: Carolyn Reyes-Guzman, Robert M. Bray, Valerie L. Forman-Hoffman, and Jason Williams. "Overweight and Obesity Trends Among Active Duty Military Personnel: A 13-Year Perspective." *American Journal of Preventive Medicine* 48, no. 2 (2015): 145–153.

Women and men in the military depend on the limited food available to them during training and service. Military installations frequently have low-cost, fast foods for purchase, and their dining facilities offer foods that lack nutrition but are energy-dense. These meals may meet the high caloric needs of personnel, but they are often excessive and promote weight gain during service.[7] Although the Pentagon has updated initiatives related to fitness, improving diets is still critical to improving health. By promoting the production of healthier foods, the Farm Bill could do much more to encourage good nutrition among service members and their families.

AGROTERRORISM

Threats to agricultural production are also an issue of national security. The concept of agroterrorism—attacks against agricultural targets—received national attention in December 2004 when the Secretary of Health and Human Services, Tommy Thompson, delivered this bombshell in his speech announcing his resignation from President George W. Bush's first-term cabinet: "For the life of me, I cannot understand why the terrorists have not attacked our food supply, because it is so easy to do."[8]

Indeed, many experts are pointing to vulnerabilities in highly concentrated as well as hard-to-defend farming systems—whether animal feeding operations, thousand-acre monoculture fields, or mega-processing facilities. One microbe can contaminate millions of eggs in a confined feeding operation where 250,000 hens are crammed six to a battery cage. One strain of wheat rust can devastate 5,000 acres of a genetically identical grain crop when the airborne fungus sucks the life out of plant stems and rapidly spreads.

In 2004, the Rand National Defense Research Institute assessed the susceptibility of the modern food chain to biological terrorism in a report titled "Hitting America's Soft Underbelly." Among many concerns, it described problems associated with contagious diseases spreading in dairies crowded with ten thousand animals. The danger lies in the frequent commingling of herds, as well as the tremendous speeds at which animals are processed and foods are distributed throughout the population. It warned that "the rapid transfer of livestock in this manner increases the risk that pathogenic agents will spread well beyond the locus of a specific outbreak before health officials become aware that a problem exists."[9] As superbugs become more resistant to our available antibiotics, this risk only grows.

The Congressional Research Service prepared a separate report in 2004 titled "Agroterrorism: Threats and Preparedness" that further outlined risks to the nation's economy, health, and food security from attacks on agriculture. Animals and plants represent hard-to-secure secondary targets with a critical shock factor. Contamination is highly possible, the authors suggested, in concentrated animal operations, shipments of food grains, and food ingredients that are routinely mixed together during processing. It specifically stated that diseases could infect livestock in confinement operations more quickly than those in pastures.[10] The Federal Bureau of Investigation warned in 2012 that foot and mouth disease poses "the most serious danger for latent, ongoing effects and general socioeconomic and political disruption."[11] It is highly contagious and if introduced by terrorists, it could devastate our livestock and food supply. All these findings support the idea that the Farm Bill should preference pasture-based agriculture over concentrated animal feeding operation management.

Other perils are economic. Because agricultural exports contribute significantly to the US economy, national security could be affected if foreign consumer confidence in the safety of American foods is shaken. A weakened economy could then lead to civil unrest. Those are but two of dozens of reports addressing the connections between food safety and national security.

Concentration of production and ownership also presents national defense concerns. First, a small number of operations produce, distribute, and process the nation's food. Modern feeding operations that are considered large have at least 1,000 beef cattle, 82,000 laying hens, 10,000 hogs, and 125,000 broiler chickens.[12] The packing plants that process those animals have become increasingly consolidated, with the slaughter lines running at alarming speeds; many slaughter up to 400 cattle per hour.[13]

Agriculture has also become geographically specialized. The top three hog-producing states (Iowa, North Carolina, and Minnesota) produce about 58 percent of US hogs.[14] The top three chicken-producing states (Georgia, Arkansas, and Alabama) produce 39 percent of US chickens.[15] More than half of the leafy greens in the United States are grown in California's Salinas Valley and are packaged in warehouses that many compare to massive salad bowls.[16] In heavily concentrated production systems, disease can spread quickly and possibly go unnoticed until entire herds or fields are contaminated. Unpredictable weather events such as floods, drought, heat, and extreme cold also present major disruptions in the food supply.

Despite mounting evidence about the dangers of an overly centralized and industrialized food system, most reactions follow predictable lines. None address the root problems of scale, lack of diversity, unhygienic production conditions in animal factories, geographic concentration of food production, or heavy dependence on fossil fuels. Instead, the government focuses on increasing monitoring capabilities to detect outbreaks before they spread out of control. For example, after an avian flu outbreak on poultry farms in the Southeast in 2017, the USDA's Animal and Plant Health Inspection Service launched a thorough investigation into the epidemiology and biosecurity conditions that created the problem and continued to monitor the farms after the fact. But it failed to acknowledge that better living conditions could have prevented the outbreak in the first place.[17]

One exception is the Know Your Farmer, Know Your Food (KYF2) initiative, instated by the 2008 Farm Bill, which supported local food production from all departments of the USDA. KYF2 focused on increasing regional infrastructure (see chapter 23 for full description). Since the program began in 2009, the USDA has invested $1 billion in regional food projects and supported a doubling of the nation's farmers markets.[18] While USDA Secretary Tom Vilsack intended for the program to become institutionalized in the USDA, it ended after the 2008 bill expired.[19] Other programs allowed the USDA to award $40 million in grants and $50 million in loans to support local food systems, however, through programs such as the Local Food Promotion Program and the Farmers Market Promotion Program.[20]

RETURN TO THE VICTORY GARDEN?

Today's grocery stores typically turn over their entire inventory 16.4 times per year.[21] If national food distribution networks were disrupted, supermarkets would have less than one month's worth of stock on hand to sustain local residents. In such a scenario, regional and local farms would have to become primary food sources. Taking food security into account, Farm Bill programs might also encourage citizens to supply part of their own food with home gardens.

Prior to the trend of agricultural industrialization after World War II, local food production was regarded as an invaluable part of daily life on the home front. Following First Lady Eleanor Roosevelt's example of installing a garden on White House grounds, "victory gardens" became popular installations in backyards, vacant lots, public parks, and apartment rooftops. Citizens were motivated to take pressure off the public food supply by growing produce of their own. Extension agents provided gardeners with seed, fertilizer, and tools.[22] By 1943, the USDA had exceeded its target of supporting eighteen million victory gardens. At their peak popularity, home gardens supplied 40 percent of the nation's produce, generating roughly 125 pounds of food for every American.[23] Today, only about one-third of US households have home gardens, although the number grew by 17 percent from 2008 to 2013 as citizens responded to rising food prices and concerns about agrochemicals (figure 42).[24]

Future Farm Bills could improve food security by launching a modern-day victory garden program—or a home-garden extension service—with a goal of inspiring another 20 million new suburban and urban gardens by 2030. The growing popularity of home and urban gardening among the millennial generation indicates that this goal might be easily met.

THERAPEUTIC FARMING

Rural areas are home to just 14 percent of the country's population yet provide nearly one-half of all

Figure 42

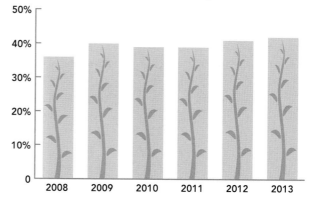

US Home Food Gardens
Household Participation

Data are based on a national sample of 42 million households.

Source: "Garden to Table: A 5-Year Look at Food Gardening in America." National Gardening Association. 2014.

military recruits—who return as veterans.[25,26] New programs are using farming as a tool for rehabilitation, re-entry into civilian life, and career changes.

The Arcadia Center for Sustainable Food and Agriculture in Virginia, just outside the nation's capital, supports veterans to begin careers in agriculture. Similar to the Beginning Farmer and Rancher Development Program, this project trains veterans to enter the field by helping them find land, market their products, and develop business skills.

Working with nature can be profoundly therapeutic for people with posttraumatic stress disorder, depression, or mental illness. Growing food and connecting with consumers provide farmers with a positive mission and sense of purpose. To that end, 2008 Farm Bill dollars from the Risk Management Agency were used to fund a series of veteran-to-farmer educational retreats around the country.

Source: "Sow the Seeds of Victory! Posters from the Food Administration during World War I," National Archives Identifier 512498.

The 2014 Farm Bill created a new status for veteran farmers to receive low-interest loans, apply for grants, and receive extra payments for conservation.[27]

Similarly, local foods are being used to rehabilitate veterans inside military hospital dining halls. Veterans Administration (VA) hospitals in Martins-burg, Virginia, and San Francisco, California, are purchasing fresh produce from local farmers to supply their cafeterias. By replacing frozen, canned, and dehydrated fruits and vegetables with local produce, these and other VA hospital cafeterias are attempting to maximize the healing qualities—superior vitamins and micronutrients—of fresh, particularly organic, foods. Many are beginning to host farmers markets at the hospital for patients and visitors, improving connections to local producers. They may also be contributing to a more diversified and resilient food system in their areas. The next logical step would be to encourage the purchase of local food from veteran farmers at these institutions.

FORWARD-LOOKING DEFENSE

The Farm Bill and the USDA can help safeguard national security with programs that improve military nutrition, decentralize livestock production, and expand regional food production and distribution. The Department of Defense could also play a powerful role by funding an upgrade in school nutrition programs to improve the health of future recruits. In fact, there is a recent precedent. Since 2002, the Department of Defense Fresh Fruit and Vegetable Program has been offering financial, administrative, and other assistance to public school cafeterias for farm-to-school programs that provide fruits and vegetables produced within the state.[28] It's time that food and agriculture systems are not only perceived as potential risks to national security. Healthy food production, access, and affordability must be acknowledged and fully funded as essential parts of forward-looking national security.

PART V

THE FUTURE OF FOOD POLICY

22. Ecosystem-Based Agriculture

RURAL AMERICA TODAY IS IN AN AGE OF MONOCULTURE. Farmers reap ever-growing harvests of annual crops by planting hybrid varieties, pumping them up with fossil fuel-based fertilizers, and managing them with pesticides and industrial machinery. A drive through monoculture farm country can appear eerily sterile, with feed corn, soybeans, wheat, or cotton as far as the eye can see, uninterrupted by so much as an acre of natural habitat. Annual crops farmed so intensively exact a steep toll: the elimination of biodiversity and the continual erosion and depletion of soil.

In response to grave concerns that the industrial food system will eventually collapse, a new vision for agriculture is emerging: the age of perennials. This idea rests on a transition to deep-rooted, diverse communities (i.e., polycultures) of long-lived perennial plants that cover and permanently protect the soil and do not need to be reseeded annually. Rather than being industrially imposed on the landscape, a perennial mixture would be designed to capture the ecosystems' processes of the wild that existed long before sodbusting, tilling, and swamp draining became standard management practices. Renewable resources like sunshine, groundwater, and organic nutrients would drive the production process.

According to the Land Institute in Salina, Kansas, the goals of perennial farming include:

- Extending the productive life of soils from the current tens or hundreds of years to thousands or tens of thousands of years;
- Developing resilience to extreme rainfall events, droughts, and insect and pest pressures;

- Reducing land runoff that creates coastal dead zones with disastrous effects on fisheries;
- Maintaining quality of surface water and groundwater;
- Building food security while addressing climate change, population growth, water scarcity, and biodiversity loss.[1]

STARTING WITH GRASS

We already have one common perennial agriculture system: hay and pasture–based grazing operations. Pastures can comprise a variety of perennials, such as timothy, orchard grass, clover, and alfalfa. Some farms and ranches are exclusively devoted to grass-fed livestock production, whereas others rotate pastures with row crops to restore the soil, prevent pest buildups, and diversify their crops. Increasingly, orchardists and vintners are turning to permanent ground cover and incorporating livestock grazing during certain times of the year. A broad range of experts sees an expansion of such farming systems as essential for regions like the Upper Mississippi River watershed, where decades of massive soil loss and leaching of nutrients from industrial corn and soybean operations have resulted in one of the world's largest dead zones in the Gulf of Mexico.

Since its diagnostic study began in 1998, Minnesota's Chippewa River Watershed Project has been researching this problem. Scientists have documented that perennial plants reduce soil sediments and agricultural nutrients in surrounding watersheds. If just 10 percent of critical lands in the Chippewa River watershed were converted to rotations of pastures and perennial crops and habitat, water quality would improve measurably throughout surrounding waterways.[2]

Critics frequently argue that shifting to such diversified agriculture is a luxury the world can no longer afford—that only chemical- and technology-intensive farming can provide the food necessary for a growing population. Peer-reviewed studies increasingly show the opposite, however. Sustainable agriculture systems are not just highly productive; they also have other benefits, such as a reduced carbon footprint, reduced toxic chemicals, soil loss prevention, habitat protection, and beauty.[3,4]

Modern organic, biodynamic, and rotational grazing practitioners have developed sophisticated and profitable farming systems using a growing base of knowledge about the interplay of ecology and farming. This marriage of specialties is referred to as *agroecology*. A defining principle of agroecology is designing food production around on-farm renewable energy exchanges rather than the extractive energy resources like petroleum-based fuels and agrochemicals so important in the age of monoculture. The production of dairy and beef cattle, swine, and poultry on small- and large-scale pasture operations has made great strides. Animals are being raised in appropriate numbers and are not solely dependent on distant sources of subsidized feeds. As in a healthy ecosystem, their wastes become soil nutrients rather than toxic by-products that contaminate watersheds. These innovations have been achieved with just a fraction of the research budget allocated to conventional agriculture.

THE NEXT STEP: PERENNIAL GRAINS

Scientists are now tackling a new frontier in agroecology: perennial grains. Perennials have many ecological advantages over annual crops. Because they live longer and develop deep roots over time, perennial plants have greater access to groundwater than do annual plants. In addition, those deep root systems make perennials less susceptible to wind and rain, protecting the soil from erosion. This trait is critical as agriculture has been expanded to steep hillsides and low-lying wetlands not suitable to annual crops.

Innovative research has been under way for decades at the Salina, Kansas–based Land Institute, Washington State University, and other institutions around the world to breed food crops with wild perennial relatives. The goal is to develop commercially viable perennial grains, oilseeds, and other crops that could form the foundation of enduring farming practices that don't compromise the soil, poison the environment, or degrade water quality. One can imagine, for example, a farm field dominated by perennial wheat or sunflowers that can remain productive for many years, without the need for annual tilling, reseeding, or applying heavy doses of chemicals.

The next leap forward in agroecology may not be that far off. According to the Land Institute's Global Inventory Project, research in Canada, Australia, China, and the United States suggests that perennialization of major grain crops like wheat, rice, sorghum, and sunflowers can be developed within the next several decades.[5] One of its most recent successes is Kernza wheat, which several prominent businesses on the West Coast (such as Patagonia Provisions) are already supporting. General Mills also announced plans to invest in the development of Kernza wheat. Its organic brand, Cascadian Farms, will soon be made with this grain.

The perennialization of animal agriculture and cropping systems, although critical, is not an end point. To be truly sustainable, farming practices must appropriately fit the land they occupy and cannot fall into the same land-abuse patterns that monoculture systems have. Just as in native grasslands or rainforests, future farming systems must be made up of combinations of perennials that function symbiotically and are highly productive and resilient to drought, floods, and pests. This approach requires an understanding of how agriculture can be adapted to the unique structure and functions of local ecosystems.

An ecosystem can remain healthy only if its species and habitats have not been picked apart by the excessive expansion and intensification of agriculture. Watersheds must remain functional without overdrafting of groundwater or discharging of nitrogen and other nutrients or poisoning by pesticides. Woodlands, shrublands, and other contiguous habitats must continue to flourish as agriculture is adapted to an area's natural ecology. American conservationist Aldo Leopold perhaps said it best and most succinctly: "A good farm is one where the wild flora and fauna have lost acreage without losing existence."[6]

TOWARD A FIFTY-YEAR FARM BILL

To spark this system-wide shift in food production, we need to reimagine the landscape itself: corn and soybean fields steadily replaced by permanent ground cover, much of it used for the grazing of animals. In the long run, newly developed perennial crops will increasingly replace annual grains and oilseeds. These complex perennial food production systems will be less dependent on fossil fuels, more resilient to weather, and better able to capture soil carbon from the atmosphere and provide wildlife habitat.

Just as it did in the days of the Dust Bowl, when the United States faced devastating soil losses, the Farm Bill presents the country's primary tool for ushering in a new generation of agricultural policy and land stewardship. It is, after all, the main economic tool we have to account for the noneconomic factors that the market alone does not protect: stewardship and health. Because it is renewed every five to seven years, the Farm Bill also presents a path that can be assessed and updated at regular intervals. And with its countrywide reach and mission to safeguard the food system, the US Department of Agriculture (USDA) is poised to take on such a forward-thinking effort as the perennialization of food production.

A coalition of organizations and sustainable farming advocates, led by the Land Institute's founder Wes Jackson, author Wendell Berry, and farmer-philosopher Fred Kirschenmann, has called for perennialization to become a focus of Farm Bill spending over the next fifty years (figure 43). USDA funding, drawn from budgets for crop subsidies, conservation, and research, could jump-start this urgently needed transition. The USDA, which has a network of research and extension services, a sizable budget, and interactions with tens of thousands of farmers and landowners, could take the lead, as it previously did with the industrialization of farming and more recently with its hefty investments in the ethanol industry. Just as cellulosic ethanol is now considered the next generation of sustainable bio-fuels, perennial food crops could certainly shape the USDA's research agenda for many decades to come.

Of course, this transition would require a major course correction in the Farm Bill itself. Its writers must confront the inevitable outcomes of continuing to mine the soil, deplete groundwater, and pollute waterways as if they are unlimited resources. Finally, they must acknowledge the Farm Bill's unique potential to support long-term solutions to many problems associated with food production. Jackson and the 50-Year Farm Bill coalition outlined the following goals to drive future food and farm policy:

- Maintain soil, soil fertility, and soil biodiversity;
- Reduce greenhouse gas emissions and dependence on fossil fuels;
- Conserve and detoxify water supplies;
- Reduce/minimize nitrogen runoff;
- Promote profitable and healthy farms and rural communities;
- Maintain high yields of healthful food.[7]

Transitioning from the age of monoculture to the age of perennials and ecosystem-based farming will be a long process. Acreage for pasture and forage crop rotations will increase. Annual feed grain crop acreage will decline, to be gradually replaced by land devoted to new perennial grains as they become commercially viable and widely available. The Land Institute's "A 50-Year Farm Bill" asserted that such a revolution in farming would be attainable if only we choose to realign priorities to achieve it: "These changes lie well within the capacities of American farmers working the world's best soils, and all can be achieved on current levels of federal

Figure 43

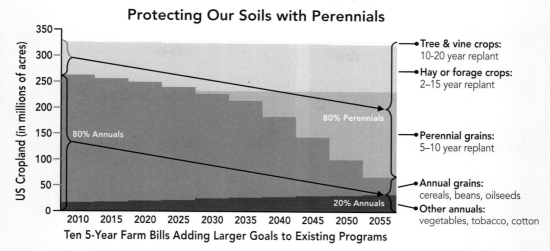

Farm Bill: 2060 Vision
Protecting Our Soils with Perennials

Tree & vine crops:
10-20 year replant

Hay or forage crops:
2–15 year replant

80% Perennials

Perennial grains:
5–10 year replant

80% Annuals

Annual grains:
cereals, beans, oilseeds

Other annuals:
vegetables, tobacco, cotton

20% Annuals

Ten 5-Year Farm Bills Adding Larger Goals to Existing Programs

Y-axis: US Cropland (in millions of acres); X-axis: 2010 2015 2020 2025 2030 2035 2040 2045 2050 2055

2010: Hay or grazing operations continue as they exist. Preparations for subsidy changes begin.

2015: Subsidies become incentive to substitute perennial grass in rotations for feed grain in meat, egg, and milk production.

2020: The first perennial wheat, Kernza™, is farmer-ready for limited acreage.

2030: Educate farmers and consumers about new perennial grain crops.

2045: New perennial grain varieties are ready for expanded geographical range. Perennial varieties for grazing and hay may also expand.

2055: High-value annual crops are mainly grown on the least erodible fields as short rotations between perennial crops.

Source: Land Institute, "A 50-Year Farm Bill," 2009.

funding. It is a question of realigning incentives so that the self-interests of the farmer coincide with the collective long-term interests of the nation."[8]

Our diets must eventually adapt to perennial agriculture also. Public health advocates already concur that we simply cannot continue eating and producing food the way we have been. Pasture-raised animals contain more nutrients that are favorable to human health than do grain-fed animals. These nutrients include omega-three fatty acids, conjugated linoleic acids, beta-carotene, and other vitamins.[9,10] Perennial grains and forages might also offer nutritional advantages.

Fifty years may not be enough time for a complete transformation of the food system, although many argue that the challenges are so urgent that we simply have no time to waste. A large-scale shift away from confined livestock systems to grass-based perennial pasture systems is a crucial starting point. The next revolution in agriculture—producing perennial food crops that function sustainably over time like grasslands or forest ecosystems—is also within reach. Federal policy makers would be wise to invest heavily in turning this research into reality on the ground.

A 50-Year Farm Bill

Wes Jackson and Wendell Berry

The extraordinary rainstorms last June caused catastrophic soil erosion in the grain lands of Iowa, where there were gullies 200 feet wide. But even worse damage is done over the long term under normal rainfall—by the little rills and sheets of erosion on incompletely covered or denuded cropland, and by various degradations resulting from industrial procedures and technologies alien to both agriculture and nature.

Soil that is used and abused in this way is as nonrenewable as (and far more valuable than) oil. Unlike oil, it has no technological substitute—and no powerful friends in the halls of government.

Agriculture has too often involved an insupportable abuse and waste of soil, ever since the first farmers took away the soil-saving cover and roots of perennial plants. Civilizations have destroyed themselves by destroying their farmland. This irremediable loss, never enough noticed, has been made worse by the huge monocultures and continuous soil-exposure of the agriculture we now practice.

To the problem of soil loss, the industrialization of agriculture has added pollution by toxic chemicals, now universally present in our farmlands and streams. Some of this toxicity is associated with the widely acclaimed method of minimum tillage. We should not poison our soils to save them.

Industrial agriculture has made our food supply entirely dependent on fossil fuels and, by substituting technological "solutions" for human work and care, has virtually destroyed the cultures of husbandry (imperfect as they may have been) once indigenous to family farms and farming neighborhoods.

Clearly, our present ways of agriculture are not sustainable, and so our food supply is not sustainable. We must restore ecological health to our agricultural landscapes, as well as economic and cultural stability to our rural communities.

For 50 or 60 years, we have let ourselves believe that as long as we have money we will have food. That is a mistake. If we continue our offenses against the land and the labor by which we are fed, the food supply will decline, and we will have a problem far more complex than the failure of our paper economy. The government will bring forth no food by providing hundreds of billions of dollars to the agribusiness corporations.

Any restorations will require, above all else, a substantial increase in the acreages of perennial plants. The most immediately practicable way of doing this is to go back to crop rotations that include hay, pasture and grazing animals.

But a more radical response is necessary if we are to keep eating and preserve our land at the same time. In fact, research in Canada, Australia, China and the United States over the last 30 years suggests that perennialization of the major grain crops like wheat, rice, sorghum and sunflowers can be developed in the foreseeable future. By increasing the use of mixtures of grain-bearing perennials, we can better protect the soil and substantially reduce greenhouse gases, fossil-fuel use and toxic pollution.

Carbon sequestration would increase, and the husbandry of water and soil nutrients would become much more efficient. And with an increase in the use of perennial plants and grazing animals would come more employment opportunities in agriculture—provided, of course, that farmers would be paid justly for their work and their goods.

Thoughtful farmers and consumers everywhere are already making many necessary changes in the production and marketing of food. But we also need a national agricultural policy that is based upon ecological principles. We need a 50-year farm bill that addresses forthrightly the problems of soil loss and degradation, toxic pollution, fossil-fuel dependency and the destruction of rural communities.

This is a political issue, certainly, but it far transcends the farm politics we are used to. It is an issue as close to every one of us as our own stomachs.

This op-ed originally appeared in the January 4, 2009, New York Times. *Wes Jackson is a plant geneticist and president emeritus of the Land Institute in Salina, Kansas. Wendell Berry is a farmer and writer in Kentucky.*

23. Local Food

Local food production
is a dynamic vehicle for
public health, job creation,
resource protection, and
food security, but Farm Bill
policies have been relatively
slow to catch on.

MORE AMERICANS CARE ABOUT THE SOURCE OF THEIR FOOD today than ever before. As part of a burgeoning local food movement, they are seeking out organically grown fruits and vegetables and pasture-raised meat, eggs, and dairy products. They want to leverage their food dollars to support their local economies, family farmers, and high standards of animal welfare, and they also want to consume the best-tasting foods available. They are turning farmers markets and community gardens into dynamic social hubs in urban areas and pushing municipalities to change laws to allow for more urban farming.

Local food production is a dynamic vehicle for public health, job creation, resource protection, and food security, but Farm Bill policies have been relatively slow to catch on to support it. Soon, though, it may be impossible for Washington policy makers to ignore a cultural phenomenon sweeping across cities throughout the country. Consider some of the trends in the rapidly evolving local food movement:

- The United States had more than 8,000 farmers markets in 2017, up from 2,746 in 1998 (figure 44).[1]

- In 2017, more than 42,000 schools had farm-to-school programs to purchase locally grown food snacks and lunches for students. In 2001, there were just six such programs.[2]

- Sales of local foods totaled more than $8.7 billion in 2015; almost 35 percent of those sales were direct to consumers.[3]

- Cities and rural areas around the country have developed more than 300 food hubs that serve as centers for storing, processing, and distributing foods grown in surrounding rural areas.[4]

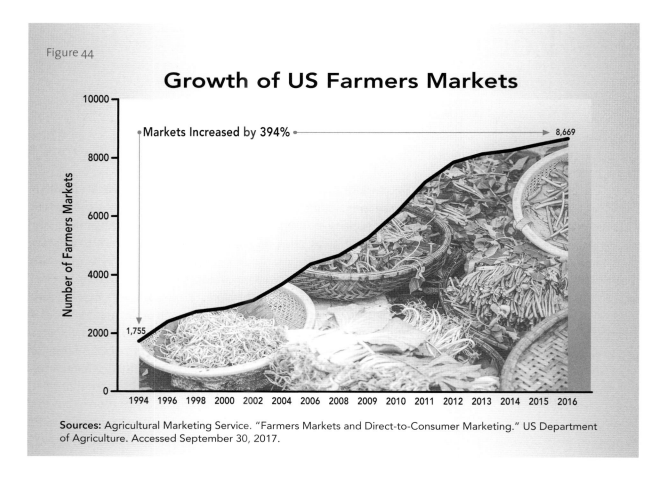

Figure 44

Growth of US Farmers Markets

Markets Increased by 394%

8,669

1,755

Number of Farmers Markets

1994 1996 1998 2000 2002 2004 2006 2008 2009 2010 2011 2012 2013 2014 2015 2016

Sources: Agricultural Marketing Service. "Farmers Markets and Direct-to-Consumer Marketing." US Department of Agriculture. Accessed September 30, 2017.

SHORTENING FOOD SUPPLY CHAINS

New business models have vastly increased the amount of local food consumed, particularly in urban areas. Community supported agriculture arrangements engage members who pay a monthly or annual fee to a farm in return for a farm share of seasonal produce and foods like eggs, grass-fed meats, and honey, usually supplied weekly. Data from the US Department of Agriculture (USDA) 2012 Census of Agriculture counted 12,617 farms that sold directly to consumers through such arrangements.[5] Farm-to-school programs are similarly changing schools' purchasing options to give preference to local farmers. That means more fresh fruits and vegetables rather than frozen and processed ingredients. Farmers markets have expanded customer bases for producers and offered opportunities for consumers to participate in a local food economy. Meanwhile, local producers in northern climates are using high-tunnel greenhouse systems to extend the growing season for local greens and other high-value crops.

Some Farm Bill grants and loans help shorten supply chains. Initiatives like the Farmers Market Promotion Program, Senior Farmers' Market Nutrition Program, and Value-Added Producer Grants have been around for at least several Farm Bill cycles, long enough to sizably increase the number of markets and the production necessary to supply them. But truly increasing local food will require significant investment in infrastructure: processing facilities where produce can be prepared, dried, and packaged; multispecies slaughter facilities where regional livestock can be processed; hubs where foods can be stored centrally before distribution; new retail outlets, especially in areas where fresh food is limited; and skilled workers and people who actually want to invest in and perform this work. USDA-funded programs such as Specialty Crop Block Grants and the Community Facilities Direct Loan and Grant Program are just beginning to address such needs. For example, one program works to put more fresh foods into inner-city convenience stores. Revolving and forgivable loans are another means by which policy makers can spur innovation and build infrastructure at the state and local levels.

The local food movement is challenging the Farm Bill's underlying conception of rural development. Is an urban farmers market that opens new business opportunities for producers who live outside the city technically "rural development"? What about a grant that helps a rural dairy set up a cheese-making facility in a county that is heavily urbanized? Current Farm Bill definitions related to rural development pose funding limitations for counties that have both dense urban populations and a balanced rural sector capable of diversified local food production. The very idea of rural development—long a goal of Farm Bill food program promoters—may become a pressure point for change as the clamor for increased local food production gets louder.

These efforts underlie a broader public discussion about the best way to feed a surging global population. The conventional agriculture industry has, for the most part, shunned (and sometimes aggressively attacked) the regional food movement as elitist and boutique. Its supporters argue that local agriculture is unable to meet the needs of a rapidly changing world. Local food advocates are pushing against that charge. They view diversified regional food production as a necessary shift away from a food system that is almost totally reliant on heavily centralized, large-scale producers and distributors. Rather than a threat, local food advocates see regional production as an essential alternative to complement our current industrial system.

Ramping up regional food production is important for the economy and public health. Jobs around the country depend on fruit and vegetable crops grown in just a few states—California and Florida, in particular. If severe weather in either of those states threatened supplies, the economic toll would be widespread. Similarly, the cost of shipping foods across the country could easily grow if petroleum were to become scarcer. Spreading production to more states could stabilize our supply and could well be necessary if Americans started eating according to the Dietary Guidelines for Americans. An additional 13 million acres of fruit and vegetable production would be required if people met these recommendations.[6]

With increasingly uncertain weather, unstable energy costs, contamination, and a host of other concerns, urban areas are looking to scale up local food production as a basic element of food security. Local governments, food councils, nongovernmental organizations, and others are working to boost local supplies of fruits and vegetables and to establish food outlets in neighborhoods where access is limited.

🐄 KNOW YOUR FARMER, KNOW YOUR FOOD

The public's growing interest in connecting with farmers has not been entirely lost on the USDA. Over the lifetime of the 2008 Farm Bill, Deputy Secretary of Agriculture Kathleen Merrigan launched the Know Your Farmer, Know Your Food (KYF2) initiative to put local agriculture on the USDA's agenda. KYF2 was a task force charged with breaking down traditional interagency silos to support local food production. Even though the program had no office, staff, or distinct budget, it immediately began to breathe new life into a bureaucracy gripped by the inertia of supporting commodity agriculture for decades. Specific goals of the KYF2 task force included:

- Stimulating community economic development;
- Fostering new opportunities for farmers and ranchers;
- Promoting locally and regionally produced foods;
- Cultivating healthy eating habits and educated, empowered consumers;
- Expanding access to affordable, fresh, and local food;

- Demonstrating the connection between food, agriculture, community, and the environment.

The team identified existing programs that could fund local food initiatives, such as Value-Added Producer Grants and the Business and Industry Guaranteed Loan Program. It increased the number of farmers markets that accept electronic Supplemental Nutrition Assistance Program (SNAP) benefits. It helped disadvantaged farmers and young people get involved in agriculture through USDA outreach and education programs. The group also identified areas that lacked nearby slaughter and processing facilities—a critical need in an era of concentrated meat-packing and processing operations.

The KYF2 initiative created a subcommittee focused on studying and promoting food hubs. These hubs are central locations where crops are aggregated, stored, processed, and distributed (figure 45). The business management structures for food hubs vary widely: some are private, some are nonprofit organizations, and some are extensions of food cooperatives. Food hubs service farmers on the one hand—many of whom may be too small to supply traditional wholesalers—and wholesale consumers on the other—such as restaurants and schools that are interested in sourcing local products. For small growers who do not own refrigerated trucks or warehouse spaces, food hubs can provide necessary infrastructure and marketing support. Likewise, for purchasers seeking local foods, a food hub can provide a steady supply of products that are otherwise hard to source.

There are now more than 300 food hubs operating across the United States. According to a 2015

How Local Food Hubs Support Farms, Businesses, and Communities

Food Aggregation
Local Food Hub purchases food from more than 40 local farmers, ensuring a fair price.

Food Distribution
Local Food Hub distributes food to schools, hospitals, institutions, markets and restaurants.

Farmer Services
Local Food Hub provides services to partner producers including accounting, sales, marketing and education.

Local Food Campaign
Using a savvy marketing campaign, Local Food Hub promotes the value of buying and eating locally.

Production Planning
Local Food Hub works with farmers and buyers to coordinate growing and match supply with demand.

Food Donations
Local Food Hub donates more than 5% of warehouse sales to local food banks and community groups.

Food Production
The farm produces more than six acres of organically grown food for distribution and donation.

Food Donations
25% of the food grown at the farm is donated to local food banks, hunger organizations and community groups.

Local Food Hub

Farmer Training
Local Food Hub hosts free workshops on organic and sustainable growing methods for participation farmers.

Community Engagement
Local Food Hub engages the community through volunteer programs, events, classes and creative partnerships.

The Local Food Hub is an organization in Charlottesville, Virginia that helps to connect the community with its local food resources in a multitude of ways.

Apprenticeships
An annual eight-month program enables young people to learn sustainable and organic growing methods.

Internships
An annual summer internship brings local high-school youth to the farm where they learn farm training and job skills.

Source: Barham, Jim. "Regional Food Hubs: Understanding the Scope and Scale of Food Hub Operations." April 19, 2011. USDA Agricultural Marketing Service.

survey by Michigan State University and the Wallace Center, food hubs employ an average of 17 people, work with an average of 115 farmers and producers, and generate an average of $3.3 million in revenue.[7] In addition, 49 percent accept SNAP benefits, helping make local, fresh foods more accessible to people with limited access and low income.[8] Local food advocates hope that the food hub model will continue to expand rapidly as a crucial boon to regional production.

The KYF2 initiative also spawned partnerships outside of the USDA. Nonprofit organizations across the nation, for example, are designing nutrition incentive programs to connect low-income families with small farmers through farmers markets. These programs help people receiving federal nutrition assistance in the form of SNAP or Women, Infants, and Children (WIC) vouchers attend farmers markets and use their assistance dollars to purchase healthy food—in many cases doubling their purchasing power when they buy fruits and vegetables. In California, Roots of Change (ROC) helped create the California Market Match Consortium (CMMC), which included 8 local nongovernmental organizations in 17 counties and benefited more than 840 individual small farmers selling specialty crops at 134 farmers markets, 70 of which offer incentives.[9] Over a two-year period, ROC and its regional partners raised nearly $250,000 in matching money, which was distributed in $5 and $10 contributions to SNAP and WIC recipients who bought fresh fruits, vegetables, and nuts at participating farmers markets.[10] This practice not only puts healthy food on people's tables; it also boosts local farmer income. The Ecology Center now oversees the CMMC, aiming to standardize operations across the state. Similar networks are managed by Market Umbrella in New Orleans, Fair Food Network in Michigan, and Wholesome Wave in several states on the East Coast. Together, these organizations are collecting data—such as weight loss and other health indicators—to share with Congress to create a permanent federal program that ushers in an effective approach to nutrition assistance across the nation. Partially resulting from the success of these programs, the 2014 Farm Bill included a $100 million Food Insecurity Nutrition Incentives grant program to encourage healthy purchases with SNAP benefits.

Although the umbrella initiative ended with the new administration in 2017, the many programs it promoted continue. The same representatives from the USDA meet every two weeks and are now called the Local Food Task Force. The compass that KYF2 helped develop on the USDA website still shows the USDA and other federal investments in local and regional food systems since 2009 (figure 46). Overall, the USDA spent more than $1 billion to increase the availability of organic food products as well as on more than 40,000 local and regional food business and infrastructure projects between 2009 and 2015.[11]

CITIES TAKING CHARGE

In 2010, Seattle took a unique approach to addressing the federal Farm Bill. Richard Conlin, president of the Seattle City Council, assembled a group that included healthcare practitioners, farmers, retailers, and other civic leaders such as Dennis Hayes, organizer of the first Earth Day. They drafted a set of food system principles, beginning with the idea that the Farm Bill should address concerns such as

Figure 46

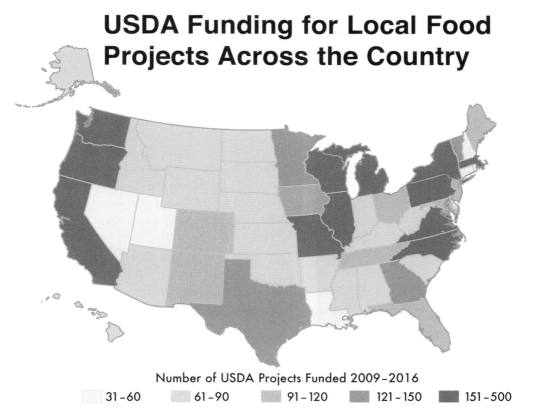

USDA Funding for Local Food Projects Across the Country

Number of USDA Projects Funded 2009–2016

31–60   61–90   91–120   121–150   151–500

Source: US Department of Agriculture. Agricultural Marketing Service. "Local Food Compass Map." Accessed September 30, 2017.

social justice and community development. The resulting Seattle Farm Bill Principles (figure 47) prioritize solutions to their circumstances in the Pacific Northwest: fighting an obesity crisis, increasing knowledge about healthy foods, building farm-to-school and school garden programs, and increasing availability of local foods. The exercise was intended as a learning experience and teaching tool rather than an extended campaign, but the idea caught

fire, and in May 2011, the City of Seattle officially ratified the principles.

By taking on the Farm Bill as a local priority, cities may soon challenge the USDA with a whole set of new priorities around urban agriculture.

Figure 47

Seattle Farm Bill Principles
Supporting Healthy Farms, Food, and People

GUIDANCE FOR THE 2012 FARM BILL

1 Health-Centered Food System

The driving principle of the Farm Bill must be the relationship of food and ecologically sound agriculture to public health. Food that promotes health includes fruits, vegetables, whole grains, nuts, seeds, legumes, dairy, and lean protein. Improving the health of the nation's residents must be a priority in developing policies, programs, and funding.

2 Sustainable Agricultural Practices

Promote farming systems and agricultural techniques that prioritize the protection of the environment so that the soil, air, and water will be able to continue producing food long into the future. Integral to both domestic and global agricultural policies should be agricultural techniques and farming practices that enhance environmental quality, build soil and soil fertility, protect natural resources and ecosystem diversity, improve food safety, and increase the quality of life of communities, farmers, and farm workers.

3 Community and Regional Prosperity and Resilience

Enhance food security by strengthening the viability of small and mid-scale farms, and increasing appropriately scaled processing facilities, distribution networks, and direct marketing. Develop strategies that foster resiliency, local innovation, interdependence, and community development in both rural and urban economies. Opportunities that create fair wage jobs are key to a strong economy.

4 Equitable Access to Healthy Food

Identify opportunities and reduce barriers by developing policies and programs that increase the availability of and improve the proximity of healthy, affordable, and culturally relevant food to urban, suburban, and rural populations. Protect the nation's core programs that fight food insecurity and hunger while promoting vibrant, sustainable agriculture.

5 Social Justice and Equity

The policies reflected in the Farm Bill impact the lives and livelihoods of many people, both in the U.S. as well as abroad. Develop policies, programs, and strategies that support social justice, worker's rights, equal opportunity, and promote community self-reliance.

6 Systems Approach to Policymaking

It is essential to reduce compartmentalization of policies and programs, and to approach policy decisions by assessing their impact on all aspects of the food system, including production, processing, distribution, marketing, consumption, and waste management. Consider the interrelated effects of policies and align expected outcomes to meet the goal of a comprehensive health-focused food system.

The Seattle Farm Bill Principles were initiated by Seattle City Council President Richard Conlin as part of the Seattle Local Food Action Initiative. These principles were intended to guide a farm bill and drafted in 2012, though the subsequent bill wasn't finalized until 2014. They still provide relevant guidance for our next farm bill.

Cities across the country immediately began taking notice. Duluth, Minnesota, adapted the principles for itself. Philadelphia, Salt Lake City, New York City, and Minneapolis established working groups in the lead-up to the 2012 Farm Bill reauthorization. The New York City Food and Farm Bill Working Group, for example, gathered more than one hundred food-related organizations to emphasize issues such as good environmental stewardship in the subsequent Farm Bill. In November 2011, the National League of Cities passed a resolution, based on the Seattle Farm Bill Principles, supporting healthy food, public health, and sustainability. This organization serves as a resource for more than sixteen hundred dues-paying members and reaches tens of thousands of other cities and towns through advocacy and networking programs.

These efforts to develop a vibrant agriculture at the intersection of urban and rural areas are moving swiftly. By taking on the Farm Bill as a local priority, cities may soon challenge the USDA with a whole set of new priorities around urban agriculture. These discussions are already extending far beyond SNAP benefits and healthy food access. New York City, for example, has been incentivizing farmers in surrounding rural areas since 1992 to ensure that its water supply is protected far upstream, a policy that saves millions of dollars in mechanical filtration costs. Air pollution from farms and animal feeding operations is another critical issue for city policy makers, as is the preservation of beauty and wildlife in a region. Many cities are working to contain sprawl and prevent subdivisions from gobbling up remaining productive lands. Farm Bill funding sources like the Farm and Ranch Lands Protection Program could help urban areas protect surrounding farmland and open space, work already being led by land trusts and other organizations in many areas of the country.

LOCAL EFFORTS TO CUT BACK ON WASTE

Finally, local businesses and nonprofit organizations are stepping up to reduce food waste. The USDA estimated in 2015 that the wasted food in homes and restaurants amounts to more than $90 billion and costs consumers $370 per person per year, with protein foods contributing more than a third of this value.[12] Americans throw away an estimated 25 percent of the food they buy.[13] That more than 12 percent of Americans experience food insecurity and 61 percent do not have $1,000 in savings to cover a potential emergency further exemplifies the need to reduce waste.[14,15]

According to the Harvard Food Law and Policy Clinic, the Farm Bill could incorporate many strategies to reduce consumer waste that have not previously been part of national agricultural policy. A national awareness campaign could help consumers understand issues like proper food storage, sell-by dates, and home composting.[16] Many businesses and nonprofit organizations have independently adopted new models to sell surplus or imperfect foods at discount rates, often targeting low-income neighborhoods. Imperfect Produce, for example, has grown rapidly out of Emeryville, California, and sells "ugly" produce at a deep discount. The Daily Table in Dorchester, Massachusetts, was founded by former Trader Joe's president Doug Rauch to sell groceries and prepared meals made from surplus foods that can be more affordable to food-insecure people in that Boston neighborhood. Such initiatives could be prioritized by the existing Community Food Project grants under the Nutrition title or by the Local Food Promotion Program under the Specialty Crops and Horticulture title.[17] In addition, eligibility for Value-Added Producer Grants could be expanded to include nonprofit organizations that adopt such models or expand to urban regions.[18]

The Farm Bill's Miscellaneous title could also include language to amend the Emerson Act to provide liability protection to food service establishments that donate surplus or imperfect food directly rather than through a nonprofit organization to increase the feasibility of donations for businesses of all sizes.[19] And for the majority of consumers who are confused by date labels on food products, the Farm Bill could incorporate language to require states to standardize labels to "Best If Used By," indicating the time frame for optimal quality, or "Use By," indicating safety, from the minimum of ten different labels currently used across the industry.[20] That is the most cost-effective solution analyzed by the nonprofit ReFED to reduce food waste, potentially diverting 390,000 tons per year and yielding $1.8 billion per year in value.[21] Although the Food Marketing Institute and the Grocery Manufacturers Association have launched a voluntary industry initiative, incorporating a requirement in the Farm Bill would provide uniformity that could significantly reduce waste.

Local bans on organic waste from entities that produce a large volume have also proven effective. In Massachusetts, for example, businesses that generate more than 1 ton of organic waste per year are not allowed to throw it away, forcing these enterprises to reduce the waste they generate, recycle the material, or use a combination of the two strategies. Massachusetts General Hospital, one of the nation's top hospitals, qualifies for this ban and in 2015 began to partner with the company Agri-Cycle and local Stonyvale Farm to collect, deliver, and digest its organic waste, producing biogas to return to the grid and fertilizer and compost for Stonyvale. Grant funding made available through the Farm Bill could support other state or local governments to implement such a ban.[22]

Efforts championed by the KYF2 initiative, the Seattle Farm Bill Principles, and numerous food policy charters are just the start of a burgeoning local agriculture revolution. The goal is not to simply expand farmers markets so that elite urban consumers can buy expensive organic foods. It's about saving small farms before they disappear altogether and supporting health, environmental sustainability, and social equity. Rural and urban constituencies need each other. By supporting regional food production, we become healthier, happier, more engaged, and more secure citizens.

Expanding local food production does not mean the end of trade or large-scale production. With more mouths to feed and a less stable climate, we will need an unfathomable range of sustainable food systems to thrive.

Because our Farm Bill dollars are finite, we must decide how to best spend them. As more city dwellers and suburbanites realize how federal food and agriculture policies actually affect them, the Farm Bill may no longer be perceived as a group of arcane programs that help midwestern corn farmers and provide SNAP benefits to the poor. The Farm Bill may become, in the near future, a local food bill, too.

24. A Citizen's Farm Bill

Reforming food and farm policy is an ongoing cultural and political process, a series of give-and-takes that stretches from the checkout stand to the voting booth.

THE FARM BILL IS ONE OF THOSE SUBJECTS TO WHICH, once you start pulling a string, you find the whole world attached. That's because the Farm Bill sets the rules of the game, influencing not only what we eat, but also who grows it, under what conditions, and to some extent, how much it costs. The agribusinesses and lobbyists that have essentially written those rules for our legislators in recent decades deserve the lion's share of the responsibility for creating the tangle of problems in our food system.

The good news is that many of the ideas needed to turn the tables and create a healthy food and farming system largely already exist. They share a common condition: most are ignored, marginalized, or underfunded by current Farm Bill programs—still, some momentum exists. The movement to create a nourishing, environmentally regenerative, and affordable food system is becoming a unifying issue of our time. People from all walks of life—including citizens, food consumers, business owners, professionals, doctors, nurses, students, teachers, and parents—have enormous influence. Every day, many of us choose to support—or not—a particular aspect of the food and farming sector through our purchases. Every day, we can speak up for improving land stewardship or basic nutritional health in our workplaces, schools, and communities. Every Farm Bill cycle, we can demand that our representatives not barter away their votes.

We can join or take active leadership positions in advocacy organizations. Many early efforts that at one time seemed minimally effective or merely symbolic later emerged as models for change, reproduced in one place after another. Some have inspired mainstream movements—such as organic farming or pasture-based livestock production—that are influencing food policy at state, national, and even international levels.

Conditions now call for a bold new Farm Bill—a true Food Bill. Program titles must become more deeply integrated so that they don't work at cross-purposes, for example, enabling destructive practices on one hand and attempting to compensate with underfunded conservation efforts on the other. Subsidies should stop undermining the nation's nutrition goals. All government subsidies—whether for crops, insurance, research, marketing, or anything else—should come with related commitments to the health of our citizens and the long-term health of the land.

Common sense demands that the narrow self-interests of corporate agribusiness must yield to a broader vision. Local and regional food systems should be expanded immediately, to cut down on food miles and to preserve family farms and create jobs. Concentrated animal production should be reduced, to curb global warming and to end egregious harms being done to animals and rural communities. Real eligibility limits should be levied on subsidy recipients, to end corporate welfare for undeserving landowners and to make funds available for other urgent programs. Funding to help communities preserve farmland should be increased, to preserve open space and to invest in jobs in rural areas.

It's time to question whether the industrial mega-farm model is the only way to feed a growing global population or whether it's even possible for such a system to survive without costly government supports and unsustainable environmental practices. It's time for citizens to see that Farm Bill politics are local politics. It's time for policies that are taking a toll on the land, making unhealthy food unrealistically cheap, and tearing the fabric of rural communities to change. It's time for better, smarter solutions. The time has come for a citizen's Farm Bill.

25. Twenty-Five Solutions

1. Mandatory conservation compliance for taxpayer-funded crop or revenue insurance.

2. Expanded infrastructure for local and regional food supply chains, including small-scale livestock processing.

3. More support for farm-direct distribution, including farm-to-school, farm-to-hospital, farm-to-healthcare provider, community-supported agriculture, and farmers markets.

4. Food labeling that informs consumers how items are produced, including whether or not they contain genetically modified organisms or animals raised in confinement systems.

5. Establishment of a fifty-year Farm Bill focused on perennial, ecologically based farming.

6. Farm Bill crop supports that align with our Dietary Guidelines for Americans.

7. A shift away from subsidizing surplus production toward rewarding measurable, per-acre stewardship practices.

8. Farm supports that function as safety nets, loans, and stewardship incentives, and not as direct giveaways.

9. Income eligibility limits on farm supports, including crop insurance with no loopholes.

10. Fair prices for all crops maintained by a re-established grain reserve and other supply management programs.

11. Federal matching grant program for counties or cities that create local Farm Bills to promote agricultural land preservation, riparian zone enhancement, and crop diversification.

12. Healthy school lunch programs tied to nearby farms and school gardens that teach children where food comes from.

13. Farm and ranchland preservation that buffers communities against sprawl, saves wildlife habitat, and prevents agricultural lands from development.

14. Preservation of native prairies and functional grasslands, with penalties for those who plow them up.

15. Incentives for a grass-based livestock economy with a goal of shifting 50 percent away from feedlots by 2050.

16. Reduction of farm-related greenhouse gas emissions through shifts to perennial and organic agriculture, including a $1 billion per year healthy soils initiative to increase soil carbon, water capture, and retention.

17. A thirty-year program to invest in solutions to the problems of food waste, with a new Food Waste Reduction title to fund it.

18. Elimination of corn ethanol standards and institution of ecological standards for bioenergy crops.

19. Elimination of anticompetitive practices in livestock, including captive supply, which now allows meat-packing monopolies to own and slaughter their own animals.

20. Funding of more on-the-ground technical conservation assistance and enforcement through the Natural Resources Conservation Service.

21. Farm-scale renewable energy and energy conservation projects.

22. Scaled-up investments in crop rotation, cover crops, and other alternatives to synthetic fertilizers.

23. Improved conditions for all food system workers with program funding from a Labor title.

24. Restoration of native pollinator habitat and invasive species removal added to conservation goals.

25. Food aid reform that enables recipient nations to purchase local or regional crops rather than commodities from US agribusinesses.

26. A Vision of Sustainable Food

THE FARM BILL MAY BE DRIVEN BY ACRONYMS AND TECHNICAL PROGRAM LANGUAGE, but what we are essentially talking about is an amazing opportunity to shape our world. The nearly $100 billion annual budget that we spend on food and agriculture is a chance to do things better, more fairly, and to compensate for values that the market does not recognize.

As we consider how this massive public resource might be redirected, let's not lose sight of the poetic outcomes we hope to achieve: protecting the natural world while we farm; promoting health and providing sustenance, especially for our children and those in need; creating a culture that values farmers, workers, and vibrant rural farming communities; and leading the world by example through a commitment to stewardship, research and innovation, fairness, and health.

Let's turn the Farm Bill on its head and, for a moment, reimagine it with broad brushstrokes. Let's think fifty years into the future, as has been done in an excellent paper spearheaded by the Land Institute (see chapter 22). That's roughly ten Farm Bills into the future and roughly how long ago it's now been since Secretary of Agriculture Earl Butz and the US Department of Agriculture (USDA) told American farmers to "get big or get out."

The policies put in place during that time changed the trajectory of American food and farming. Mandatory set-asides were abandoned. Supply management mechanisms that guarantee prices were slowly dismantled. The food stamp program was hitched to the Farm Bill. Conservation dollars began to be pilfered for production-boosting infrastructure. The biggest players and their beneficiaries began to write the rules that determine our economics of agriculture. We can, however, choose to write different rules and create policies that put food and farming on a new path. It is not very difficult to imagine a time in America's future when the sun rises over a vastly different agricultural landscape. Here are a few ideas about what that landscape could look like:

- *If you're too big, get out.* Future Farm Bills can place real limits on income eligibility for crop insurance and price supports rather than offer open checkbooks to the biggest operations that tragically distort markets. We need every cent of that $100 billion for all the good work that has to be done.

- *No subsidization without social obligation.* The Dust Bowl and Great Depression that spawned early Farm Bill programs should never be far from our minds. Conservation programs and requirements, once cornerstones of farm policy, have slowly eroded away. If we are going to use taxpayer dollars to support farming businesses, the public must receive something of real value in return. We have a lot to ask: zero soil erosion, clean air and water entering and leaving farms, optimal biodiversity protection, and programs that shift away from heavily polluting practices.

- *Transition from fossil fuel–based monocultures to agroecology.* Future agricultural systems can be far more locally adapted, intelligence based, and rich in labor, skills, and knowledge to optimize exchanges of energy and nutrients between domestic farming and the natural world. The so-called alternative agriculture of the present—diversified organic operations, grass pastures, and humanely raised livestock operations—should lead our food system. Fifty years, two generations of new farmers, and ten Farm Bills of consistent programs to support these production methods would put us in uncharted territory. If we pursue real change—rotational grazing systems, no-till organic farming, and perennial polyculture crops that provide new ways to raise grains, oilseeds, energy, and fibers—we can protect the soil with deep-rooted plants and slowly take over tens and then hundreds of millions of acres. They will replace the dueling banjos of chemically drenched corn and soybeans that dominate American agriculture.

- *Far-reaching conservation incentives.* Ten percent of America's land should always be in the Conservation Reserve Program, with increasing protection of large, contiguous acres; 10 percent, then 25, 50, and eventually 100 percent of farms can incorporate cover crops and permanent ground cover on portions of farms. Measurable gains in soil carbon and soil organic matter can be rewarded as we give true value to a truly nonrenewable resource.

- *A cultural shift at the USDA.* The USDA can move its focus from feeding the world with industrial agriculture to leading the world with practices that can be locally applied so that we can feed ourselves without destroying the planet.

Specific changes to Farm Bill titles could include:

- A *Labor title* that offers programs to support millions of farm workers without whom food production would be impossible.

- A *transparency initiative* to improve labeling and production information systems that teach consumers about the true costs of production.

- An *Urban Agriculture title* to support the growth of the vibrant inner-city food production movement.

- A *Food Waste Reduction title* dedicated to solving the dilemma that nearly 40 percent of all the country's food currently produced goes uneaten and often ends up in landfills.

- A *Livestock title*, renamed the *Animal Husbandry title*, to focus once again on diverse breeds and complex issues of grazing, feeds, animal health, regional processing, and ensuring fair markets and an end to meat-packer monopolies.

- A *Species Restoration and Predator Coexistence program* to replace the current Animal Damage Control program, which spends $100 million each year to trap, poison, and attempt to eradicate species such as coyotes, mountain lions, wolves, bears, and redwing blackbirds.

- To top it off, our Dietary Guidelines for Americans and requirements for federal nutrition programs will, for once, be supported by the policies that make eating a healthy diet easier and more affordable.

Talking about policy in a way that energizes people may be as important as the changes we demand. Let's think carefully about the kind of future we envision and then advocate for those poetic outcomes.

ACTIVIST TOOL KIT

LOCAL FARM BILL ORGANIZING

Become a Farm Bill organizer. Inform yourself about the bill. Get together with local groups working on the bill. Set up a table at your farmers market. Include the Farm Bill in your teaching about food policy, food studies, or agriculture. Here are some solid suggestions gathered from experienced Farm Bill organizers. Get busy!

Learn about the Farm Bill. Learn to "crack the code" of Farm Bill lingo. The US Department of Agriculture has a lot of useful information, including the full text of the bill itself and specialized reports.

Adopt a local food charter. Check out the Seattle Farm Bill Principles and the Healthy Food Declaration or draft a new one of your own.

Bring local officials up to speed. A local Farm Bill agenda can easily begin with a community group. Political leaders are more likely to engage once they understand that the movement is legitimate.

Communicate with your representatives. Meet with your elected representatives to discuss your commitment to local food and see if you can work together. Members of the Senate Committee on Agriculture, Nutrition, and Forestry and the House Committee on Agriculture have to hear clearly and often from their districts about emerging priorities.

Be clear about the connections. What foodshed or geographical region are you discussing? What are the specific needs? How will buying locally help address local needs?

Create outreach and educational opportunities. Communicate to your community members why they have an interest in the outcome of Farm Bill debates. Look over the Environmental Working Group's Farm Subsidy Database and other search engines to familiarize yourself with spending in your state.

Build coalitions. Identify the many constituencies affected by local food systems: family farms, public health offices, economic development groups, local schools, government agencies, charities, food policy councils, and social justice movements. Develop partnerships to spread the word.

Think beyond Washington. Much of the decision making and project funding is done at the state level. Consider volunteering for a state technical committee such as the Natural Resources Conservation Service.

Take the long view. Change rarely happens over the span of just one Farm Bill. Learn about how previous gains were made—and realize that they must be supported and defended throughout the long processes of appropriation, implementation, rulemaking, and so on.

USDA AGENCIES AND FARM BILL PROGRAMS

Familiarize yourself with the work of agencies and programs from recent Farm Bills that have a record of achievement. A number of important programs have been created to promote a healthy food and farming system. See if they can be applied or expanded to your area of influence.

Agricultural Marketing Service
- Farmers Market and Local Food Promotion Programs
- Federal-State Marketing Improvement Program
- Specialty Crop Block Grant Program

Farm Service Agency
- Farm Loan Programs
- Farm Storage Facility Loan Program

Food and Nutrition Service
- Senior Farmers' Market Nutrition Program
- Supplemental Nutrition Assistance Program
- Special Supplemental Nutrition Program for Women, Infants, and Children
- WIC Farmers' Market Nutrition Program

National Institute of Food and Agriculture
- Agriculture and Food Research Initiative—Improved Sustainable Food Systems
- Agriculture and Food Research Initiative—Agricultural Economics and Rural Communities
- Beginning Farmer and Rancher Development Program
- Community Food Projects Competitive Grant Program
- Small Business Innovation Research Program
- Sustainable Agriculture Research and Education

Natural Resources Conservation Service
- Conservation Stewardship Program
- Conservation Technical Assistance
- Environmental Quality Incentives Program
- Agricultural Conservation Easement Program

Risk Management Agency
- Risk Management Education Partnership Program

Rural Development
- Business and Industry Guaranteed Loan Program
- Community Facilities Grant Programs
- Rural Business Development Grant Program
- Rural Microentrepreneur Assistance Program
- Value-Added Producer Grants

GET CONNECTED

STEP 1.   STAY UP TO DATE. The Food and Farm Bill field is complex and constantly evolving. Check these websites to learn more about the issues and stay up to date with the latest news and changes:

Center for Rural Affairs
Lyons, NE
(402) 687-2100
www.cfra.org

Environmental Working Group
Washington, DC
(202) 667-6982
www.ewg.org

Farm Bill Budget Visualizer
Baltimore, MD
www.jhsph.edu/clf/programs/visualizer/

Farmdoc
www.farmdoc.illinois.edu/

Institute for Agriculture and Trade Policy
Minneapolis, MN
(612) 870-0453
www.iatp.org

National Sustainable Agriculture Coalition
Washington, DC
(202) 547-5754
www.sustainableagriculture.net

Watershed Media
Healdsburg, CA
(707) 431-2936
www.watershedmedia.org
www.foodfightbook.org

STEP 2.   GET INVOLVED. Assembled here is a list of organizations, agencies, educational institutes, and other entities to help you find organizations in your field of interest or your area to work with.

CONSERVATION GROUPS

American Forest Foundation
Washington, DC
(202) 765-3660
www.forestfoundation.org

Defenders of Wildlife
Washington, DC
(800) 385-9712
www.defenders.org

Environmental Defense Fund
New York, NY
(800) 684-3322
www.edf.org

Green Cities California
www.greencitiescalifornia.org

Izaak Walton League of America
Gaithersburg, MD
(301) 548-0150
www.iwla.org

Natural Resources Defense Council
New York, NY
(212) 727-2700
www.nrdc.org

Soil and Water Conservation Society
Ankeny, IA
(515) 289-2331
www.swcs.org

Wild Farm Alliance
Watsonville, CA
(831) 761-8408
www.wildfarmalliance.org

Xerces Society
Portland, OR
(503) 232-6639
www.xerces.org

SUSTAINABLE AGRICULTURE

Alabama Sustainable Agriculture Network
Birmingham, AL
(256) 743-0742
www.asanonline.org

American Farmland Trust
Washington, DC
(202) 331-7300
www.farmland.org

The Berry Center
New Castle, KY
(502) 845-9200
www.berrycenter.org

California Climate and Agriculture Network
Sebastopol, CA
(707) 329-6374
www.calclimateag.org

Dakota Rural Action
Brookings, SD
(605) 697-5204
www.dakotarural.org

Ecological Farming Association
Soquel, CA
(831) 763-2111
www.eco-farm.org

Farm Aid
Cambridge, MA
(617) 354-2922
www.farmaid.org

Florida Organic Growers
Gainesville, FL
(352) 377-6345
www.foginfo.org

Glynwood Center
Cold Spring, NY
(845) 265-3338
www.glynwood.org

GRACE Communications
New York, NY
(212) 726-9161
www.gracelinks.org

The Land Institute
Salina, KS
(785) 823-5376
www.landinstitute.org

Land Stewardship Project
Minneapolis, MN
(612) 722-6377
www.landstewardshipproject.org

Less = More
Sierra Club Michigan Chapter
www.moreformichigan.org

Marin Carbon Project
Point Reyes Station, CA
www.marincarbonproject.org

Michael Fields Agricultural Institute
East Troy, WI
(262) 642-3303
http://michaelfields.org/

Missouri Rural Crisis Center
Columbia, MO
(573) 449-1336
www.morural.org

National Center for Appropriate Technology
Butte, MT
(800) ASK-NCAT
www.ncat.org

National Center for Appropriate Technology:
Sustainable Agriculture Project
(800) 346-9140
www.attra.ncat.org

National Family Farm Coalition
Washington, DC
(202) 543-5675
www.nffc.net

National Farmers Union
Washington, DC
(202) 554-1600
www.nfu.org

Northeast-Midwest Institute
Washington, DC
(202) 544-5200
www.nemw.org

Northeast Sustainable Agriculture Working Group
Kingston, NY
(845) 501-0191
www.nesawg.org

Northern Plains Sustainable Agriculture Society
LaMoure, ND
(701) 883-4304
www.npsas.org

Organic Trade Association
Washington, DC
(202) 403-8520
www.ota.com

Pesticide Action Network North America
Berkeley, CA
(510) 788-9020
www.panna.org

Rural Advancement Foundation International–USA (RAFI)
Pittsboro, NC
(919) 542-1396
www.rafiusa.org

Socially Responsible Agriculture Project
Salem, OR
(844) 367-7727
www.sraproject.org

Worldwatch Institute
Washington, DC
(202) 745-8092
www.worldwatch.org

HEALTHY FOOD SYSTEMS AND ANTI-HUNGER

Ample Harvest
www.ampleharvest.org

Berkeley Food Institute
Berkeley, CA
(510) 643-8821
www.food.berkeley.edu

Bread for the World
Washington, DC
(202) 639-9400
www.bread.org

California Food Policy Advocates
Oakland, CA
(510) 433-1122
www.cfpa.net

Center for Food Safety
Washington, DC
(202) 547-9359
www.centerforfoodsafety.org

Change Food
New York, NY
www.changefood.org

Congressional Hunger Center
Washington, DC
(202) 547-7022
www.hungercenter.org

Fair Food Network
Ann Arbor, MI
(734) 213-3999
www.fairfoodnetwork.org

Farmers Market Coalition
(888) FMC-8177
www.farmersmarketcoalition.org

Feeding America
Chicago, IL
(800) 771-2303
www.feedingamerica.org

Food and Water Watch
Washington, DC
(202) 683-2500
www.foodandwaterwatch.org

Food Animal Concerns Trust
Chicago, IL
(773) 525-4952
www.foodanimalconcernstrust.org

Food Routes
Millheim, PA
(814) 349-9856
www.pasa.org

Green Lands Blue Waters
www.greenlandsbluewaters.net

National Farm to School Network
(847) 917-7292
Chicago, IL
www.farmtoschool.org

Northwest Farm Bill Action Group
Seattle, WA
www.nwfoodfight.org

Roots of Change
San Francisco, CA
(415) 391-0545
www.rootsofchange.org

Slow Food USA
Brooklyn, NY
(718) 260-8000
www.slowfoodusa.org

The Food Trust
Philadelphia, PA
(215) 575-0444
www.thefoodtrust.org

Wholesome Wave
Bridgeport, CT
(203) 226-1112
www.wholesomewave.org

Why Hunger New York, NY
(212) 629-8850
www.whyhunger.org

EDUCATION AND BEGINNING FARMER PROGRAMS

Agriculture and Land-Based Training Association (ALBA)
Salinas, CA
(831) 758-1469
www.albafarmers.org

California FarmLink
Aptos, CA
(831) 425-0303
www.californiafarmlink.org

Center for Ecoliteracy
Berkeley, CA
(510) 845-4595
www.ecoliteracy.org

Community Alliance with Family Farmers
Davis, CA
(530) 756-8518
www.caff.org

Leopold Center for Sustainable Agriculture
Ames, IA
(515) 294-3711
www.leopold.iastate.edu

Midwest Organic and Sustainable Education Service (MOSES)
Spring Valley, WI
(715) 778-5775
www.mosesorganic.org

National Young Farmers' Coalition
Hudson, NY
518-643-3564
www.youngfarmers.org

Sustainable Agriculture and Food Systems Funders (SAFSF)
Santa Barbara, CA
(805) 687-0551
www.safsf.org

UC Sustainable Agriculture Research and Education Program
Davis, CA
(530) 752-3915
www.asi.ucdavis.edu/programs/sarep

USDA Sustainable Agriculture Research and Education (SARE)
College Park, MD
www.sare.org

INTERNATIONAL TRADE AND GLOBALIZATION

Global Development and Environment Institute at Tufts University
Medford, MA
(617) 627-3530
www.ase.tufts.edu/gdae

International Forum on Globalization
San Francisco, CA
(415) 561-7650
www.ifg.org

Local Futures
East Hardwick, VT
(802) 472 3505
www.localfutures.org

Oxfam
Oxford, England
44 (0) 1865 47 3727
www.oxfam.org.uk

World Trade Organization (WTO)
Geneva, Switzerland
41 (0) 22 739 51 11
www.wto.org

RENEWABLE ENERGY

Alternative Energy Resources Organization
Helena, MT
(406) 443-7272
www.aeromt.org

Clean Coalition
Menlo Park, CA
(650) 308-9046
www.clean-coalition.org

Climate Central
Princeton, NJ
(609) 924-3800
www.climatecentral.org

Earthworks
Washington, DC
(202) 887-1872
www.earthworks.org

Energy Foundation
San Francisco, CA
(415) 561-6700
www.ef.org

Environmental Law and Policy Center (ELPC)
Chicago, IL
(312) 673-6500
www.elpc.org

Rocky Mountain Institute
Boulder, CO
(303) 245-1003
www.rmi.org

Union of Concerned Scientists
Cambridge, MA
(617) 547-5552
www.ucsusa.org

GOVERNMENT AGENCIES

Agricultural Marketing Service
Washington, DC
See website for individual program contact
information
www.ams.usda.gov

Association of Clean Water Administrators
Washington, DC
(202) 756-0605
www.acwa-us.org

Congress
Washington, DC
See website for instructions on how to write to
your representatives and senators
www.congress.org

Congressional Research Service
Washington, DC
www.loc.gov/crsinfo/about/
CRS reports can be found at these websites:
University of North Texas
https://digital.library.unt.edu/explore
/collections/CRSR/
Council for Science and Environment
www.ncseonline.org/programs/science
-policy/crs-reports

Economic Research Service
Washington, DC
(202) 694-5050
www.ers.usda.gov

National Agricultural Statistics Service
Washington, DC
(800) 727-9540
www.nass.usda.gov

Natural Resources Conservation Service
Washington, DC
See website for local contact information
www.nrcs.usda.gov

United States Department of Agriculture
Washington, DC
See website for contact information for
individual agencies
www.usda.gov

POLICY

Agricultural Policy Analysis Center
Knoxville, TN
(865) 974-7407
www.agpolicy.org

American Farm Bureau Federation
Washington, DC
(202) 406-3600
www.fb.org

Chicago Council on Global Affairs
Chicago, IL
(312) 726-3860
www.thechicagocouncil.org

Farm Aid
Cambridge, MA
(800) FARM-AID
www.farmaid.org

Food First
Oakland, CA
(510) 654-4400
www.foodfirst.org

Food Research and Action Center
Washington, DC
(202) 986-2200
www.frac.org

National Agricultural Law Center
Fayetteville, AR
(479) 575-7646
www.nationalaglaw.org

Organic Farming and Research Foundation
Santa Cruz, CA
(831) 426-6606
www.ofrf.org

Public Citizen
Washington, DC
(202) 588-1000
www.citizen.org

ChangeLab Solutions
Oakland, CA
(510) 302-3380
www.changelabsolutions.org

Rudd Center for Food Policy and Obesity
Hartford, CT
(860) 380-1000
www.uconnruddcenter.org

W. K. Kellogg Foundation
Battle Creek, MI
(269) 968-1611
www.wkkf.org

World Resources Institute
Washington, DC
(202) 729-7600
www.wri.org

PUBLIC HEALTH AND NUTRITION

Academy of Nutrition and Dietetics
Chicago, IL
(800) 877-1600
www.eatright.org

Alliance for a Healthier Generation
Portland, OR
888-KID-HLTH
www.healthiergeneration.org

American Public Health Association
Washington, DC
(202) 777-2742
www.apha.org

Center for a Livable Future
Baltimore, MD
(410) 223-1811
www.jhsph.edu/clf

Center for Science in the Public Interest
Washington, DC
(202) 332-9110
www.cspinet.org

Food Democracy Now
Clear Lake, IA
(515) 207-2761
www.fooddemocracynow.org

MIT Collaborative Initiatives
Cambridge, MA
(617) 252-0003
www.collaborativeinitiatives.org

Partnership for a Healthier America
Washington, DC
(202) 842-9001
www.ahealthieramerica.org

Public Health Institute: Center for Wellness and Nutrition
  Sacramento, CA
  (916) 265-4042
  www.centerforwellnessandnutrition.org

Physicians Committee for Responsible Medicine
  Washington, DC
  (202) 686-2210
  www.pcrm.org

Prevention Institute
  Oakland, CA
  (510) 444-7738
  www.preventioninstitute.org

Society for Nutrition Education and Behavior
  Indianapolis, IN
  (800) 235-6690
  www.sneb.org

United Fresh Produce Association
  Washington, DC
  (202) 303-3400
  www.unitedfresh.org

STEP 3.   TAKE IT TO THE HILL. Tell the people in charge of the Farm Bill what you want our country's food policy to look like. Check to see if your senators or representative sits on one of the key committees listed below. Remember that committee membership changes each election cycle, so keep checking back!

House Committee on Agriculture—Oversight of all US policy related to agriculture.

House Subcommittee on Commodity Exchanges, Energy, and Credit—Policies, statutes, and markets relating to commodity exchanges; agricultural credit; rural development; energy; rural electrification.

House Subcommittee on Conservation and Forestry—Policies and statutes relating to resource conservation, forestry, and all forests under the jurisdiction of the Committee on Agriculture.

House Subcommittee on General Farm Commodities and Risk Management—Policies, statutes, and markets relating to commodities, including barley, cotton, cottonseed, corn, grain sorghum, honey, mohair, oats, other oilseeds, peanuts, pulse crops, rice, soybeans, sugar, wheat, and wool; the Commodity Credit Corporation; risk management policies and statutes, including Federal Crop Insurance; producer data and privacy issues.

House Subcommittee on Livestock and Foreign Agriculture—Policies, statutes, and markets relating to all livestock, poultry, dairy, and seafood, including all products thereof; the inspection, marketing, and promotion of such commodities and products; aquaculture; animal welfare; grazing; foreign agricultural assistance and trade promotion.

House Subcommittee on Nutrition—Policies and statutes relating to nutrition, including the Supplemental Nutrition Assistance Program and domestic commodity distribution and consumer initiatives.

House Subcommittee on Biotechnology, Horticulture, and Research—Policies, statutes, and markets relating to horticulture, including fruits, vegetables, nuts, and ornamentals, bees, and organic agriculture; policies and statutes relating to marketing and promotion orders; pest and disease management; bioterrorism; adulteration and quarantine matters; research, education, and extension; biotechnology.

House Committee on Appropriations—Funding allocations for specific programs during each fiscal year.

Senate Committee on Agriculture, Nutrition, and Forestry—Oversight of all US policy related to agriculture.

> **Senate Subcommittee on Commodities, Risk Management, and Trade**—Production of agricultural crops, commodities, and products; farm and ranch income protection and assistance, including safety net programs and farm credit; commodity price support programs; insurance and risk protection, freshwater food production; agricultural trade; foreign market development; futures, options, and derivatives.

> **Senate Subcommittee on Conservation, Forestry, and Natural Resources**—Conservation, protection, and stewardship of natural resources and the environment; state, local, and private forests; general forestry; pesticides.

> **Senate Subcommittee on Livestock, Marketing, and Agriculture Security**—Animal welfare; inspection and certification of plants, animals, and products; plant and animal diseases and health protection; domestic marketing and product promotion; marketing orders and regulation of agricultural markets.

> **Senate Subcommittee on Nutrition, Agricultural Research, and Specialty Crops**—Domestic and international nutrition, food assistance, and hunger prevention; school and child nutrition programs; local and healthy food initiatives; food and agricultural research, education, economics, and extension.

> **Senate Subcommittee on Rural Development and Energy**—Rural economic revitalization and quality of life; rural job and business growth; rural electrification, telecommunications, and utilities; renewable energy production and energy efficiency improvement on farms and ranches and in rural communities; innovation in the use of agricultural commodities and materials.

Senate Committee on Appropriations—Funding allocation for specific programs during each fiscal year.

NOTES

Chapter 1

1. Robert A. Hoppe, *America's Diverse Family Farms, 2017 Edition,* EIB-185 (Washington, DC: USDA Economic Research Service, 2017), https://www.ers.usda.gov/publications/pub-details/?pubid=86197.

2. *Crops* (Washington, DC: USDA Economic Research Service, May 8, 2018), https://www.ers.usda.gov/topics/crops/.

3. Timothy A. Wise, "Agricultural Dumping under NAFTA: Estimating the Costs of U.S. Agricultural Policies to Mexican Producers," Working Paper No. 09-08 (Medford, MA: Global Development and Environment Institute at Tufts University, 2010).

4. Timothy A. Wise, *The Cost to Mexico of U.S. Corn Ethanol Expansion*, Working Paper No. 12-01 (Medford, MA: Global Development and Environment Institute at Tufts University, May 2012).

5. Sophia Murphy, *A Return to Low Commodity Prices and U.S. Dumping* (Minneapolis, MN: Institute for Agriculture and Trade Policy, October 20, 2016), https://www.iatp.org/blog/201610/a-return-to-low-commodity-prices-and-us-dumping.

6. Food and Nutrition Service, "Supplemental Nutrition Assistance Program," US Department of Agriculture, updated June 2017, https://www.fns.usda.gov/pd/supplemental-nutrition-assistance-program-snap.

7. Alisha Coleman-Jensen, Christian Gregory, and Matthew Rabbitt, *Key Statistics and Graphics* (Washington, DC: USDA Economic Research Service, 2017), https://www.ers.usda.gov/topics/food-nutrition-assistance/food-security-in-the-us/key-statistics-graphics.aspx#foodsecure.

Chapter 2

1. Alisha Coleman-Jensen et al., "Household Food Security in the United States in 2014," Report No. 194 (Washington, DC: USDA Economic Research Service, September 2015).

2. Essayist and farmer Wendell Berry has written: "The global 'free market' is free to the corporations precisely because it dissolves the boundaries of the old national colonialisms, and replaces them with a new colonialism without restraints or boundaries. It is pretty much as if all the rabbits have now been forbidden to have holes, thereby 'freeing' the hounds." "The Total Economy," in *Citizenship Papers* (Washington, DC: Shoemaker and Hoard, 2003), 66.

Chapter 3

1. Renée Johnson, "Previewing a 2018 Farm Bill," CRS Report R44784, Congressional Research Service, March 15, 2017.

2. Ferd Hoefner, Sustainable Agriculture Coalition, "Farm Bill Primer," PowerPoint presentation, September 2005.

3. The American farm lobby is politically secure thanks to the overrepresentation of rural America in the Senate and makes slightly more than $50 million worth of political donations in each election cycle. The food and nutrition programs—with their backing from urban representatives—historically have provided the "critical mass" of political support for the omnibus bill from outside of Farm Belt states.

4. Daren Bakst, Josh Sewell, and Brian Wright, "Addressing Risk in Agriculture" (Washington, DC: Heritage Foundation, September 8, 2016), http://www.heritage.org/agriculture/report/addressing-risk-agriculture.

5. Environmental Working Group, "Commodity Subsidies in the United States Totaled $183.7 Billion from 1995–2016," accessed May 28, 2018, https://farm.ewg.org/progdetail.php?fips=00000&progcode=totalfarm&page=conc&regionname=theUnitedStates.

6. USDA Office of Budget and Program Analysis, "FY 2016 Budget Summary and Annual Performance Plan," https://www.obpa.usda.gov/budsum/fy16budsum.pdf.

7. According to the USDA, 1.73 billion tons of soil was lost in 2007, the most recent year for which there is data. However, there are concerns that this number does not represent the true amount of soil loss. Many believe that major crop expansion for ethanol and export markets may be contributing to increased soil loss. "RCA Appraisal 2011: Soil and Water Resources Conservation Act," United States Department of Agriculture, March 2011, ftp://ftp-fc.sc.egov.usda.gov/NHQ/rca/2011_RCA_Appraisal_Pre_Publication_Copy.pdf, 3-2.

8. Brenda Carlson, email message to Christina Badaracco, June 20, 2017.

9. John Cawley and Chad Meyerhoefer, "The Medical Care Costs of Obesity: An Instrumental Variables Approach," *Journal of Health Economics* 31, no. 1 (2012): 219–30; Eric A. Finkelstein et al., "Annual Medical Spending Attributable to Obesity," *Health Affairs* 28, no. 5 (2009), doi.org/10.1377/hlthaff.28.5.w822.

Chapter 4

1. According to one long-time Farm Bill observer, about one-third of the members of the Agriculture Committees are new representatives and senators who have been assigned to the task and are eager to be released from these committees as soon as possible.

2. National Sustainable Agriculture Coalition, "Farm, Food, and Conservation Communities Urge Congress to Respect Farm Bill Process," February 22, 2017, http://sustainableagriculture.net/blog/groups-oppose-reopening-farmbill/.

3. National Sustainable Agriculture Coalition, "Agriculture Appropriations Chart Fiscal Year 2015," http://sustainableagriculture.net/wp-content/uploads/2008/09/NSAC-FY-2015-Ag-Appropriations-Chart-Legal-Size-w-PBR1.pdf. Ironically, slashing EQIP funding hurts relatively environmentally friendly operations more than the worst offenders. See "Paying the Polluters" in chapter 8.

4. Jonathan Copess, Gary Schnitkey, and Nick Paulson, "Sequestration and Farm Program Payments," *FarmDoc Daily* 5 (September 2015): 167, http://farmdocdaily.illinois.edu/2015/09/sequestration-and-farm-program-payments.html.

5. Tiffany Stecker, "Appropriations: House Agriculture Bill Guts Farm Bill Energy Programs—Advocates," E&E News, June 19, 2015, https://www.eenews.net/eedaily/stories/1060020525?t=https%3A%2F%2Fwww.eenews.net%2Fspecial_reports %2Fbudget_ 2016%2Fstories%2F1060020525.

Chapter 5

1. Quoted in "Ownership Matters: Three Steps to Ensure a Biofuels Industry That Truly Benefits Rural America," David Morris, based on a speech to the Minnesota Ag Expo in Morton, Minnesota, January 25, 2006.

2. Elizabeth Corcoran, "The Answer on the Wind," *San Francisco Chronicle*, January 8, 2006, M1.

3. Quoted in Howard Zinn, "Self-Help in Hard Times," *A People's History of the United States* (New York: Harper and Row, 1980), 389.

4. The longest period of relative parity between farm prices and manufacturing prices was 1911–1914, the years leading up to World War I, and this period was used to determine the price parity index. For an extended analysis, see John C. Culver and John Hyde, *American Dreamer: The Life and Times of Henry A. Wallace* (New York: Norton, 2000), 56.

5. Culver and Hyde, *American Dreamer*, 99.

6. Michael Pollan, *The Omnivore's Dilemma: A Natural History of Four Meals* (New York: Penguin, 2006), 48.

7. Office of Budget and Program Analysis, "FY 2017 Budget Summary," US Department of Agriculture, https://www.obpa.usda .gov/budsum/fy17budsum.pdf.

8. An excellent account of this period can be found in Culver and Hyde, *American Dreamer*.

9. Pollan, *Omnivore's Dilemma*, 49.

10. Scott Marlow, *The Non-Wonk Guide to Understanding Federal Commodity Payments* (Pittsboro, NC: Rural Advancement Foundation International, 2005).

11. It was estimated that Farm Bill spending during these troubled times had a multiplier effect of seven. That is, every $1 of government funds spent on farm and food policies generated $7 in the overall economy. See Culver and Hyde, *American Dreamer*, for more details.

12. Richard Manning, *Against the Grain: How Agriculture Hijacked Civilization* (New York: North Point Press, 2004), 171.

13. Bernard De Vito, quoted in Mark Arax and Rick Wartzman, *The King of California* (New York: Public Affairs, 2003), 186.

14. Written in 1924, referenced in Arax and Wartzman, *King of California*, 375.

Chapter 6

1. Paul Conkin, *A Revolution Down on the Farm: The Transformation of American Agriculture since 1929* (Lexington: University Press of Kentucky, 2008), 98.

2. The Soviets, with the cooperation of large grain companies, quietly purchased large amounts of grain at preinflationary prices in the early 1970s. Prices soared after the Soviet grain deal was announced, but most farmers had already sold their grain at low prices.

3. Daniel Imhoff, ed., *The CAFO Reader: The Tragedy of Industrial Animal Factories* (Healdsburg, CA: Watershed Media, 2010).

4. National Agricultural Statistics Service, "2012 Census Highlights," Report ACH12-4, US Department of Agriculture, modified March 2015, https://www.agcensus.usda.gov/Publications/2012/Online_Resources/Highlights/Hog_and_Pig_Farming/.

5. One of the most notorious incidents of this era involved the shooting of banker Rudy Blythe and chief loan officer Deems Thulin by James Jenkins and Steven Jenkins in Ruthton, Minnesota, in 1983. The bank had foreclosed on the father and son's dairy operation, and the Jenkins took their rage out on unsuspecting bank officials. See Paul Levy, "Twenty Years after the Ruthton Banker Killings: Desperation Still Simmers," *Star Tribune*, October 20, 2003.

6. Michael Pollan, *The Omnivore's Dilemma: A Natural History of Four Meals* (New York: Penguin, 2006), 52–53.

7. Pollan, *Omnivore's Dilemma*.

8. Conkin, *Revolution Down on the Farm*, 132–33.

9. Organic Trade Association, "Maturing U.S. Organic Sector Sees Steady Growth of 6.4 Percent in 2017," April 2018, https://www.ota.com/news/press-releases/20201.

10. Catherine Greene, "Organic Provisions in the 2014 Farm Act," USDA Economic Research Service, updated April 2017, https://www.ers.usda.gov/topics/natural-resources-environment/organic-agriculture/organic-provisions-in-the-2014-farm-act/.

11. Greene, "Organic Provisions."

12. National Agriculture Statistics Service, "2012 Census Highlights," ACH12-3, US Department of Agriculture, updated May 2017, https://www.agcensus.usda.gov/Publications/2012/Online_Resources/Highlights/Farm_Demographics/.

13. Economic Research Service, "Food Dollar Application," US Department of Agriculture, updated March 2018, https://data.ers.usda.gov/reports.aspx?ID=17885&reportPath=/FoodDollar/Real.

14. Mary Hendrickson and William Heffernan, "Concentration of Agricultural Markets," Department of Rural Sociology, University of Missouri, April 2007, web edition.

15. National Agricultural Statistics Service, "Farms, Land in Farms, and Livestock Production 2012 Summary," US Department of Agriculture, February 2013.

16. National Agricultural Statistics Service, "Farms, Land in Farms."

17. Mark Drabenstott, "Do Farm Payments Promote Rural Economic Growth?," *Main Street Economist*, Federal Reserve Bank of Kansas City, March 2005, 4.

18. Phil Davies, "Trouble on the Farm," *fedgazette,* Federal Reserve Bank of Minneapolis, April 12, 2017, https://minneapolisfed.org/publications/fedgazette/trouble-on-the-farm.

19. Traci Bruckner, "Agricultural Subsidies and Farm Consolidation," *American Journal of Economics and Sociology* 75, no. 4 (2016): 645–46, http://onlinelibrary.wiley.com/doi/10.1111/ajes.12151/full.

Chapter 7

1. Dennis Roth, "Food Stamps: 1932–1977: From Provisional and Pilot Programs to Permanent Policy," USDA Economic Research Service, modified August 2015, https://pubs.nal.usda.gov/sites/pubs.nal.usda.gov/files/foodstamps.html.

2. R. Douglas Hurt, "The Great Plains during World War II," University of Nebraska–Lincoln, 2008, http://plainshumanities.unl.edu/homefront/agriculture.html.

3. Hurt, "The Great Plains," 8.

4. Regina A. Galer-Unti, *Hunger and Food Assistance Policy in the United States* (New York: Garland, 1995).

5. Joanne Guthrie, "National School Lunch Program," USDA Economic Research Service, October 5, 2016, https://www.ers.usda.gov/topics/food-nutrition-assistance/child-nutrition-programs/national-school-lunch-program.aspx.

6. "Congress Overhauls Food Stamp Program," *CQ Almanac* 33 (1977): 457–70, http://library.cqpress.com/cqalmanac/cqal77-1203222.

7. Office of Budget and Program Analysis, "FY 2016 Budget Summary and Performance Plan," US Department of Agriculture, 2016, https://www.obpa.usda.gov/budsum/fy16budsum.pdf.

8. Economic Research Service, "Key Statistics and Graphics," US Department of Agriculture, updated October 4, 2017, https://www.ers.usda.gov/topics/food-nutrition-assistance/food-security-in-the-us/key-statistics-graphics/#insecure.

9. Steven Carlson et al., "SNAP Works for America's Children," Center on Budget and Policy Priorities, September 2016, https://www.cbpp.org/research/food-assistance/snap-works-for-americas-children#_ftn1.

10. James Mabil and Jim Ohls, "Supplemental Nutrition Assistance Program Participation Is Associated with an Increase in Household Food Security in a National Evaluation," *Journal of Nutrition* 145, no. 2 (2015): 344–51.

11. Stephanie Ettinger de Cuba et al., "The SNAP Vaccine: Boosting Children's Health," Children's Health Watch, February 2012, http://childrenshealthwatch.org/the-snap-vaccine-boosting-childrens-health/.

12. Edward Frongillo, Diana Jyoti, and Sonya Jones, "Food Stamp Program Participation Is Associated with Better Academic Learning among School Children," *Journal of Nutrition* 136, no. 4 (2006): 1077–80.

13. Hilary Hoynes, Diane Whitmore Schanzenbach, and Douglas Almond, "Long-Run Impacts of Childhood Access to the Safety Net," *American Economic Review* 106, no. 4 (2016): 903–34.

14. Peter Pringle, ed., *A Place at the Table: The Crisis of 49 Million Hungry Americans and How to Solve It* (New York: Public Affairs, 2013).

15. The USDA's Thrifty Food Plan is a tool intended to help individuals on food assistance have a healthy diet. TFP is meant to "represen[t] a minimal cost diet based on up-to-date dietary recommendations, food composition data, food habits, and food price information." TFP is also the basis for maximum food assistance allotments. See Andrea Carlson et al., "Thrifty Food Plan 2006," US Department of Agriculture Center for Nutrition Policy and Promotion, April 2007, http://www.cnpp.usda.gov/Publications/FoodPlans/MiscPubs/TFP2006Report.pdf.

16. Carlson et al., "Thrifty Food Plan 2006."

17. Tatiana Andreyeva, Amanda Tripp, and Marlene Schwartz, "Dietary Quality of Americans by Supplemental Nutrition Assistance Program Participation Status: A Systematic Review," *American Journal of Preventative Medicine* 49, no. 4 (2015): 594–604.

18. Food and Nutrition Service, "Diet Quality of Americans by SNAP Participation Status: Data from the National Health and Nutrition Examination Survey, 2007–2010," US Department of Agriculture, May 2015.

Chapter 8

1. Natural Resources Conservation Service, "USDA to Invest in Prairie Pothole Landscape Effort," US Department of Agriculture, accessed June 2017, https://www.nrcs.usda.gov/wps/portal/nrcs/detail/national/home/?cid=STELPRDB1245728.

2. "Cover Crops and CAFOS: An Analysis of 2016 EQIP Spending," January 12, 2017, *National Sustainable Agriculture Coalition*, http://sustainableagriculture.net/blog/eqip-fy2016-analysis/.

3. Steve Davies, "Senators from Drought-Ridden States Seek More Help from USDA," July 5, 2017, *Agri-Pulse,* https://www.agri-pulse.com/articles/9497-senators-from-drought-ridden-states-seek-more-help-from-usda.

4. Davies, "Senators from Drought-Ridden States."

5. Ronald Reynolds, "The Conservation Reserve Program and Duck Production in the U.S. Prairie Pothole Region," in *Fish and Wildlife Benefits of Farm Bill Conservation Programs, 2000–2005 Update,* US Department of Agriculture Natural Resources Conservation Service and Farm Service Agency, 35.

6. The 2002 Farm Bill provided funding for an additional 1 million acres of wetland set-asides and restoration, mostly in the southeastern bottomland forests that should never have been farmed in the first place.

7. "The lower 48 states had an estimated 220 million acres of wetlands and streams in precolonial times, but 115 million acres of them had been destroyed by 1997." In John Heilprin, "U.S. Reports Increase in Wetland Acreage: Bush Administration Figures Are Disputed as Being Misleading," Associated Press, *San Francisco Chronicle,* March 31, 2006, A2.

8. More than 80 percent of species use aquatic habitats at some point in their life cycle. Creek corridors are probably the single most important wildlife linkages because they connect all other habitats and lie at the heart of an ecosystem.

9. Natural Resources Conservation Service, "Restoring America's Wetlands: A Private Lands Conservation Success Story," US Department of Agriculture, https://www.nrcs.usda.gov/Internet/FSE_DOCUMENTS/stelprdb1045079.pdf.

10. Representative Ron Kind's "Healthy Farms, Foods, and Fuels Act of 2006" called for a doubling of water protection incentives to $2 billion per year and a restoration of 3 million acres of wetlands.

11. Sixty percent of EQIP funds were committed to livestock operations.

12. Natural Resources Conservation Service, "Wetlands Reserve Program," accessed June 2017, https://www.nrcs.usda.gov/wps/portal/nrcs/main/national/programs/easements/wetlands/.

13. Megan Stubbs, "Agricultural Conservation: A Guide to Programs," CRS Report for Congress R40763, Congressional Research Service, April 17, 2018, https://fas.org/sgp/crs/misc/R40763.pdf.

14. "2014 Farm Bill Drill Down: The Bill by the Numbers," *National Sustainable Agriculture Coalition,* February 4, 2014, http://sustainableagriculture.net/blog/2014-farm-bill-by-numbers/.

15. "Environmental Quality Incentives Program," Environmental Working Group, updated 2017, https://conservation.ewg.org/about_eqip.php.

16. National Sustainable Agriculture Coalition, "What Is in the 2014 Farm Bill for Sustainable Farms and Food Systems?," January 2014, http://sustainableagriculture.net/blog/2014-farm-bill-outcomes/#LRFS.

Chapter 9

1. Thomas Fogarty, "Freedom to Farm? Not Likely," *USA Today,* January 2, 2002, https://usatoday30.usatoday.com/money/covers/2002-01-03-bcovthu.htm.

2. Daryll Ray and Harwood Schaffer, "The 1996 'Freedom to Farm' Farm Bill," *MidAmerica Farmer Grower* 35, no. 3 (2014).

3. Scott Marlow, "The Non-Wonk Guide to Understanding Federal Commodity Payments" (Pittsboro, NC: Rural Advancement Foundation International–USA, 2005), 3.

4. Marlow, "The Non-Wonk Guide."

5. US Government Accountability Office, "Agricultural Conservation: USDA Needs to Better Ensure Protection of Highly Erodible Cropland and Wetlands," Report GAO-03-418, 2003.

6. Dan Morgan, "The Farm Bill and Beyond," Economic Policy Paper Series (Washington, DC: German Marshall Fund of the United States, January 2010), 13.

Chapter 10

1. Dottie Rosenbaum, "Farm Bill Contains Significant Domestic Nutrition Improvements," Center on Budget and Policy Priorities, July 1, 2008, http://www.cbpp.org/cms/?fa=view&id=358.

2. Alisha Coleman-Jensen, "Food Insecurity in U.S. Households Essentially Unchanged from 2013, but Down from 2011 High," US Department of Agriculture, September 9, 2015, https://www.usda.gov/media/ blog/2015/09/9/food-insecurity-us -households-essentially-unchanged-2013-down-2011-high.

3. National Sustainable Agriculture Coalition, "2014 Farm Bill Drill-Down: The Bill by the Numbers," February 4, 2014, http:// sustainableagriculture.net/blog/2014-farm-bill-by-numbers/.

4. Renée Johnson et al., "The 2008 Farm Bill: Major Provisions and Legislative Action," CRS Report for Congress RL34696, Congressional Research Service, updated November 6, 2008.

5. Economic Research Service, "Agricultural Act of 2014: Highlights and Implications," US Department of Agriculture, updated April 3, 2017, https://www.ers.usda.gov/agricultural-act-of-2014-highlights-and-implications/.

6. Economic Research Service, "Agricultural Act of 2014."

7. Economic Research Service, "Agricultural Act of 2014."

8. "Industry Statistics and Projected Growth," Organic Trade Association, updated 2017, https://www.ota.com/resources /market-analysis.

9. "The Cost of Organic Food," *Consumer Reports,* March 19, 2015, https://www.consumerreports.org/cro/news/2015/03 /cost-of-organic-food/index.htm.

10. Dominika Średnicka-Tober et al., "Higher PUFA and n-3 PUFA, Conjugated Linoleic Acid, α-Tocopherol and Iron, but Lower Iodine and Selenium Concentrations in Organic Milk: A Systematic Literature Review and Meta- and Redundancy Analyses," *British Journal of Nutrition* 115 (2016): 1043–60.

Chapter 11

1. Environmental Working Group, "2014 Farm Subsidy Database," http://farm.ewg.org/region.php?fips=00000.

2. Randy Schnepf, "Farm Safety-Net Payments Under the 2014 Farm Bill: Comparison by Program Crop," Congressional Research Service, August 11, 2017.

3. Colin O'Neill, "Are Billionaires Getting Crop Insurance Subsidies? We Still Don't Know," Environmental Working Group, April 28, 2016, http://www.ewg.org/agmag/2016/04/are-billionaires-getting-crop-insurance-subsidies-we-still-don-t-know.

4. Robert Hoppe, "Structure and Finances of U.S. Farms: Family Farm Report, 2014 Edition," USDA Economic Research Service, December 2014, https://www.ers.usda.gov/publications/pub-details/?pubid=43916.

5. Environmental Working Group, "2014 Farm Subsidy Database."

6. "Government Payments by Program," USDA Economic Research Service, updated February 7, 2018, https://data.ers.usda.gov/reports.aspx?ID=17833.

7. "Highlights from the February 2018 Farm Income Forecast," USDA Economic Research Service, updated February 20, 2018, https://www.ers.usda.gov/topics/farm-economy/farm-sector-income-finances/highlights-from-the-farm-income-forecast.

8. Timothy Wise, "Understanding the Farm Problem: Six Common Errors in Presenting Farm Statistics," Global Development and Environment Institute, Tufts University, March 2005, 12.

9. "United States Top Recipients 1995–2014," Environmental Working Group Farm Subsidy Database, accessed July 1, 2017, http://farm.ewg.org/top_recips.php?fips=00000&progcode=totalfarm&regionname=theUnitedStates.

10. Michael Langemeier, "Farm Machinery Costs and Custom Rates," May 2017, Purdue Center for Commercial Agriculture, https://ag.purdue.edu/commercialag/Pages/ Resources/Management-Strategy/Machinery-Economics/Farm-Machinery-Costs-and-Custom-Rates.aspx.

11. Don Dodson, "How Much Is That Combine in the Window?," November 2, 2014, *News-Gazette* (Champaign, IL), http://www.news-gazette.com/news/business/2014-11-02/how-much-combine-window.html.

12. Associated Press, "Prince Gets Texas' Biggest Farm Subsidy: $2.2 Million Granted on Holdings Larger than Lichtenstein," *Los Angeles Times*, December 9, 1986, http://articles.latimes.com/1986-12-09/news/mn-1880_1_farm-subsidy.

13. Dan Chapman, Ken Foskett, and Megan Clarke, "How Savvy Growers Can Double, or Triple, Subsidy Dollars," *Atlanta Journal-Constitution*, October 2, 2006.

14. Dan Chapman, Ken Foskett, and Megan Clarke, "How Your Tax Dollars Prop Up Big Growers and Squeeze the Little Guy," *Atlanta Journal-Constitution,* October 1, 2006.

15. Forrest Laws, "GAO Report Sheds Little Light on Payment Limit Rules," Southwest Farm Press, July 1, 2004.

16. "Options for Reducing the Deficit: 2017 to 2026," Congressional Budget Office, December 2016, https://www.cbo.gov/publication/52142.

17. Anne Weir Schechinger, "Congressional Budget Office: Farm Subsidies Costing Taxpayers $7.5 Billion More than Expected," Environmental Working Group, June 30, 2017, http://www.ewg.org/agmag/2017/06/congressional-budget-office-farm-subsidies-costing-taxpayers-75-billion-more-expected.

18. "Milking Taxpayers," *The Economist*, February 12, 2015, http://www.economist.com/news/united-states/21643191-crop-prices-fall-farmers-grow-subsidies-instead-milking-taxpayers.

19. Environmental Working Group, "Members of Congress Collect at Least $9.5 Million in Farm Subsidies," June 2016, http://www.ewg.org/agmag/2016/06/members-congress-collect-least-95-million-farm-subsidies.

20. "Milking Taxpayers."

21. Elanor Starmer and Timothy Wise, "Feeding at the Trough," Tufts University Global Development and Environment Institute, Policy Brief No. 07-03, December 2007.

22. Food and Water Watch and Public Health Institute, "Beyond Subsidies: Dispelling Common Myths about Public Health and the Farm Bill," Summer 2011.

23. Patrick Canning, "A Revised and Expanded Food Dollar Series: A Better Understanding of Our Food Costs," ERR-114, USDA Economic Research Service, February 2011.

24. Tim Hearden, "Farm Subsidies: Industry Defends Need for Rice Aid," Capital Press, July 28, 2011, http://www.capitalpress .com/TH-subsidy-california-w-photos-infobox-072911; California Department of Food and Agriculture, "Agricultural Statistical Review," California Agricultural Resource Directory 2010–2011.

25. Heather Cooley et al., "Impacts of California's Ongoing Drought: Agriculture," Pacific Institute, August 2015; "California Agricultural Statistics Review, 2014–2015," California Department of Food and Agriculture, 2015, https://www.cdfa.ca.gov/statistics /PDFs/2015Report.pdf; "California Agricultural Statistics, Crop Year 2013," USDA National Agricultural Statistics Service, 2014.

26. Environmental Working Group, "2014 Farm Subsidy Database."

27. "2012 Census of Agriculture: Specialty Crops, Vol. 2, Part 8," USDA National Agricultural Statistics Service.

28. "2012 Census of Agriculture: Specialty Crops."

Chapter 12

1. "Who Owns US Farmland and How Will It Change?" National Sustainable Agriculture Coalition. September 2015, http:// sustainableagriculture.net/blog/total-2014-results/.

2. USDA Economic Research Service, "U.S. Agricultural Trade Data Update," updated May 4, 2018, https://www.ers.usda .gov/data-products/foreign-agricultural-trade-of-the-united-states-fatus/us-agricultural-trade-data-update/.

3. For instance, Tyson, Cargill, Swift, and National Beef Packing Co. control 83.5 percent of the beef-packing market. Smithfield, Tyson, Swift, and Hormel control 64 percent of pork packing. Cargill, Archer Daniels Midland (ADM), ConAgra, and Cereal Food Processors control 63 percent of flour processing. ADM, Bunge, and Cargill control 71 percent of the soybean crushing market. Similar statistics unfold for corn, soybean oil, poultry, turkey, and many other markets. Richard C. Longworth, *Caught in the Middle: America's Heartland in the Age of Globalism* (New York: Bloomsbury, 2009).

4. Conkin, *A Revolution Down on the Farm: The Transformation of American Agriculture since 1929* (Lexington: University Press of Kentucky, 2008).

5. Latetia V. Moore and Frances E. Thompson, "Adults Meeting Fruit and Vegetable Intake Recommendations—United States, 2013," *Morbidity and Mortality Weekly Report* 64, no. 26 (2015): 709–13.

Chapter 13

1. Joseph Stiglitz, "Cotton Bailout: King Cotton's Tyranny: U.S. Subsidies Unfairly Cut," *Atlanta Journal Constitution*, October 8, 2006.

2. Heinz Strubenhoff, "The WTO's Decision to End Agricultural Export Subsidies Is Good News for Farmers and Consumers," *Brookings Institution*, February 8, 2016, https://www.brookings.edu/blog/future-development/2016/02/08/the-wtos-decision -to-end-agricultural-export-subsidies-is-good-news-for-farmers-and-consumers/.

3. US cotton farmers receive an average of $230 per acre in subsidies.

4. Terry Townsend, "Cotton and the 2104 Farm Bill: Proof the WTO Matters," *Choices*, July 1, 2015, https://agfax.com/2015 /07/01/cotton-2014-farm-bill-proof-wto-matters/.

5. Renée Johnson, "Previewing a 2018 Farm Bill," Congressional Research Service, March 15, 2017.

6. Anne Weir Schechinger, "New USDA Subsidy Program Will Send Hundreds of Millions of Dollars to Cotton Farmers," Environmental Working Group, March 8, 2018, https://www.ewg.org/agmag/2018/03/new-usda-subsidy-program-will-send-hundreds-millions-dollars-cotton-farmers#.Wx5qGiOB2A8.

7. William Miao, "Removal of Agricultural Subsidies in New Zealand," Environmental Performance Index, Yale University, January 14, 2014, http://archive.epi.yale.edu/case-study/removal-agricultural-subsidies-new-zealand.

8. "US Reports Major Shift in Farm Subsidy Focus under 2014 Farm Bill," *Bridges* 21, no. 2 (January 26, 2017), http://www.ictsd.org/bridges-news/bridges/news/us-reports-major-shift-in-farm-subsidy-focus-under-2014-farm-bill.

9. Peter Shelton, "Can the US Farm Bill and EU Common Agricultural Policy Address 21st Century Global Food Security?," International Food Policy Research Institute, July 23, 2014.

10. Dieter Helm, "Agriculture after Brexit," *Oxford Review of Economic Policy* 33, no. S1 (2017): S124–33.

11. Mark A. McMinimy, "TPP: American Agriculture and the TransPacific Partnership (TPP) Agreement," Congressional Research Service, August 30, 2016, https://fas.org/sgp/crs/misc/R44337.pdf.

12. Leslie Shaffer, "Former US Trade Representative: Ditching TPP 'Devastating' for Farmers," *CNBC*, January 24, 2017, http://www.cnbc.com/2017/01/23/former-us-trade-representative-ditching-tpp-devastating-for-farmers.html.

Chapter 14

1. John Pickford, "New Zealand's Hardy Farm Spirit," *BBC News*, October 16, 2004, http://news.bbc.co.uk/2/hi/programmes/from_our_own_correspondent/3747430.stm.

2. Pickford, "New Zealand's Hearty Farm Spirit."

3. Laura Sayre, "Farming without Subsidies?," Rodale Institute, March 20, 2003, http://www.newfarm.org/features/0303/newzealand_subsidies.shtml.

4. Stephen T. Morris, "Sheep and Beef Cattle Production Systems," in *Ecosystem Services in New Zealand—Conditions and Trends*, J. R. Dymond, ed. (Lincoln, New Zealand: Manaaki Whenua Press, 2013).

5. Ramesh Baskaran, Ross Cullen, and Sergio Colombo, "Estimating Values of Environmental Impacts of Dairy Farming in New Zealand," https://researcharchive.lincoln.ac.nz/bitstream/handle/10182/4797/baskaran_nzae_09.pdf;sequence=1.

6. New Zealand Winegrowers, "Annual Report 2016," *New Zealand Wine*, 2016, https://www.nzwine.com/en/news-media/statistics-reports/new-zealand-winegrowers-annual-report/.

7. Sayre, "Farming without Subsidies?"

8. World Bank, *Global Economic Prospects 2004: Realizing the Development Promise of the Doha Agenda* (Washington, DC: World Bank Publications, 2003).

9. Vangelis Vitalis, "Agricultural Subsidy Reform and Its Implications for Sustainable Development: The New Zealand Experience," *Environmental Sciences* 4, no. 1 (2007): 21–40.

10. "New Zealand's Two-Way Trade with China More than Triples over the Decade," *Stats New Zealand*, March 1, 2018, https://www.stats.govt.nz/news/new-zealands-two-way-trade-with-china-more-than-triples-over-the-decade.

11. "Trade with China Nearly Tripled in Past Decade," *Stats New Zealand*, September 6, 2016, http://www.stats.govt.nz/browse_for_stats /industry_sectors/imports_and_exports/trade-china-tripled-decade.aspx.

12. Baskaran, Cullen, and Colombo, "Estimating Values of Environmental Impacts."

13. Zhaohai Bai et al., "Global Environmental Costs of China's Thirst for Milk," *Global Change Biology* 24, no. 5 (2018): 2198–2211.

14. Jasmijn de Boo, "New Zealand's Dirty Dairy," *Huffington Post*, February 13, 2018, https://www.huffingtonpost.com/jasmijn -de-boo/new-zealands-dirty-dairy_b_14717214.html?guccounter=1.

Chapter 15

1. Eric A. Finkelstein et al., "Annual Medical Spending Attributable to Obesity: Payer-and Service-Specific Estimates," *Health Affairs* 28, no. 5 (2009): w822–31.

2. Dana Gunders, "Wasted: How America Is Losing Up to 40 Percent of Its Food from Farm to Fork to Landfill," National Resources Defense Council Issue Paper, August 2012.

3. ReFED, "27 Solutions to Food Waste," accessed February 17, 2018, http://www.refed.com/?sort=economic-value-per-ton.

4. ReFED, "27 Solutions to Food Waste."

5. Erwan Monier, Liyu Xu, and Richard Snyder, "Uncertainty in Future Agro-Climate Projections in the United States and Benefits of Greenhouse Gas Mitigation," *Environmental Research Letters* 11, no. 5 (2016).

6. "Sources of Greenhouse Gas Emissions," US Environmental Protection Agency, updated April 14, 2017, https://www.epa.gov /ghgemissions/sources-greenhouse-gas-emissions.

7. Emily Broad Leib et al., "Opportunities to Reduce Waste in the 2018 Farm Bill," Harvard Food Law and Policy Clinic, May 2017, https://furtherwithfood.org/wp-content/uploads/2017/05/Food-Waste-in-the-Farm-Bill-report_v10.pdf.

8. Food policy councils are coalitions of local stakeholders and government representatives who discuss stressors on the local food system and work together to promote healthy and sustainable food policies while increasing awareness among local citizens.

Chapter 16

1. Agency for Healthcare Research and Quality, "Medical Expenditure Panel Survey," US Department of Health and Human Services, accessed May 28, 2018, https://meps.ahrq.gov/data_stats/quick_tables_results.jsp?component=1&subcomponent=0 &tableSeries=2&year=.

2. Food insecurity means that a household had limited or uncertain availability of food or limited or uncertain ability to acquire acceptable foods in socially acceptable ways (i.e., without resorting to emergency food supplies, scavenging, stealing, or other unusual coping strategies). Mark Nord et al., "Household Food Security in the United States, 2009," USDA Economic Research Service, web edition.

3. "Overweight in Children," American Heart Association, July 5, 2016, http://www.heart.org/HEARTORG/HealthyLiving /HealthyKids/ChildhoodObesity/Overweight-in-Children_UCM_304054_Article.jsp#.WWo68tPytE4.

4. "Obesity and Overweight," CDC National Center for Health Statistics, updated May 3, 2017, https://www.cdc.gov/nchs /fastats/obesity-overweight.htm.

5. "Chronic Diseases: The Leading Causes of Death and Disability in the United States," Centers for Disease Control and Prevention, updated June 28, 2017, https://www.cdc.gov/chronicdisease/overview/index.htm.

6. "Shifts Needed to Align with Healthy Eating Patterns," *Current Eating Patterns in the United States*, 2016, https://health.gov/dietaryguidelines/2015/guidelines/chapter-2/current-eating-patterns-in-the-united-states/.

7. Hester Jeon, "Fizzling Out: Soda Producers Will Refresh Product Lines to Decelerate Falling Demand," *IBISWorld Industry Report*, November 2013, http://studylib.net/doc/8071516/ibisworld-industry-report-31211a-soda.

8. US Department of Agriculture and US Department of Health and Human Services, "Dietary Guidelines for Americans, 2010" (Washington, DC: US Government Printing Office, 2010).

9. "Food Marketing to Kids," Public Health Law Center, updated 2017, http://www.publichealthlawcenter.org/topics/healthy-eating/food-marketing-kids.

10. "Out of Balance: Marketing of Soda, Candy, Snacks, and Fast Foods Drowns Out Healthful Messages," Consumers Union and California Pan-Ethnic Health Network, September 2005.

11. "Childhood Obesity Facts," Centers for Disease Control and Prevention, updated January 25, 2017, https://www.cdc.gov/healthyschools/obesity/facts.htm.

12. Kenneth E. Thorpe, *The Future Costs of Obesity: National and State Estimates of the Impact of Obesity on Direct Health Care Expenses* (Minnetonka, MN: United Heath Foundation, November 2009), 2.

13. Adam Gilden Tsai, David F. Williamson, and Henry Glick, "Direct Medical Cost of Overweight and Obesity in the United States: A Quantitative Systematic Review," *Obesity Reviews: An Official Journal of the International Association for the Study of Obesity* 12, no. 1 (2011): 50–61.

14. Gary Paul Nabhan, *Why Some Like It Hot: Food, Genes, and Cultural Diversity* (Washington, DC: Island Press, 2004), 175–77.

15. "Nutrient Content of the U.S. Food Supply, 1909–2010," USDA Center for Nutrition Policy and Promotion, 2014, https://www.cnpp.usda.gov/USFoodSupply-1909-2010.

16. "Summary Findings," USDA Economic Research Service, updated January 9, 2017, https://www.ers.usda.gov/data-products/food-availability-per-capita-data-system/summary-findings/.

17. "Agriculture Fact Book 2001–2002," USDA, Economic Research Service, chap. 2, web edition.

18. Drew Desilver, "What's on Your Table? How America's Diet Has Changed Over the Decades," Pew Research Center, December 13, 2016, http://www.pewresearch.org/fact-tank/2016/12/13/whats-on-your-table-how-americas-diet-has-changed-over-the-decades/.

19. "Dietary Guidelines for Americans, 2010," USDA Center for Nutrition Policy and Promotion, January 2011, A-2.

20. Karen R. Siegel, Kai McKeever Bullard, and Giuseppina Imperatore, "Association of Higher Consumption of Foods Derived from Subsidized Commodities with Adverse Cardiometabolic Risk among US Adults," *Journal of the American Medical Association* 176, no. 8 (2016): 1124–32.

21. Food and Water Watch and Public Health Institute, "Beyond Subsidies: Dispelling Common Myths about Public Health and the Farm Bill," White Paper, 2011.

22. Physicians Committee for Responsible Medicine, "Agricultural Policies versus Health Policies," 2011, http://www.pcrm.org /health/reports/agriculture-and-health-policies-ag-versus-health.

23. "Dairy Data," USDA Economic Research Service, updated July 13, 2017, https://www.ers.usda.gov/data-products/dairy-data/.

24. "Table 1. Top Food Sources of Saturated Fats among U.S. Population, 2005–2006 NHANES," National Cancer Institute Division of Cancer Control and Population Sciences, updated May 2016, https://epi.grants.cancer.gov/diet/foodsources/.

25. Michael Moss, "While Worrying about Fat, U.S. Pushes Cheese Sales," *New York Times*, November 6, 2010, web edition.

26. Heather Schoonover and Mark Muller, "Food without Thought: How U.S. Farm Policy Contributes to Obesity," Institute for Agriculture and Trade Policy, 2006.

27. Leah Zerbe, "Factory Farms Use 30 Million Pounds of Antibiotics a Year (and You're Eating Some of It)," Rodale News, December 21, 2010, web edition.

28. Center for Veterinary Medicine, "2015 Summary Report on Antimicrobials Sold or Distributed for Use in Food-Producing Animals," US Food and Drug Administration, December 2016, https://www.fda.gov/downloads/ForIndustry/UserFees/Animal DrugUserFeeActADUFA/UCM534243.pdf.

29. "About Antimicrobial Resistance," Centers for Disease Control and Prevention, updated April 6, 2017, https://www.cdc.gov /drugresistance/about.html.

30. Zerbe, "Factory Farms."

31. "Antimicrobial Resistant," Centers for Disease Control and Prevention, updated June 12, 2017, https://www.cdc.gov/drug resistance/index.html.

32. Laura Jeffers, "How You Can Avoid Low-Level Arsenic in Rice and Chicken," Cleveland Clinic Health Essentials, February 10, 2015, https://health.clevelandclinic.org/2015/02/how-you-can-avoid-low-level-arsenic-in-rice-and-chicken/.

33. Keeve E. Nachman et al., "Roxarsone, Inorganic Arsenic, and Other Arsenic Species in Chicken: A U.S.-Based Market Basket Sample," *Environmental Health Perspectives* 121, no. 7 (2013): 818–24.

34. Kristin Ohlson, "Dirt First," *Orion Magazine*, April 2016.

35. Dan Charles, "The Gulf of Mexico's Dead Zone Is the Biggest Ever Seen," *The Salt*, National Public Radio, August 3, 2017, http://www.npr.org/sections/thesalt/2017/08/03/541222717/the-gulf-of-mexicos-dead-zone-is-the-biggest-ever-seen.

36. Grace Communications Foundation, "Waste Management," accessed May 4, 2018, http://www.sustainabletable.org/906 /waste-management.

37. Lee Bergquist and Kevin Crowe, "Manure Spills in 2013 the Highest in Seven Years Statewide," *Milwaukee Journal Sentinel*, December 5, 2013.

38. "2016 Cover Crop Survey Analysis," USDA Sustainable Agriculture Research and Education and Conservation Technology Information Center, accessed August 9, 2017, http://www.sare.org/Learning-Center/Topic-Rooms/Cover-Crops/Cover-Crop -Surveys.

39. Mark Bittman et al., "How a National Food Policy Could Save Millions of American Lives," *Washington Post*, November 7, 2014.

Chapter 17

1. Steve Carlson and Zoe Neuberger, "WIC Works: Addressing the Nutrition and Health Needs of Low-Income Families for 40 Years," *Center on Budget and Policy Priorities*, updated March 29, 2017, https://www.cbpp.org/research/food-assistance/wic-works-addressing-the-nutrition-and-health-needs-of-low-income-families.

2. "Healthy School Lunches Improve Kids' Habits," *Pew Charitable Trusts*, April 14, 2016, http://www.pewtrusts.org/en/research-and-analysis/issue-briefs/2016/04/healthy-school-lunches-improve-kids-habits.

3. New America, "The Real Benefits of SNAP," *SNAP to Health*, accessed May 28, 2018, https://www.snaptohealth.org/snap/the-real-benefits-of-the-snap-program/

4. Adam Drewnowski and Petra Eichelsdoerfer, "Can Low-Income Americans Afford a Healthy Diet?," *Nutrition Today* 44, no. 6 (2010): 246–49.

5. Drewnowski and Eichelsdoerfer, "Can Low-Income Americans Afford a Healthy Diet?"

6. Elizabeth Condon et al., "Diet Quality of Americans by SNAP Participation Status: Data from the National Health and Nutrition Examination Survey, 2007–2010," prepared by Walter R. McDonald & Associates, Inc. and Mathematica Policy Research for the USDA Food and Nutrition Service, May 2015.

7. Zach Conrad et al., "Cardiometabolic Mortality by Supplemental Nutrition Assistance Program Participation and Eligibility in the United States," *American Journal of Public Health* 107, no. 3 (2017): 466–74.

8. Anna H. Grummon and Lindsey Smith Taillie, "Nutritional Profile of Supplemental Nutrition Assistance Program Household Food and Beverage Purchases," *American Journal of Clinical Nutrition* 106, no. 1 (2017): 1433–42.

9. "Healthier Food, Healthier People," *PCRM Good Medicine*, Summer 2017.

10. Steven Kull et al., "Americans on SNAP Benefits," University of Maryland School of Public Policy Program for Public Consultation, April 2017.

11. Sara Berg, "AMA Backs Comprehensive Approach Targeting Sugary Drinks," *AMA Wire*, June 14, 2017, https://wire.ama-assn.org/ama-news/ama-backs-comprehensive-approach-targeting-sugary-drinks.

12. Rebecca L. Rivera et al., "SNAP-Ed (Supplemental Nutrition Assistance Program–Education) Increases Long-Term Food Security among Indiana Households with Children in a Randomized Controlled Study," *Journal of Nutrition* 146, no. 11 (2016): 2375–82.

13. Sharon Sugerman et al., "California Adults Increase Fruit and Vegetable Consumption from 1997–2007," *Journal of Nutrition Education and Behavior* 43, no. 4 (2011): S96–S103.

14. Renée Johnson, *The U.S. Trade Situation for Fruit and Vegetable Products,* Congressional Research Service, RL34468, December 1, 2016.

15. "Food Access Research Atlas Documentation," updated December 5, 2017, https://www.ers.usda.gov/data-products/food-access-research-atlas/documentation/.

16. Triada Stampas and William Guillaume Koible, "New York City's Meal Gap 2016 Trends Report," Food Bank for New York City, accessed May 4, 2018, https://www.foodbanknyc.org/wp-content/uploads/Meal-Gap-Trends-Report-2016.pdf.

17. A. Bryce Hoflund, "Urban and Rural Food Deserts in Nebraska," University of Nebraska at Omaha, November 2014.

18. A. Bryce Hoflund, "Urban and Rural Food Deserts in Nebraska."

19. "Rural KS. Grocery Stores Closing," *Topeka (KS) Capital-Journal*, May 22, 2010, web edition.

20. Office of Budget and Program Analysis, "FY 2016 Budget Summary and Annual Performance Plan," US Department of Agriculture, 2016.

21. Office of Budget and Program Analysis, "FY 2018 Budget Summary," US Department of Agriculture, 2018.

22. "Agricultural Production and Prices," USDA Economic Research Service, updated May 5, 2017, https://www.ers.usda.gov/data-products/ag-and-food-statistics-charting-the-essentials/agricultural-production-and-prices/.

23. Mechel S. Paggi and Jay E. Noel, "The U.S. 2008 Farm Bill: Title X and Related Support for the U.S. Specialty Crop Sector," *Choices*, 3rd quarter 2008, web edition.

Chapter 18

1. "The Energy Independence and Security Act: Charting a New Direction for America's Energy Policy," United States Senate Committee on Energy and Natural Resources, web edition, accessed September 21, 2011.

2. US Energy Information Administration, "Oil: Crude and Petroleum Products Explained," updated May 8, 2017, https://www.eia.gov/energyexplained/index.cfm?page=oil_imports.

3. Craig Cox and Andrew Hug, "Driving Under the Influence: Corn Ethanol and Energy Security," Environmental Working Group, June 2010.

4. Robert Wisner, "Ethanol Usage Projections and Corn Balance Sheet," Iowa State University Agricultural Marketing Resource Center, updated December 2015, https://www.extension.iastate.edu/agdm/crops/outlook/cornbalancesheet.pdf.

5. US Energy Information Administration, "Frequently Asked Questions," updated March 2017, https://www.eia.gov/tools/faqs/faq.php?id=27&t=10.

6. Frances Thicke, *A New Vision for Iowa Food and Agriculture* (Fairfield, IA: Mulberrry Knoll, 2010), 95.

7. Alternative Fuels Data Center, "Maps and Data—Global Ethanol Production," US Department of Energy, updated May 2017, https://www.afdc.energy.gov/data/.

8. Robert Rapier, "A Cellulosic Ethanol Milestone," *Forbes,* April 2016, https://www.forbes.com/sites/rrapier/2016/04/26/a-cellulosic-ethanol-milestone/#5c9e8f981072.

9. Craig Cox, personal communication, August 2017.

10. Rapier, "A Cellulosic Ethanol Milestone."

11. Sena Christian, "Is Cellulosic Ethanol the Next Big Thing in Renewable Fuels?," *Earth Island Journal*, January 2015, http://www.earthisland.org/journal/index.php/elist/eListRead/is_cellulosic_ethanol_the_next_big_thing_in_renewable_fuels/.

12. J. E. Campbell, D. B. Lobell, and C. B. Field, "Greater Transportation Energy and GHG Offsets from Bioelectricity than Ethanol," *Science* 324, no. 5930 (May 22, 2009): 1055–57.

13. Christopher R. Knittel, "Corn Belt Moonshine: The Costs and Benefits of U.S. Ethanol Subsidies," American Enterprise Institute, 2011.

14. Paul W. Gallagher, Winnie C. Yee, and Harry S. Baumes, "2015 Energy Balance for the Corn-Ethanol Industry," USDA Office of the Chief Economist, February 2016.

15. Alexander E. Farrell et al. "Ethanol Can Contribute to Energy and Environmental Goals," *Science* 311, no. 5760 (2006): 506–508.

16. Tad W. Patzek, "Thermodynamics of the Corn-Ethanol Biofuel Cycle," *Critical Reviews in Plant Sciences* 23, no. 6 (2004): 519–567.

17. Thicke, *A New Vision*, 95.

18. "ADM Hit by Vote on Ethanol Subsidies; Shares Are Likely Oversold," *Forbes*, June 2011, https://www.forbes.com/sites/ycharts /2011/06/24/adm-hit-by-vote-on-ethanol-subsidies-shares-are-likely-oversold/#266dfca716e7.

19. Renewable Fuels Institute, "Changing the Climate: Ethanol Outlook 2008," February 2008, http://www.ethanolrfa.org/wp -content/uploads/2015/09/RFA_Outlook_2008.pdf.

20. Cox, personal communication.

21. Colin A. Carter and Henry I. Miller, "Corn for Food, Not Fuel," *New York Times,* July 2012, http://www.nytimes.com /2012/07/31/opinion/corn-for-food-not-fuel.html.

22. James Conca, "It's Final—Corn Ethanol Is of No Use," *Forbes*, April 2014, https://www.forbes.com/sites/jamesconca /2014/04/20/its-final-corn-ethanol-is-of-no-use/#a0a4a6767d35.

23. "Findings," USDA Economic Research Service, updated August 8, 2017, https://www.ers.usda.gov/topics/farm-economy /bioenergy/findings/#impacts.

24. Christopher K. Wright and Michael C. Wimberly, "Recent Land Use Change in the Western Corn Belt Threatens Grasslands and Wetlands," *Proceedings of the National Academy of Sciences* 110, no. 10 (2013): 4134–39.

25. Mark Z. Jacobson, "Effects of Ethanol (E85) versus Gasoline Vehicles on Cancer and Mortality in the United States," *Environmental Science and Toxicology* 41, no. 11 (2007): 4150–57.

26. Tom Philpott, "Reviving a Much-Cited, Little-Read Sustainable-Ag Masterpiece," *Grist,* 2007, https://grist.org/article/soil/.

Chapter 19

1. Peter Huber and Mark Mills, *The Bottomless Well: The Twilight of Fuel, the Virtue of Waste, and Why We Will Never Run Out of Energy* (New York: Basic Books, 2005), 7.

2. Patrick Canning and Sarah Rehkamp, "The Relationship between Energy Prices and Food-Related Energy Use in the United States," drawn from *The Role of Fossil Fuels in the U.S. Food System and the American Diet*, USDA Economic Research Service, June 2017, https://www.ers.usda.gov/amber-waves/2017/june/the-relationship-between-energy-prices-and-food-related-energy -use-in-the-united-states/.

3. Estimates of this ratio vary from 6:1 to more than 20:1. The average of all these estimates is around 10:1, which has become the most commonly cited figure. See Simon Fairlie, *Meat: A Benign Extravagance* (White River Junction, VT: Chelsea Green, 2010).

4. Michael Bomford, personal correspondence.

5. Bomford, personal correspondence, interpreting Nathan Pelletier et al., "Comparative Life Cycle Environmental Impacts of Three Beef Production Strategies in the Upper Midwestern United States," *Agricultural Systems* 103, no. 6 (July 2010): 380–89.

6. Claudia Hitaj and Shellye Suttles, "Trends in U.S. Agriculture's Consumption and Production of Energy: Renewable Power, Shale Energy, and Cellulosic Biomass," USDA Economic Research Service, EIB 159, August 2016.

7. Megan Stubbs, "Renewable Energy Programs in the 2008 Farm Bill," Congressional Research Service, December 20, 2010.

8. "2008 Farm Bill Side-by-Side: Title IX: Energy," USDA Economic Research Service, accessed September 14, 2011, web edition.

9. "2008 Farm Bill Side-by-Side."

10. Andy Olsen et al., "Farm Energy Success Stories," Environmental Law and Policy Center, January 2014.

11. "Rural Energy for America Program," National Sustainable Agriculture Coalition, updated October 2016, http://sustainable agriculture.net/publications/grassrootsguide/renewable-energy/renewable-energy-energy-efficiency/.

12. "USDA—Rural Energy for America Program (REAP) Grants," Database of State Incentives for Renewables and Efficiency, updated February 2016, http://programs.dsireusa.org/system/program/detail/917.

13. Olsen et al. "Farm Energy Success Stories."

14. "Frequent Questions about Livestock Biogas Projects," US Environmental Protection Agency, updated October 2016, https://www.epa.gov/agstar/frequent-questions-about-livestock-biogas-projects.

15. "Frequent Questions."

16. Dana Gunders, "Wasted: How America Is Losing Up to 40 of Its Food from Farm to Fork to Landfill," National Resources Defense Council Issue Paper, August 2012.

17. ReFED, "27 Solutions to Food Waste," accessed February 17, 2018, http://www.refed.com/?sort=economic-value-per-ton.

18. ReFED, "27 Solutions."

19. ReFED, "27 Solutions."

20. Support for reducing waste closer to the point of consumption will be addressed in chapter 23.

21. Harvard Food Law and Policy Clinic, "Opportunities to Reduce Food Waste in the 2018 Farm Bill," May 2017.

22. Harvard Food Law and Policy Clinic, "Opportunities to Reduce Food Waste."

23. Economic Research Service, "Fertilizer Use and Markets," USDA, updated November 9, 2016, https://www.ers.usda.gov/topics /farm-practices-management/chemical-inputs/fertilizer-use-markets/.

24. Mark Ribaudo, "Reducing Agriculture's Nitrogen Footprint: Are New Policy Approaches Needed?," *Amber Waves*, September 2011, web edition.

25. Ryan Stockwell and Eliav Bitan, "Future Friendly Farming," National Wildlife Federation, August 2011, http://www.nwf.org /~/media/PDFs/Wildlife/FutureFriendlyFarmingReport.pdf.

26. Pete Smith and Mercedes Bustamante, coordinating lead authors, "Agriculture, Forestry and Other Land Use (AFOLU)," chapter 11 in *Climate Change 2014: Mitigation of Climate Change: Contribution of Working Group III to the Fifth Assessment Report of the Intergovernmental Panel on Climate Change*, ed. O. Edenhofer et al. (Cambridge, UK, and New York: Cambridge University Press, 2014), https://www.ipcc.ch/report/ar5/wg3/.

27. "Sources of Greenhouse Gas Emissions," US Environmental Protection Agency, updated April 2017, https://www.epa.gov/ghgemissions/sources-greenhouse-gas-emissions.

28. Johannes Kotschi and Karl Müller-Sämann, "The Role of Organic Agriculture in Mitigating Climate Change: A Scoping Study," International Federation of Organic Agriculture Movements, May 2004.

29. Stephen Russell, "Everything You Need to Know about Agricultural Emissions," World Resources Institute, May 2014, http://www.wri.org/blog/2014/05/everything-you-need-know-about-agricultural-emissions.

30. Helene York, "What's the Fairest Way to Eat Food?," *The Atlantic*, December 22, 2009, https://www.theatlantic.com/health/archive/2009/12/whats-the-fairest-way-to-eat-food/32432/.

31. Christopher L. Weber and H. Scott Matthews, "Food-Miles and the Relative Climate Impacts of Food Choices in the United States," *Environmental Science and Technology* 42 (2008): 3508.

32. Ann Perry, "Putting Dairy Cows Out to Pasture: An Environmental Plus," *Agricultural Research,* May-June 2011, 18–19.

33. Quoted in Perry, "Putting Dairy Cows Out to Pasture," 19.

34. Jane M-F Johnson et al. "Agricultural Opportunities to Mitigate Greenhouse Gas Emissions," *Environmental Pollution* 150 (2007): 113.

35. Paul Hanley, "Study Debunks Myths on Organic Farms," *Star Phoenix*, September 27, 2011, web edition.

36. "Soil Carbon and Organic Farming," Soil Association, November 2009, web edition.

37. "The Clean Power Plan: Keeping Climate Progress on Track," Natural Resources Defense Council, June 2016.

38. "Lazard's Levelized Cost of Energy Analysis—Version 9.0," Lazard, 2015, https://www.lazard.com/perspective/levelized-cost-of-energy-analysis-90/.

Chapter 20

1. Roger Classen, "Do Farm Programs Encourage Native Grassland Losses?," *Amber Waves*, September 2011, 2.

2. Tyler J. Lark, J. Meghan Salmon, and Holly K. Gibbs, "Cropland Expansion Outpaces Agricultural and Biofuel Policies in the United States," *Environmental Research Letters* 10, no. 4 (2015): 1–11.

3. National Sustainable Agriculture Coalition, "2014 Farm Bill Drill Down: Conservation—Easements, CRP, and Energy," February 10, 2014, http://sustainableagriculture.net/blog/2014-farm-bill-acep-crp-energy/.

4. Sean L. Maxwell et al., "Biodiversity: The Ravages of Guns, Nets and Bulldozers," *Nature* 636 (August 10, 2016): 144.

5. Lori Ann Burd, "EPA Analysis: 97 Percent of Endangered Species Threatened by Two Common Pesticides," Center for Biological Diversity, April 7, 2016, https://biologicaldiversity.org/news/press_releases/2016/pesticides-04-07-2016.html.

6. American Farmland Trust, "Farmland," 2017, https://www.farmland.org/our-work/areas-of-focus/farmland.

7. Sustainable Agriculture Coalition, "No Time for Delay: A Sustainable Agriculture Agenda for the 2007 Farm Bill," 2006, 10.

8. Justin Fritscher, "USDA to Invest $4 Million for Honey Bee Food Sources on Private Lands," USDA Natural Resources Conservation Service, October 6, 2015, https://www.nrcs.usda.gov/wps/portal/nrcs/detail/national/newsroom/releases/?cid=nrcseprd405226.

9. Natural Resources Conservation Service, "Greater Sage Grouse," USDA, updated 2016, https://www.nrcs.usda.gov/wps/portal/nrcs/detail/national/plantsanimals/fishwildlife/?cid=stelprdb1047022.

10. Natural Resources Conservation Service, "Greater Sage Grouse," 49.

11. Arthur Allen addressed this issue in "The Conservation Reserve Enhancement Program," in *Fish and Wildlife Benefits of Farm Bill Conservation Programs, 2000–2005 Update*, ed. J. B. Haufler, Wildlife Society Technical Review 05-2, October 2005, 123.

12. "2007 Natural Resources Inventory," Natural Resources Conservation Service, April 2010, web edition.

13. Ronald E. Reynolds, "The Conservation Reserve Program and duck production in the United States' Prairie Pothole Region," in *The Conservation Reserve Program—Planting for the Future: Proceedings of a National Conference*, ed. A. W. Allen and M. W. Vandever (Fort Collins, CO: US Geological Survey, Biological Resources Discipline, Scientific Investigations Report 2005–5145, 2005), 144–48.

14. Stephen J. Brady, "Highly Erodible Land and Swampbuster Provisions of the 2002 Farm Act," in *Fish and Wildlife Benefits of Farm Bill Conservation Programs, 2000–2005 Update*," ed. J. B. Haufler, Wildlife Society Technical Review 05-2, October 2005, 12.

15. Interagency Agricultural Projections Committee, "USDA Agricultural Projections to 2026," February 2017, https://www.usda.gov/oce/commodity/projections/USDA_Agricultural_Projections_to_2026.pdf.

16. Economic Research Service, "Conservation," USDA, updated April 18, 2017, https://www.ers.usda.gov/agricultural-act-of-2014-highlights-and-implications/conservation/.

17. Hannah J. Ryan, "Long-Time Advocate for Conservation, Randy Gray, Receives Prestigious Award," *Intermountain West Joint Venture*, May 20, 2013, https://iwjv.org/news/long-time-advocate-conservation-randy-gray-receives-prestigious-award.

18. Christopher K. Wright and Michael C. Wimberly, "Recent Land Use Change in the Western Corn Belt Threatens Grasslands and Wetlands," *Proceedings of the National Academy of Sciences* 110, no. 10 (2013): 4134–39.

19. Farm Service Agency, "Conservation Reserve Program Annual Summary and Enrollment Statistics FY 2012," US Department of Agriculture, 2012, https://www.fsa.usda.gov/Assets/USDA-FSA-Public/usdafiles/Conservation/PDF/summary12.pdf.

20. Douglas Johnson, "Grassland Bird Use of Conservation Reserve Program Fields in the Great Plains," *Fish and Wildlife Benefits of Farm Bill Conservation Programs, 2000-2005 Update*, ed. J. B. Haufler, Wildlife Society Technical Review 05-2, October 2005, 26.

21. Jonathan Foley, "The Other Inconvenient Truth: The Crisis in Global Land Use," October 5, *Yale Environment 360*, 2009, https://e360.yale.edu/features/the_other_inconvenient_truth_the_crisis_in_global_land_use.

22. US Committee of the North American Bird Conservation Initiative, "2014 Farm Bill Field Guide to Fish and Wildlife Conservation," April 2015.

23. National Sustainable Agriculture Coalition, "Analysis of CSP Enrollment in FY 2017," December 2017.

24. Tom H. Oliver et al., "Biodiversity and Resilience of Ecosystem Functions," *Cell* 30, no. 11 (2015): 673–84.

25. Fritscher, "USDA to Invest $4 Million."

26. Nicholas W. Calderone, "Insect Pollinated Crops, Insect Pollinators and US Agriculture: Trend Analysis of Aggregate Data for the Period 1992–2009," *PLOS One* 7 no. 5 (2012): e37235.

27. Nathalie Steinhauer et al., "Colony Loss 2016–2017: Preliminary Results," Bee Informed, August 28, 2017, https://beeinformed.org/results/colony-loss-2016-2017-preliminary-results/.

28. J. O. Whitaker Jr., "Food of the Big Brown Bat *Eptesicus fuscus* from Maternity Colonies in Indiana and Illinois," *American Midland Naturalist* 134, no. 2 (1995): 346–50.

29. Cris D. Hein and Michael R. Schirmacher, "Impact of Wind Energy on Bats: A Summary of Our Current Knowledge," *Human–Wildlife Interactions* 10, no. 1 (2016): 19–27.

30. Justin G. Boyles et al., "Economic Importance of Bats in Agriculture," *Science* 332, no. 6025 (2011): 41–42.

31. The Land Institute, "A 50-Year Farm Bill," June 2009, https://landinstitute.org/wp-content/uploads/2016/09/FB-edited-7-6-10.pdf.

32. Marc Ribaudo, "Reducing Agriculture's Nitrogen Footprint: Are New Policy Approaches Needed?," *Amber Waves*, September 2011, web edition.

33. Walter V. Reid, "Capturing the Value of Ecosystem Services to Protect Biodiversity," in *Managing Human-Dominated Ecosystems*, ed. Victoria Hollowell (St. Louis, MO: Botanical Garden Press, 2001), 197–225.

Chaper 21

1. Robert Gottlieb, *Food Justice* (Cambridge, MA: MIT Press, 2014), 87.

2. Division of Preventive Medicine, "2011 Annual Report," Walter Reed Army Institute of Research, Silver Spring, MD, 2011.

3. John M. Shalikashvili et al., "Mission: Readiness, Military Leaders for Kids," September 21, 2010, http://cdn.missionreadiness.org/CNR-Sign-On-Letter-2.pdf.

4. Division of Preventive Medicine, "2011 Annual Report."

5. "Obesity Takes Its Toll on the Military," Associated Press, July 5, 2005.

6. Task Force on Defense Personnel, "Health, Health Care, and a High-Performance Force," Bipartisan Policy Center, March 2017, https://cdn.bipartisanpolicy.org/wp-content/uploads/2017/03/BPC-Defense-Health-Care.pdf.

7. Marian Tanofsky-Kraff et al., "Obesity and the US Military Family," *Obesity* 21, no. 11 (2013): 2205–20.

8. Robert Pear, "U.S. Health Chief, Stepping Down, Issues Warning," *New York Times*, December 4, 2004.

9. Peter Chalk, "Hitting America's Soft Underbelly," Rand National Defense Research Institute, 2004, https://www.rand.org/pubs/monographs/MG135.readonline.html.

10. Jim Monke, "Agroterrorism: Threats and Preparedness," Congressional Research Service, August 13, 2004.

11. Dean Olson, "Agroterrorism: Threats to America's Economy and Food Supply," *FBI Law Enforcement Bulletin*, February 2012, https://leb.fbi.gov/2012/february/agroterrorism-threats-to-americas-economy-and-food-supply.

12. Natural Resources Conservation Service, "Animal Feeding Operations," USDA, accessed September 15, 2017, https://www.nrcs.usda.gov/wps/portal/nrcs/main/national/plantsanimals/livestock/afo/#.

13. Eric Schlosser, *Fast Food Nation: The Dark Side of the All-American Meal* (New York: Houghton Mifflin, 2002).

14. "State Rankings by Hogs and Pigs Inventory," National Pork Board, updated July 8, 2016, http://www.pork.org/pork-quick-facts/home/stats/structure-and-productivity/state-rankings-by-hogs-and-pigs-inventory/.

15. National Agricultural Statistics Service, "Poultry—Production and Value 2016 Summary," USDA, April 2017, http://usda.mannlib.cornell.edu/usda/current/PoulProdVa/PoulProdVa-04-28-2017.pdf.

16. "Facts, Figures, and FAQs," Monterey County Farm Bureau, accessed September 15, 2017, http://montereycfb.com/index.php?page=facts-figures-faqs.

17. Lisa Schnirring, "USDA: Environmental Spread, Multiple Entries Likely Fueled US H7N9 Outbreaks," University of Minnesota Center for Infectious Disease Research and Policy, June 23, 2017, http://www.cidrap.umn.edu/news-perspective/2017/06/usda-environmental-spread-multiple-entries-likely-fueled-us-h7n9-outbreaks.

18. Brie Mazurek, "Remembering the Obamas' Food Legacy," Center for Urban Education about Sustainable Agriculture, January 20, 2017, https://cuesa.org/article/remembering-obamas%E2%80%99-food-legacy.

19. Renée Johnson et al., "The Role of Local Food Systems in U.S. Farm Policy," Congressional Research Service, July 17, 2014, http://nationalaglawcenter.org/wp-content/uploads/assets/crs/R42155.pdf.

20. Renée Johnson, "The Role of Local Food Systems in U.S. Farm Policy," Congressional Research Service, February 18, 2016, https://fas.org/sgp/crs/misc/R44390.pdf.

21. "Grocery Stores Industry," CSIMarket, Inc., updated 2017, https://csimarket.com/Industry/industry_Efficiency.php?ind=1305.

22. USDA National Institute of Food and Agriculture website.

23. A. Bryan Endres and Jody M. Endres, "Homeland Security Planning: What Victory Gardens and Fidel Castro Can Teach Us in Preparing for Food Crises in the United States," *Food and Drug Law Journal* 64, no. 2 (2009): 405–39.

24. "Garden to Table: A 5-Year Look at Food Gardening in America," National Gardening Association, 2014, https://garden.org/special/pdf/2014-NGA-Garden-to-Table.pdf.

25. Economic Research Service, "Overview," USDA, updated June 15, 2017, https://www.ers.usda.gov/topics/rural-economy-population/population-migration/.

26. "Rural America Supplies More Recruits to the Military," Wessel's Living History Farm, accessed September 15, 2017, http://www.livinghistoryfarm.org/farminginthe70s/life_07.html.

27. Abby Wendle, "From War to Plow: Why USDA Wants Veterans to Take Up Farming," National Public Radio, March 3, 2015, http://www.npr.org/sections/thesalt/2015/03/03/390251255/from-war-to-plow-why-usda-wants-veterans-to-take-up-farming.

28. Marion Kalb and Deborah Shore, "Department of Defense Farm to School Program: Frequently Asked Questions," Community Food Security Coalition, http://mda.maryland.gov/farm_to_school/Documents/dod_f2s.pdf.

Chapter 22

1. The Land Institute, "A 50-Year Farm Bill," June 2009, https://landinstitute.org/wp-content/uploads/2016/09/FB-edited-7-6-10.pdf.

2. Judy Swenson, "CRWP, LSP Test New Strategy," October 14, 2010, http://www.montenews.com/article/20101014/NEWS/310149940.

3. Lauren C. Ponisio and Paul R. Ehrlich, "Diversification, Yield and a New Agricultural Revolution: Problems and Prospects," *Sustainability* 8, no. 11 (2016): 1118.

4. Claire Kremen, "Reframing the Land-Sparing/Land-Sharing Debate for Biodiversity Conservation," *Annals of the New York Academy of Sciences* 1355 (2015): 52–76.

5. Timothy E. Crews et al., "Going Where No Grains Have Gone Before: From Early to Mid-Succession," *Agriculture, Ecosystems and Environment* 223 (2016): 223–38.

6. Aldo Leopold, "Biotic Farming," *Journal of Forestry*, September 1939.

7. The Land Institute, "A 50-Year Farm Bill."

8. Dan Imhoff, "Overhauling the Farm Bill: Planting for the Future with Perennials," *The Atlantic*, March 12, 2012, https://www.theatlantic.com/health/archive/2012/03/overhauling-the-farm-bill-planting-for-the-future-with-perennials/254423/.

9. H. D. Karsten et al., "Vitamins A, E and Fatty Acid Composition of the Eggs of Caged Hens and Pastured Hens," *Renewable Agriculture and Food Systems* 25, no. 1 (2010): 45–54.

10. Cynthia A. Daley et al., "A Review of Fatty Acid Profiles and Antioxidant Content in Grass-Fed and Grain-Fed Beef," *Nutrition Journal* 9, no. 10 (2010): 1–12.

Chapter 23

1. Agricultural Marketing Service, "Farmers Markets and Direct-to-Consumer Marketing," USDA, updated January 31, 2018, https://www.ams.usda.gov/services/local-regional/farmers-markets-and-direct-consumer-marketing.

2. National Farm to School Network, "About Farm to School," accessed February 19, 2018, http://www.farmtoschool.org/about/what-is-farm-to-school.

3. National Agricultural Statistics Service, "2012 Census of Agriculture Highlights: Direct Farm Sales of Food," USDA, December 2016.

4. National Good Food Network Food Hub Collaboration, "Counting Values: Food Hub Financial Benchmarking Study," 2014.

5. National Agricultural Statistics Service, "2012 Census of Agriculture Highlights."

6. Jean C. Buzby, Hodan Farah Wells, and Gary Vocke, "Possible Implications for US Agriculture from Adoption of Select Dietary Guidelines," USDA Economic Research Service, 2006.

7. Jill Hardy et al., *Findings of the 2015 National Food Hub Survey* (East Lansing, MI: Michigan State University Center for Regional Food Systems and The Wallace Center at Winrock International, 2016), http://foodsystems.msu.edu/resources/2015-food-hub-survey.

8. John Fisk and James Barham, "Food Hubs 101, Appendix," National Good Food Network Food Hub Collaboration, 2014.

9. Farmers' Markets America, "Market Match: SNAPing Up Benefits for Farmers and Shoppers," 2013.

10. Michael Dimock, personal correspondence.

11. USDA Office of Communications, "USDA Reports Record Growth in U.S. Organic Producers," news release, April 4, 2016, https://www.usda.gov/media/press-releases/2016/04/04/usda-reports-record-growth-us-organic-producers.

12. Center for Nutrition Policy and Promotion, "Let's Talk Trash," USDA, September 2015.

13. Jonathan Bloom, *American Wasteland: How America Throws Away Nearly Half of Its Food (and What We Can Do About It)* (Cambridge, MA: Da Capo Press, 2010).

14. Economic Research Service, "Key Statistics and Graphs," USDA, updated October 4, 2017, https://www.ers.usda.gov/topics/food-nutrition-assistance/food-security-in-the-us/key-statistics-graphics.aspx.

15. Taylor Tepper, "Most Americans Don't Have Enough Savings to Cover a $1K Emergency," *Bankrate,* January 18, 2018, https://www.bankrate.com/banking/savings/financial-security-0118/.

16. Harvard Food Law and Policy Clinic, "Opportunities to Reduce Food Waste in the 2018 Farm Bill," May 2017.

17. Harvard Food Law and Policy Clinic, "Opportunities to Reduce Food Waste."

18. Harvard Food Law and Policy Clinic, "Opportunities to Reduce Food Waste."

19. Harvard Food Law and Policy Clinic, "Opportunities to Reduce Food Waste."

20. Harvard Food Law and Policy Clinic, "Opportunities to Reduce Food Waste."

21. ReFED, "27 Solutions to Food Waste," accessed February 17, 2018, http://www.refed.com/?sort=economic-value-per-ton.

22. Harvard Food Law and Policy Clinic, "Opportunities to Reduce Food Waste."

GLOSSARY

adjusted gross income   An income formula that determines eligibility for subsidy payments. At present, millionaires and nonfarmers are welcome.

Agricultural Conservation Easement Program (ACEP)   A program that helps landowners, farmers, and Native American tribes protect agricultural lands by preventing conversion to nonagricultural usage and protect or enhance wetlands by purchasing easements. It was initiated by the 2014 Farm Bill.

appropriations   The annual process of allocating funds to specific programs within the Farm Bill and all other legislation. Programs can be funded at any level, regardless of what was authorized by the legislation.

authorization   The writing and approval of legislation, theoretically determining how funds should be allocated. However, programs may or may not actually be funded at the authorized level.

base acreage   Historical planting records calculated by averaging the previous five years for wheat or feed grains, or the previous three years for cotton and rice, plus land idled through an acreage-reduction or acreage-diversion program. The result determines the amount of subsidy payments.

beginning farmer/rancher   A person with fewer than ten years of experience operating a farm or ranch.

budget reconciliation   The process of changing authorized spending levels without reauthorizing an entire bill. This process can take place at any time, even in legislation intended to last for a set number of years.

cellulosic ethanol   Ethanol made from inedible plants or inedible parts of edible plants, including grasses, leftover corn stalks, and woody materials.

Change in Mandatory Program Spending (ChIMPS)   A political term for when committees revise promised budgets for a program, usually to a lower amount.

Child Nutrition Act   A federal law originally passed in 1966 to assure the health of the nation's children. The School Breakfast Program, Special Milk Program, and Special Supplemental Nutrition Program for Women, Infants, and Children are among the programs included in the act.

concentrated animal feeding operation (CAFO) A term developed by the Environmental Protection Agency to define animal factory farms with more than one thousand "animal units" kept more than forty-five days per year. It is regulated as a potential point source of pollution under the Clean Water Act.

Conservation Reserve Program (CRP)   A program offering financial incentives to eligible farmers who agree to idle part of their land so as to prevent soil erosion, increase wildlife habitat, improve water quality, and reduce the damage of floods and other natural disasters.

Conservation Stewardship Program (CSP)   A green payment program that rewards landowners for habitat protection, chemical reduction, energy conservation, and other environmentally directed efforts.

counter-cyclical payments   A program that provides financial stability and security to farmers producing certain crops like wheat, corn, upland cotton, and peanuts by making up any gap between the market price of the crop and a set target price.

cover crops   Crops planted between harvests that protect and restore nitrogen and other nutrients in the soil.

crop rotation   A practice of changing crops between seasons to break disease cycles and naturally restore organic matter and nutrients to the soil.

direct payments   Automatic payments formally established in 2002 and eliminated in 2014 for landowners who formerly produced commodity crops. They did not need to be farming or producing commodity crops to receive the payments.

disaster assistance   Payments that compensate growers for weather-related losses.

disincentive programs   Penalties that deny landowners or farmers federal subsidies if they plow erosion-prone grasslands (Sodbuster or Sodsaver) or drain or alter wetlands (Swampbuster) to expand crop acreage.

distiller's dried grains with solubles (DDGS) The residual grains left over from corn ethanol production that are fed to livestock.

Environmental Quality Incentives Program (EQIP) Financial and technical assistance to farmers to improve soil, water, plant, animal, and air-related resources on agricultural land; unfortunately, a significant portion of these funds go to CAFO operations.

Farmers' Market Nutrition Program (FMNP) A program associated with the Special Supplemental Nutrition Program for Women, Infants, and Children, with an emphasis on providing access to local fresh produce.

flat-funding See **Changes in Mandatory Program Spending (ChIMPS)**.

food crop ethanol A biofuel made from feed crops grown on arable land that could otherwise be used to grow food for humans.

food desert A fresh-food-free zone with (1) a poverty rate of 20 percent or higher or where (2) at least five hundred people or 33 percent of the population lives more than 1 mile (in an urban area) or more than 10 miles (rural area) from the nearest supermarket or large grocery store.

food hub A central location for the aggregation, processing, storage, and distribution of locally or regionally produced foods.

food security The US Department of Agriculture's term used to classify households that frequently experience hunger to varying degrees: High Food Security, Marginal Food Security, Low Food Security, Very Low Food Security.

genetically modified organism (GMO) Crop given specific attributes, such as resistance to herbicides, from genes introduced from another species.

green payments Agricultural subsidies that support conservation efforts.

Know Your Farmer, Know Your Food (KYF2) An effort within the US Department of Agriculture that promoted the strengthening of local and regional food systems and cultivated a national awareness of the value of local food systems. Although the formal initiative ended in 2017, many programs continue under the Local Food Task Force.

loan deficiency payments Subsidies that provide an influx of cash when market prices are at harvest-time lows, allowing the producer to delay the sale of the commodity until more favorable market conditions emerge.

marker bill A legislative bill used to introduce specific measures or issues into a larger legislative debate. Although not intended to ever come to a vote on the floor, a marker bill is proposed as a "placeholder" for specific aspects of a larger bill.

monoculture The repeated planting one single crop over a large area, usually with detrimental effects on biological diversity.

omnibus legislation A single piece of legislation that addresses several measures or diverse subjects.

peak oil The point at which oil production reaches its maximum rate, after which time supplies rapidly decline.

principal farm operator The person designated as most responsible for making daily decisions about the farm business and running the farm, in cases in which there is more than one person performing these tasks.

production agriculture An agribusiness term describing commodity-based industrial agriculture: predominantly corn, cotton, wheat, rice, soybeans, animal foods, and sugar.

Rural Energy for America Program (REAP)   Grants to fund on-farm renewable energy and energy conservation projects, formerly known as Section 9006 grants.

Sodbuster   A disincentive program included in the 1985 Farm Bill that withdrew federal payments from farmers who plowed up protected grasslands.

Sodsaver   A provision to deter landowners from converting grasslands, particularly native sod, to cropland in the drought- and flood-prone lands of the Prairie Pothole Region.

Special Supplemental Nutrition Program for Women, Infants, and Children (WIC)   A program that provides nutrition and other health assistance to pregnant and postpartum low-income women and their children up to five years of age found to be nutritionally at risk.

specialty crops   Farm Bill term for fruits, nuts, vegetables, dried fruits, and nursery crops.

Supplemental Nutrition Assistance Program (SNAP)   A program that helps people who cannot afford sufficient nutrition for themselves and their families to purchase food.

SNAP-Ed   A program that provides nutrition education to recipients of the Supplemental Nutrition Assistance Program to help them make healthier food choices.

Swampbuster   A disincentive program included in the 1985 Farm Bill that withdrew federal payments from farmers who drained wetlands.

target price   A price floor established by Congress for agricultural products. When the price of a good falls below this point, deficiency payments kick in.

three boxes   The World Trade Organization's three classifications of government supports to agriculture: amber (limited), blue (permitted with conditions), and green (permitted).

trade-distorting subsidy   A subsidy that artificially depresses prices for a given good, giving that country's exports a market advantage over its competition.

Watershed Rehabilitation Program (WRP) A voluntary program that provides funding to rehabilitate aging dams to promote clean water for downstream rural communities.

Wetlands Reserve Program (WRP)   A voluntary easement program that paid farmers to preserve wetlands, aiming to achieve optimal wetland function and wildlife habitat. It was moved under the ACEP program by the 2014 Farm Bill.

INDEX